ROAD RAGE

Barefoot, wearing a white tank top and dark shorts, Faye Gray stood crying at 2:30 A.M. Her shiny red Mazda RX7 lay in a ditch by the side of the road. Driving home alone, she had somehow managed to wreck her car.

A white tractor-trailer stopped. The driver was in his midtwenties and willing to give her a lift to the nearest gas station. As the truck rolled to a halt just out of sight of the gas station, Gray thanked him and opened the door.

The driver pulled her back into the truck, grabbing her shorts so hard they ripped in half. He slammed the door behind her, then struck her in the face. He punched her in the chest and abdomen, then smashed his fist into her spine. She fought back, but that only made him more angry.

He put his hands around her neck and didn't let go until she was dead.

BOOK YOUR PLACE ON OUR WEBSITE AND MAKE THE READING CONNECTION!

We've created a customized website just for our very special readers, where you can get the inside scoop on everything that's going on with Zebra, Pinnacle and Kensington books.

When you come online, you'll have the exciting opportunity to:

- View covers of upcoming books
- Read sample chapters
- Learn about our future publishing schedule (listed by publication month *and author*)
- Find out when your favorite authors will be visiting a city near you
- Search for and order backlist books from our online catalog
- Check out author bios and background information
- Send e-mail to your favorite authors
- Meet the Kensington staff online
- Join us in weekly chats with authors, readers and other guests
- Get writing guidelines
- AND MUCH MORE!

**Visit our website at
http://www.kensingtonbooks.com**

THE BABYFACE KILLER

Jon Bellini

PINNACLE BOOKS
Kensington Publishing Corp.
http://www.kensingtonbooks.com

PINNACLE BOOKS are published by

Kensington Publishing Corp.
850 Third Avenue
New York, NY 10022

All Kensington Titles, Imprints, and Distributed Lines are available at special quantity discounts for bulk purchases for sales promotions, premiums, fund-raising, and educational or institutional use. Special book excerpts or customized printings can also be created to fit specific needs. For details, write or phone the office of the Kensington special sales manager: Kensington Publishing Corp., 850 Third Avenue, New York, NY 10022, attn: Special Sales Department, Phone: 1-800-221-2647.

Pinnacle and the P logo Reg. U.S. Pat. & TM Off.

First Printing: January 2002
10 9 8 7 6 5 4 3 2 1

Printed in the United States of America

*Dedicated to all the families of
the victims of Lesley Warren*

ACKNOWLEDGMENTS

I wish to extend my gratitude to the following individuals, without whose kind support this book would not have been possible: Asheville Police Department's Ted Lambert, Spartanburg County Sheriff's Department's Carroll Amory, New York State Police's Bob Cooke and Dick Ladue, High Point Police Department's Mark McNeill, Jerry Grubb, Jeff Pate and Steve Campbell. And Monette McKinney, David Shampine, Jefferson County DA James King and Lee Hurley. Also, my literary agent Piers Murray. And, of course, Paul Dinas, my editor Karen Haas, and all the kind folk at Kensington Publishing.

"I didn't want to hurt them; I only wanted to kill them."

—David "Son of Sam" Berkowitz

Prologue

The burgundy Ford LTD and the gray Granada swerved out of the parking lot of the low-level modern redbrick police building close to the old railroad track on the barren, windswept side of town. A strike force followed in a three-vehicle convoy; it was composed of a brand-new black Pontiac van containing a five-man SWAT team, plus two black-and-white cruisers, each filled with uniformed officers.

Detective Jerry Grubb drove the LTD, his bulky frame backlit by the gleaming sun streaking across the shiny blacktop. His forehead was glistening with sweat, and what remained of his wispy blond hair was swept across his crown. As he mopped his brow with a handkerchief, he took a long, deep breath and then leaned across and snapped on the AC switch.

Grubb's cruiser smelled of stale cigarettes and sweaty people. It had carried all sorts in its time. The dashboard paint was chipped and there was a hole in the place where the large, old radio receiver had been anchored until some bright spark in the department decided it would be cheaper to issue detectives with nonprofessional walkie-talkies.

Jerry Grubb—in his early forties, but appearing at least ten years older—swung his head around to see how the convoy was keeping up. He hoped they wouldn't need the SWAT team. His partner Mark McNeill was immediately behind him in his Granada. The three detectives in Grubb's car watched in silence as he continued dabbing his sweaty brow. Then he grabbed a pack of cigarettes from the large pocket inside his door.

"Chances are he'll be expectin' us," Grubb said, lighting up.

"How come?" one of the other detectives asked.

"The woman who gave Asheville the address probably went and tipped him off."

"D'you reckon he's offed the girl at the house?"

"Maybe. But Asheville says it's not his style to stay with a woman for a week and then kill her . . ." Grubb replied, ". . . not unless he's lookin' for a one–way ticket to the death chamber."

"Is he armed?" asked one of the younger officers in the backseat.

"They reckon he's packing a forty-four Magnum Redhawk and a couple of blades. . . ." Grubb paused. "He's been at the house all week. Plans to hop a Greyhound to Florida tonight. It's now or never."

"Any dope?"

"Snorts more blow than John Belushi . . . but we're gonna try and talk him out nice 'n' easy," Grubb said, then added thoughtfully, "Just so long as he doesn't come out shootin'."

Then he took a deep breath and dunked his sweaty handkerchief back in his jacket pocket for the first time since their journey had begun. "The guy's smart," Grubb said. "Asheville pulled him in just a couple of days after he'd done his last victim.

Throttled her with his bare hands. But they couldn't hold him because they didn't have a body or witnesses. So he got himself bailed. . . . He was in the Twenty-second Infantry, Tenth Mountain Division up at Fort Drum, New York. A trained killer. He'll take us all out if we give him the chance."

As the faces of the other detectives in Grubb's LTD grew longer, Grubb patted the grip of his well-worn Glock 9mm tucked in a holster exposed by his open jacket.

"The house is next to a kindergarten and there's a family living on the other side. We can drive up to the kindergarten without him seeing us from any of the windows of the house. If he's on the front porch, we'll swamp him, no trouble. If he stays in, we hit the side door right after the SWAT team goes into the front and back. The others are holding back until we say."

"How d'you wanna get in the door?" one of the detectives asked.

"If it sounds quiet inside, we'll use the ram. If we hear any movement or gunfire, then we'll use weapons."

Grubb turned toward the officers in the back and they both patted their shotguns. A three-inch Magnum shotgun shell loaded with fine powdered lead can easily blow the lock off a door without injuring the people inside.

"What about the kids? Where are they?" one of the younger officers asked.

"The woman's sister said they could be in there with them," Grubb said. "We just don't know for sure."

They all wished the children were a million miles away. Grubb took a deep breath in through his nose before letting the air out through his teeth with a long, slow hiss. Just then his radio crackled. "You sure?" Grubb responded. "Maybe it was the family next door?" He looked at the other detective. "Deputies positioning in the area behind the house heard a baby crying."

The SWAT team's black van dropped off behind the LTD and the Granada after Grubb told them to wait on standby. The two High Point PD black-and-whites had already headed around the other side of the block where deputies were clearing properties in the immediate vicinity of the target's house.

The neighborhood got progressively more run-down as the LTD and the Granada crept down Phillips Avenue. Many of the houses looked abandoned; wrecked autos stood on bricks in a few driveways. A handful of kids hung out on street corners while old folks swept their front yards. Past a liquor store, two men emerged, swigging at bottles in brown paper bags. Three men sat talking in a 1970s gas-guzzler, maybe doing a drug deal.

As the unmarked cruisers slowed down for a stop sign, Grubb squinted and panned the sidewalk. Then he punched a button on his radio. A brief conversation followed in which deputies near the house reported they had completed clearing the kindergarten.

"Nothin' happening inside the house," one of them said over the high-pitched radio waves.

The LTD and the Granada caught three cars coming eastward at another stop sign a block away from their destination. The detectives found themselves staring up the street toward the target's house for what seemed like an eternity, but it was really only a few seconds. As the last of the three cars floated by, the LTD and the Granada crept across the road markings and swept into the kindergarten's empty driveway.

At 2:20 P.M., just two minutes after the time they had estimated, the detectives sat silently in both their cars and carried out one final check on the area. This end of Phillips was like a ghost town. There was little movement on the sidewalk. A handful of pigeons flapped into the air as Grubb buzzed down his driver-side window. Then a dog barked in the distance and broke the wall of silence. Across the street, sunlight bathed the white clapboard houses in a hot yellow glow. Grubb noticed a shiny black Kawasaki Vulcan 750 motorcycle parked in front.

"He's in."

Grubb looked across at his partner McNeill in his Granada, held his right hand up and began counting down with his fingers.

5-4-3-2-1. . . .

Six detectives emerged from the Granada and the LTD, all wearing Kevlar bullet-proof vests under their dark blue plastic High Point PD jackets, and clipped their doors quietly shut. Two officers held their Magnum shotguns pointing down alongside their thighs so as not to be easily noticed. Another one carried a door ram under his arm. All six began slowly and carefully crossing the front yard of the kindergarten. The door they were aiming for was on the left of the porch that ran around the front of the tatty, paint-peeling house.

Jerry Grubb called the house on his cell phone. A woman answered. She was expecting the call, so his introduction was brief. "He wants to come out," she told the investigator. Grubb knew they couldn't take any chances in case he was trying to trick them.

The detectives were still looking to their left and

right when they heard the door of the house squeak open. A tall white man in a blue shirt and tight Levis walked out, stretching his arms and yawning. His dark dyed hair was standing on end as he stood on the porch blinking his eyes and rubbing them. He was in his early twenties with a round, pudgy, young-looking face.

"That's him," Grubb whispered.

Then he screamed, "DO NOT MOVE! AGAINST THE WALL!"

McNeill and Grubb racked the slides on their Glocks.

"Let's do it. GO! GO! GO!" Grubb shouted into his radio.

He and McNeill took the forward positions. Just then Grubb caught his target's gaze as the man stood passively. Out of the corner of his eye, he noticed two younger detectives with shotguns drawn in the air.

"DO NOT MOVE! DO NOT MOVE!"

Grubb and McNeill jumped the five-step stairway to the porch in two leaps.

"DO NOT MOVE!"

The target stayed still, gently smiling.

"I ain't movin', sir. I ain't movin'," he said calmly and politely.

Grubb and McNeill were just two feet from him. Their Glocks pointing directly at the man. Behind them were footsteps, shadows appearing from all directions and a car squealing in the background. The SWAT team was in the yard.

The smile on his target's face got even broader. Guns cocked, at least four SWAT team members hurdled over the porch railings.

Then McNeill and Grubb dragged their man across the floor by the scruff of his collar, his limp legs bouncing off the porch steps as they headed into the yard.

Then the woman crashed out of the door with a baby in her arms. "Oh my God! Oh my God!"

"On the floor, please, ma'am!" ordered one detective.

"Anyone else in there?"

"What?"

"Anyone in the house?"

"No."

To the side of her, the target was spread-eagled in the dusty front yard.

The mother held the child tight to her, sobbing.

The prisoner looked up from the yard, still smiling.

"Are you Lesley Eugene Warren?" Detective Mark McNeill asked, pulling a wallet from the man's back pocket.

"Sure am" was the quiet response.

"This your picture on the license?" McNeill asked, flipping open the wallet.

"Yup."

Then Detective Grubb served a warrant on Lesley Eugene Warren for his arrest. "We got some officers over in Asheville wanna talk to you, Lesley."

"That's fine by me, sir," responded Warren. "I'd be more than happy to talk to them. Tell 'em to come on up."

Warren had with him $87.58 when he was arrested. He was also packing a carry-on bag containing a pair of Nike trainers, a fringe vest, a pair of rubber boots, a raincoat, a pair of suspenders and a pair of cord pants.

Lesley Warren was then thoroughly searched and the High Point detectives removed the contents of his pockets, including a set of Renault car keys.

"Who do these belong to?" Grubb asked his prisoner.

"They're mine," he answered.

Warren was handcuffed and put in a van belonging to the High Point patrol transport detective division. At 2:45 P.M., as the pickup team traveled back to High Point police headquarters on Leonard Avenue, Jerry Grubb called the Warren task force investigators two hundred miles away to tell them their man was in custody.

A collective cheer went up throughout the office when the news came through. The citizens of Asheville, North Carolina, could once more sleep easy in their beds at night.

One

The city of Asheville sits comfortably on either side of the French Broad River in a sizable valley known as the Asheville Plateau 2,340 feet above sea level between the Blue Ridge and Great Smoky Mountains in Buncombe County, one of eighteen counties that encompass Western North Carolina.

In the 1600s, the land on which Asheville now sprawls was protected land, given to the Cherokees by the king of England. After the Revolutionary War, the area was thrown open for development grants, and by 1784, pioneers had followed the Native American trails to their homes alongside the creeks and rivers that fed into the French Broad.

Incorporated by the General Assembly of North Carolina in 1797, Asheville was named after Samuel Ashe, the popular governor of North Carolina. The city rapidly became known as the regional, cultural and medical center of Western North Carolina even though its population remained relatively small. Thanks to its geographical position in the Confederacy, the town was dubbed "the Capital City of the Confederate States of America" from 1861 through 1865. During the War for Southern Independence, the County of Buncombe and Asheville even issued its own paper currency in denominations of five cents, ten cents, fifteen cents, twenty cents, twenty-five cents, fifty cents and one dollar.

On April 3, 1865, Colonel Isaac M. Kirby of the Union left East Tennessee with 1,100 men on a raid against the town. This became known as the Battle of Asheville. Three days later, Kirby's force was defeated by local militia led by Colonel G.W. Clayton. It wasn't one of the classic engagements of the War for Southern Independence, but it was vastly important to the town and county of Buncombe.

In 1880, the railroad arrived. That, combined with the technical wonders of time—electricity, telephone and telegraph—sparked a population explosion and Asheville officially became a city in 1883. Soon afterward, it was proclaimed the best place in the world for the cure of tuberculosis—then the number one killer in the nation. Sanitariums were built on all the hills surrounding the city. Many of the sick also happened to be extremely rich and their investments in Asheville led to a boom in the late 1880s, which lasted more than thirty years.

The well-documented excesses of the Roaring Twenties combined with the hardships of the Great Depression ten years later left Asheville, like many other cities, overextended and completely broke. However, over the following three decades, a combination of civic pride and mountain spirit helped the city pay off every penny of its defaulted loans.

In the 1950s came the freeways and Asheville found itself at the junction of Interstates 26 and 40. The I-240 connector route passed right through downtown and became known as the Blue Ridge Parkway. As developers once again flooded the area, Asheville preserved numerous historical city center buildings; later, these formed the backbone of the city's renaissance in the 1960s.

"It's a city with a gentle pace and hardy spirit, a city with soul in the heart of the mountains" is how residents liked to hear their hometown described.

By the mid-1960s, Asheville's culture was neither northern nor southern, nor was it mountain or flat.

It was into this supposedly eclectic society that Douglas Eugene Warren of Candler, near Asheville, and Phyllis Jean West, a native of Texas, married on December 2, 1966. The Warrens immediately settled in a trailer parked on land owned by Doug's father in a community called the Hominy Township in Candler, just northeast of Asheville.

Candler, a satellite commercial district that had long since expanded beyond the boundaries of Asheville, sat just a few miles down Highway 23. North of the town's sprawling business parks, the countryside quickly became green and luscious. Vast rolling fields and lakes were separated only by narrow country lanes running through the valleys and open pastures alongside meandering streams.

Just ten months after the Warrens' marriage, their first child, Lesley Eugene Warren, was born on October 15, 1967. However, Lesley's birth did little to quell the fiery relationship between his young parents, Phyllis and Doug. His mother later claimed she and baby Lesley were often beaten by Doug Warren during his regular fits of temper. Phyllis believed her husband's attacks on his baby son were his way of getting even with her.

Lesley Warren later told friends and relatives his father hit him with a belt before he was even old enough to stand. By the time he was able to speak, Lesley had become afraid to make any spontaneous statements in case his father punished him. By the age of three, Lesley became completely withdrawn whenever he was in the company of his parents. He was dealing with the violence by retreating into his own dreamworld.

"He never dared say anything in front of his papa," recalled Lesley's uncle Carl Russell Warren. "Only time I ever saw him smile was when we were well away from his home." Other relatives said there was little sign of happiness in Lesley's eyes. "He'd had the crap beaten out of him and he was dead inside," said his cousin Jimmy Knight. "The kid never stood a chance."

Lesley Warren escaped his parents' war zone by running into the beautiful countryside that surrounded the family's trailer home. He'd disappear for hours at a stretch, retreating into a dreamworld, which helped him escape the reality of his brutal upbringing. Rhododendron, azalea, laurel and dogwood flowers bathed the area in a rich tapestry of colors. Beyond the flowers was the forest where Lesley would pick berries and study the creatures playing in the fields and the trees. Doug and Phyllis Warren were so preoccupied with their marital problems they hardly noticed Lesley spending entire days out alone in the countryside.

"Doug said there weren't nothin' that could harm the boy out in the forest," recalled Carl Russell Warren. "And it got him out of their hair."

The pleasant year-round climate in that part of Western North Carolina was influenced by the Blue Ridge Mountains to the southeast and the Great Smokies to the northwest, tempered by occasional storms that moved eastward from the Great Plains or northward from the Gulf of Mexico. The result was moderate summers and winters separated by spectacular long, mild springs and falls. Little, lonely

Lesley Warren could wander the forest and countryside virtually any time of the day or night he
wanted. He forgot about his parents and talked to
the birds and the animals and the plants instead.
They didn't hit each other. They didn't say they
hated each other and they certainly didn't hate little
Lesley.

Despite the Warrens' marital battles, Phyllis got
pregnant with a second child, which delighted
young Lesley, who was desperate for some company.
On December 19, 1970, Laron Ray Warren was
born. The infant was immediately showered with
love and affection by Phyllis, leaving Lesley completely out in the cold. Meanwhile, Doug began
spending longer periods away from the family's
home while he traveled the state looking for work
to help pay for his young family's upkeep.

Lesley Warren reacted by retreating further and
further into a world of his own. His mother later
recalled that her son had a constantly "unreadable
baby face." Whenever she told him things, she'd
"watch them go right through him." Phyllis added,
"You would know he heard you, but what you said
wasn't going in."

When Doug Warren made one of his rare appearances in Candler, he'd spend much of his time in
the local bars. If Warren was drunk, violence soon
followed. His wife and oldest son continued to be
on the receiving end. Doug Warren treated baby
Laron like the golden child. By the time he was five
years old, Lesley Warren had been relegated to the
status of black sheep of the family.

"He was the one they blamed for everythin'.
Laron was the apple of his folks' eye, but Lesley just
couldn't do nothin' right," recalled Jimmy Knight,
a cousin.

Many years later, Lesley Warren's mom insisted that until the birth of Laron she had given Lesley more attention than her husband. She believed that Doug Warren became so resentful of this that he started lashing out at Lesley more frequently. The unhappy and tortured expression on Lesley's face seemed almost permanent to the Warrens' friends and family. "Lesley looked so unhappy everyone thought he was a miserable son of a gun. You expect a kid that age to laugh and smile a bit, but the look on his face was always sad," explained Carl Warren. As one child psychiatrist explained: "If an infant is lying there and gets hit because the father wants to get a rise out of the mother, the infant doesn't know right, wrong or indifferent. He just doesn't know."

Basically, Lesley Warren was being so consistently punished for no good reason that he'd retreated into a sea of fantasy where he blocked out all the horrors of life. The line between right and wrong was already blurring. He'd developed his own way of dealing with life. As he got older, his emotions remained those of a young child. He never learned how to develop his behavior accordingly. He didn't even have the common sense to avoid his father's brutal punishments. "Lesley didn't have coping skills. He'd lay there and be hit from nowhere for no special reason," explained child psychiatrist Dr. Bruce Welch.

The early years of Lesley Warren's life were a never-ending battle for survival. He was kicked, punched and whipped time and time again, and on most occasions had no idea why his father was doing it. It left the little boy bewildered and emotionally detached—an underlying pathology that tortured Lesley Warren virtually from the moment he was born. The only way he could cope was to separate himself from his feelings and those appalling experiences at the hands of his father.

But his father, Doug, was about to inflict an even bigger emotional scar on his eldest son.

In 1971, Lesley Warren, his baby brother, Laron, and mother, Phyllis, were sleeping over at her in-laws' house after yet another evening of fighting between his parents. Just before 2:00 A.M., Lesley was awoken by the sound of his father shouting and screaming out in the yard that separated their trailer home from his grandparents' house. Rubbing the sleep from his eyes, Lesley peered out of the bedroom window and saw his father setting fire to the trailer that had been his one and only home throughout his short life. Phyllis woke up just as the flames were licking the outside of the trailer. She called the fire department immediately. But by the time the Upper Hominy Volunteer Fire Department arrived on the scene from their station on Pisgah Highway in Candler, it was too late.

Four-year-old Lesley Warren watched as they doused the trailer in water while Doug Warren, wearing nothing but his pants, sat nearby on a wall. Phyllis Warren eventually marched out to her husband and yet another argument started. The firefighters were never told that Doug Warren had deliberately started the blaze. They presumed it was an accident.

Minutes after the blaze was finally put out, little Lesley Warren walked out into the cinder-smoking yard and asked a firefighter if he could get his things from inside the trailer. "There's nothin' left in there, son," came the reply. "Everything's burned to a cinder." All Lesley Warren's possessions—his toys, clothes, even his favorite shoes—had been destroyed. As he later recalled to one medical examiner, "I'd have been better off dead from that day onwards."

That same night, Doug Warren was banished from the family home. He never returned. The fire represented the beginning of the end for Lesley Warren. He was forever haunted by those images of his childhood possessions being reduced to ash. As his mother later recalled, "Lesley changed on that day. His face never smiled again."

Carol Pressley, next-door neighbor to Lesley Warren's grandparents, knew Doug Warren pretty well during the time Warren lived in the trailer on his parents' land. Pressley was at home the night the trailer burned down and she never forgot looking out of the window of her own house to see Doug Warren, wearing nothing but that pair of pants, sitting between the trailer and his parents' house.

One child-care specialist who later examined Lesley Warren explained, "Lesley witnessed the burning of his home at the hands of his father, and witnessed his father's expulsion from the family. He also experienced very direct and abrupt rejection from his father. He had been gifted with a high intelligence, but was crippled emotionally and his character development reflects, in part, his early traumas."

Statistics show that children with chronic disorders have a very high frequency of first-degree relatives (e.g., fathers) with alcoholism, abusive behavior and antisocial personalities. Lesley Warren's traits were to a large part caused by his father's antisocial behavior.

That fire turned the already shy toddler into a self-destructive personality. Lesley Warren stopped even playing with other children and rarely mentioned his father from that moment onward. "It was like he stepped out of this world into another one," his mother, Phyllis, later recalled.

With Doug Warren banished from the family home, Phyllis and the two young boys eventually moved to a house on nearby Ben Lippen Road. But the burned-out trailer remained in the grandparents' yard as a painful memorial to Lesley Warren of his unhappy early childhood. Sometimes the youngster would go up the street and play ball just as an excuse to go and stand and stare at the burned-out wreck. He'd flash back to all the screaming and shouting and unhappiness. By the age of seven, Lesley Warren had few friends, a sense of isolation from society and a feeling that everyone was out to get him.

Phyllis Warren began noticing that her son was constantly accepting blame for things he hadn't done. It wasn't until later she realized that little Lesley was convinced he wasn't loved anymore.

His father made little or no effort to stay in contact with his son. "I really didn't know him," Doug later admitted. "We had some problems and I didn't see him much after that."

On February 7, 1973, Lesley Warren's parents divorced. It was only many years later that Doug Warren's history of lawbreaking at that time was disclosed. Many later surmised that Lesley "inherited" certain traits from his father.

Some child-care experts even believe that Warren's father passed down to his son a "bad gene," which began manifesting itself inside Lesley Warren from an early age.

There is no doubt about Doug Warren's code of abhorrent conduct:

   1. He had been physically abusive and cruel toward his infant son Lesley.

   2. He had a pretty extensive substance-abuse history.

   3. He physically abused his wife and set fire to the family home in the process.

   4. He had numerous encounters with the law.

Those four factors demonstrated severe antisocial behavior. The biggest danger was that young Lesley might take up the mantle and prove the old saying "Like father, like son." Yet within two years of his divorce from Phyllis, Doug Warren had genuinely turned over a new leaf.

He married a woman named called Hattie and was to eventually stay married for twenty-two years and raise three more children, Joseph, Wallace and Eugene. But he never managed to repair the wounds inflicted on his first son, Lesley.

On October 12, 1973, just a few days after Lesley's sixth birthday, Phyllis Warren was granted full custody of her two young sons, Lesley and Laron, by a Buncombe County court. A restraining order was placed on Doug Warren to prevent him from in any way "harassing or molesting" his wife and their children. His only access to the boys was on each Sunday, for one hour, between the hours of 2:00 P.M. and 5:00 P.M.

Lesley Warren's inability to communicate his thoughts and feelings concerned teachers and family members alike. At the Garrett's Playland kindergarten in Candler, one member of the staff commented: "You only had to look at Lesley's face to know he was an empty book. He just didn't behave like other kids. He'd be on his own—even out in the school yard."

At home there were other danger signs. Whenever the family went out to restaurants, Lesley insisted on sitting with his back against the wall so people couldn't sneak up behind him. He also refused to go into local stores with his family or into shopping malls. Instead, he'd remain huddled up in the car anxiously awaiting their return.

Lesley Warren's uncle Carl Russell Warren saw a lot of the boy during those early years of his life. He insisted Warren's father treated his son badly and rejected him because he hadn't wanted the child in the first place.

But Carl Russell Warren also recalled that following the divorce, Doug tried to see Lesley frequently but ended up having such bad fights with his wife that the boy would run out in the yard to get away from the noise. Carl Warren was extremely sorry for his nephew because he felt Doug showed a lot of favoritism toward his younger son Laron from the moment he was born. Carl also confirmed that while Doug never laid a hand on Laron, he regularly inflicted corporal punishment on Lesley. "I often used to see bruises and other marks on Lesley where he had been beaten," Carl later recalled.

Lesley Warren had little or no real social skills, so the only way he could create attention was to get into trouble. Stealing something and then getting caught gave him a sense of purpose. It meant he was somebody even if it was for all the wrong reasons. He began by stealing at home on a relatively harmless level: taking toys from his baby brother; stealing food out of the icebox before supper was served; occasionally dipping into his mom's purse for a dollar bill. Lesley Warren quickly realized that such actions pulled his mom's attention away from his baby brother, Laron. It was a way for Lesley to assert himself on the family, to make himself feel important.

When Doug Warren's place was taken by stepfather Sam Murray, who drank heavily and eventually began disciplining Lesley, his world turned upside down. The punishments weren't as pathological or physical as those inflicted by Doug Warren, but Lesley didn't see any difference.

Back in the not-so-politically-correct 1970s, a spanking with the back of the hand might have been acceptable. But these punishments on Lesley Warren represented a relentless beating of the spirit and body on a little boy who still didn't understand what he had done wrong. They also sowed fresh seeds of anger and resentment.

Throughout this period, Lesley's mother disciplined her son by sending him to his bedroom. As child-care experts later discovered, that was an event he didn't particularly mind. In fact, Warren actively sought out that punishment so he could escape all confrontations with his family. In his room, no one was bothering him. Once again he could retreat into his own little world.

His mother believes to this day that her son deliberately sought out punishment because Lesley relished violating rules and being disobedient. It also guaranteed him a trip to his bedroom, allowing him to avoid further confrontation. "Then he'd shape up and behave fine after that," Phyllis Warren later recalled.

Lesley Warren soon began getting so nervous he regularly doubled up in pain and had to be taken to a doctor. Most times he was simply sent home and told he'd suffered a few harmless stomach cramps. However, Lesley began complaining more and more frequently about such problems. He constantly writhed in agony and claimed to have other pains all over his body. Most of the pains Warren suffered were psychosomatic. The youngster was trying to attract attention to his plight, but he didn't have the confidence to tell anyone what he truly felt.

On September 13, 1974, Lesley Warren began attending Candler's Emma Elementary School. His teacher, Payne Mundy, was disturbed when Phyllis Warren requested that she inform Lesley he did not have a father if discussions about the family ever came up at school.

Lesley Warren's elementary school record sheet with Buncombe County schools had his father's name removed and replaced with the name of Phyllis's mother, Merle West, and her security guard father, Lesley West. It also revealed that Phyllis had gotten to twelfth grade, compared with her parents, who'd both only gotten to tenth grade. On the bottom of Warren's report card was written: *"Father not to pick up."* Phyllis Warren was doing her damnedest to make sure her former husband played no part in the upbringing of their elder son.

A few weeks after the start of term, Doug Warren turned up at the classroom door, where he stood and looked in at his son in the middle of class. When teacher Payne Mundy noticed, she walked out of the class to talk to him. Warren insisted he did not want Lesley to see him. He just wanted to see how his son was, he told her. He admitted being afraid of the court order and that he didn't want to upset the child. But Lesley Warren noticed his father looking in and was very confused when he didn't want to speak to him. Payne Mundy later said that Lesley became even more withdrawn after that incident.

By the time Lesley Warren got into third grade, teacher Charlotte Spence remembered Phyllis Warren making several visits to the school during which she told the teacher there had been regular abuse in the family home before the split from his father. Lesley's teachers soon became extremely concerned by Lesley's "general state of anxiety."

In early 1975, Charlotte Spence and other teachers persuaded Phyllis Warren to take her son to see Dr. William Matthews, a clinical psychologist. Matthews immediately noted Lesley Warren became agitated under any form of pressure and suffered from tremors and tics.

Dr. Matthews later explained, "A tic in a forty-year-old executive is a lot different than a tic in a seven-year-old child. That's usually a sign of a fairly severe nervous disorder in someone that young."

Lesley Warren had a motoric tic, which meant he was suffering from a muscle spasm. It provoked a rapid, jerky movement in the young boy and led to a lot of teasing from his classmates. Matthews was so concerned by Lesley Warren's problems that he tried to probe Warren's background to find an explanation.

But the more questions Matthews asked, the more introspective young Lesley became. He hated being subjected to the sort of humiliating questions and examinations carried out by Dr. Matthews. Lesley presented a rigid and controlled impression from that moment on. "It was almost a wooden-Indian appearance. He stopped himself from any physical response," Matthews later explained.

Lesley Warren's attempts to deceive medical examiners hastened his complete withdrawal from normality. He didn't want to share his innermost feelings because he thought it would cause him more problems at home. Lesley Warren's trust of people had been destroyed by the brutality of his family. Warren admitted to Dr. Matthews he felt rejected by his father. Matthews concluded that Lesley's extensive and continually disruptive family history had started "from the time Lesley was born."

In 1978, Lesley once again visited child-care specialist Dr. Matthews following some new "behavioral problems" at school. One teacher later explained: "There were frequent incidents of antisocial behavior and a passive defiance on the part of Lesley Warren to do what he damn well pleased."

Passive defiance was summed up thusly by one specialist who saw Lesley Warren: "The perfect image that I have for passive defiance is a child who doesn't ever say "no." He just won't do what he's told. That spills over into the passive/aggressive area .. from the psychiatrists' and psychologists' perspective, we call things aggressive when they're not so obviously aggressive.

"The kind of aggression you're talking about with passive/aggressive is classic, like when you would ask a coworker or a child to do something, they won't say 'yes' or 'no,' or they may say 'yes' and not do it. They deflect it off. They can't confront people directly. That's basically the passive/aggressive style of coping with things."

Lesley Warren had become an expert at saying "yes" but never actually doing what he was told. Lesley Warren had seven more sessions with Dr. Matthews at that time and the psychiatrist noted that Warren's state of anxiety became "markedly reduced" afterward.

When Lesley Warren turned twelve he was seen by a psychotherapist named C. Jonathan Ahr after he had once again become "socially defiant and oppositional." Ahr's report later recalled: "His [War-ren's] academic performance was poor and there was generalized passive defiance which was observed in stealing, lying and difficulties in the academic set-ting." Lesley Warren's emotional problems were once again careening out of control and no one seemed able to help him over his problems.

On April 5, 1979, Lesley Warren began attending Erwin Middle School, where he at first tried his hardest to project a friendly, quiet image. At this stage, he had a chunky build and a floppy, longish hairstyle. Life at home was marginally more stable for the first time in years. Warren's academic marks were mostly in the C and D range, but under the section marked "Evaluation of Social & Personal As-sets," there were two D grades for "Dependability" and "Industriousness." Intriguingly, one of his high-est marks was a B for "Courtesy."

Warren's good manners had been hammered into him from an early age, but they were delivered in a robotic, emotionless voice. At Erwin Middle School, Lesley got into trouble whenever life at home became extremely stressful. In October 1980, Warren was given a third episode of therapy after "trying to run away from home, having what ap-peared to be low motivation and poor academic per-formance plus a strong susceptibility to influences of negative peer groups."

Dr. Matthews later recalled: "He had poor moti-vation and was again showing passive defiance of his antisocial behavior. Antisocial behavior is rule break-ing in a younger child. It's also lawbreaking behav-ior in an older youth or an adult." Lesley Warren was exhibiting antisocial behavior on virtually a full-time basis.

Even his own mother sensed that Lesley Warren

had no interest in his future development. One day she was watching television with her son when he made a chilling comment: "It wouldn't be so hard to die."

In the summer of 1980, Lesley Warren broke into his cousin's house in the Tiny Farms housing development in Leicester, near the family home in Candler, on the outskirts of Asheville. His mother believes to this day that Lesley Warren deliberately engineered the break-in so he would get caught. "To me, that was just a way of his to ask for help," she later recalled.

There are few other details known about the break-in attempt, but it was not considered serious enough to warrant a custodial sentence and Warren was let off with a caution by police.

On August 17, 1981, Lesley Warren enrolled at the Erwin High School, on Lee's Creek Road, Asheville. He was withdrawn on January 4, 1982. During that period, he missed fifteen days out of a total sixty-five days of schooling.

The year 1982 proved to be a benchmark in the bizarre development of Leslie Warren's childhood. It started with Warren—then age fourteen—being charged with writing extortion letters threatening to rape the teenage sister of one of his school friends. The letters were considered by police to be a particularly evil form of extortion.

Warren was immediately referred to the Blue Ridge Community Mental Health Center, located in Asheville. He was given a supposedly thorough and extensive evaluation, which involved numerous psychological tests.

Warren had been continually getting into trouble with the law, had been caught vandalizing school buses, stealing guns and ammunition, as well as the earlier incident of breaking and entering his cousin's house. Warren showed signs of severe depression. One doctor even gave a provisional diagnosis of Warren as being "unsocialized with depressive features." Lesley Warren was in a severely disturbed state; if something wasn't done quickly, then he could get into really serious trouble.

Warren had also begun writing a series of deeply disturbing letters that were an outpouring of emotional turmoil—to himself. The letters gave the impression, according to those who saw them, that Warren was in the midst of "self-destructive thinking and possibly disorganized or delusional thinking."

At the Blue Ridge Health Center, his first evaluation was carried out by psychology expert Dave Evers. He diagnosed Warren with "conduct disorder of adolescence and schizoid personality disorder." Evers concluded that Warren was "severely emotionally disturbed and was an imminent danger to himself or others." Evers later recalled that Warren's reaction to any anxiety at the time was to act out, that this was his only means of handling anxiety or stress. Lesley Warren's facial tic and severely bitten fingernails were once again noted.

Lesley Warren saw another psychiatrist, Dr. McDonald, at the Blue Ridge Health Center. McDonald insisted he saw no signs of psychosis in Warren but he was concerned by some "soft signs" as he later described them. McDonald saw evidence of a possible "psychotic process" and that raised alarm bells. Other doctors at Blue Ridge didn't see Warren as an immediate threat.

What they didn't realize was that from the relatively early age of fourteen, Lesley Warren's behavior was fueled by abusing drugs, including cocaine and marijuana.

A medical report on Lesley Warren in January 1982 stated: "Adjustment problems arising from the physical abuse and emotional instability in the Warrens' marriage were obvious before Lesley reached seven years old. Lesley has not developed a strong, healthy relationship with anyone, but has remained a withdrawn, highly independent lad who has learned to live with chronic fear and anxiety. However, any type of stress or change has exacerbated his symptomology. . . ."

The report continued: "At the time he entered school, and again when his mother remarried, and again at puberty, Lesley caused enough problems to be referred to treatment. Although the acute symptoms subsided after several months, Lesley's chronic maladjustment has continued. . . ."

What the report didn't mention was that at one time Lesley Warren's mother had tried to give him away to an aunt because she couldn't stand sharing her home with him.

He truly was an unwanted child.

Two

At the Blue Ridge Health Center, Lesley Warren was seen by psychologists, psychiatrists and a social worker all working as a team. The psychologists reported that Lesley had high normal intelligence with an IQ of between 115 and 125, which was considered in the bright-to-normal range and was approximately equal to or higher than the IQ of the average law student. One female psychologist described Warren as a socially detached loner and she wrote: "His needs for independence and autonomy find expression in forced control, rebellion, lack of ego defenses and an absence of just coping skills." This absence of coping skills was very significant because as the consultant warned: "He has virtually no control over his actions."

The diagnosis given to Warren at that time included the usual conduct disorder, which was directly related to his rule-breaking behavior. Warren's antisocial behavior was out of control. "He'd broken all kinds of rules. He'd vandalized things; he'd stolen things. He did a lot of obvious things to get himself into trouble and not take much care not to be caught," said one evaluator at the time.

Most significantly, following assessment, he was described as having a schizoid personality disorder. Lesley Warren was detached from everything, including his own emotions. When Warren experienced emotions, he didn't actually feel them. It was as if he were not the person suffering elation, fear, anger or whatever. He had absolutely no way of relating to it.

Lesley Warren still suffered the emotional baggage of a normal person, but he had absolutely no idea when he was getting angry. This meant he didn't really show any outward sign of what he was thinking or feeling. Lesley Warren looked cool and aloof. He felt above others because he wasn't having to suffer in the same way as they were.

Lesley Warren's biggest problem was that he didn't know how to process the emotions that others take for granted. It was inevitable that he would one day explode. Warren was charged by police over the rape threats to his classmate's sister. It also emerged that there had been other classmates threatened by Warren. It was clear Lesley Warren had been breaking the rules in all directions and behaving in a thoroughly antisocial way since the age of twelve. He even told psychologist Dave Evers that the girl he wrote the threatening letters to had been calling him up on the phone and harassing him. Evers was so convinced by Warren's account of what had happened that he recommended to Blue Ridge that authorities should determine whether or not the girl did in fact call him and say rude remarks about his parents.

But Evers did eventually concede: "My own feeling is that this is a creative figment of his imagination to justify his [Warren's] conduct." And he concluded: "I consider Lesley Warren a danger to himself and to others, as well as severely emotionally disturbed."

Lesley was just fourteen years and three months old at the time.

Other specialists who examined Warren noted that he was in many ways trying to seek punishment by his actions. One expert later explained, "He wanted punishment because he hoped that it might stop him doing even worse things." It was described as "punishment-seeking behavior." Others inside the Blue Ridge Health Center were not convinced that Lesley Warren felt so bad about his actions.

"I think that a lot of times Lesley did things to get away with them, and sometimes, especially when he was younger, he did things to get caught," said one expert who examined him at Blue Ridge.

But others still had faith in the quiet, polite youngster. "I think he had a lot of schizoid traits, and I think they're very descriptive of a lot of aspects of his personality. They're very evocative of a lot of the aspects of Lesley," one psychiatrist later recalled. "He deserved a chance in society."

The fact that Warren thrived on fear as his only emotion should have been a classic warning sign. Warren seemed to have completely missed out on joy, pleasure and anxiety. By this time, Lesley Warren was taking a wide range of medications, including two hundred milligrams of Synequon at night because he told doctors he was so depressed he couldn't sleep. It seemed a blatant contradiction in his character because in the daytime Warren was completely unaware of the damage he was causing to himself and others around him.

Just a few days after the Blue Ridge evaluations, Lesley Warren was placed in Broughton State Hospital and remained there for some months. Doctors felt they had no choice if they were to have any chance of helping Lesley Warren turn into a regular,

upstanding citizen. "At that time, he was a liability
to society, but we felt that with the right treatment
his life could be turned around," explained one psychiatric evaluator. Eventually, Broughton Park State
Hospital concluded that Warren had "serious im-
pulse-control deficiencies and inadequate rigid defenses and serious family dysfunction."

During his stay at the hospital, Warren, who was
being held in a controlled environment surrounded
by other people, still managed to cause chaos. His
behavior was described as "constantly disruptive."

"It was what you'd call antisocial behavior and
rule breaking and rule ignoring and that sort of
thing," one member of the hospital staff later recalled. Numerous mental-health experts examined
Warren at Broughton Park State Hospital. Social
worker Joan Hinshaw reported that Warren's natural father appeared to be extremely immature, unable to hold down a job and extremely jealous of
Lesley.

At Broughton Park State Hospital, Warren was
subjected to an MMPI test, which was supposed to
reveal his true psychological state. Warren tried to
trick the experts. He'd had enough of being tested
like a guinea pig and was bored of being in a mental
institution. He wanted to be free. Warren managed
to convince the MMPI testers that he was not suffering from any kind of psychosis. Psychologists later
admitted that the MMPI test results should have
been taken with a grain of salt. However, some of
Warren's problems did come to the surface and a
report compiled at the time refers to his immaturity,
naivety, self-centeredness, a complete lack of insight
into the world and elements of serious depression.

At Broughton Park State Hospital, Lesley Warren
was also given an achievement test to see if he was

performing at his school-grade level. The test involved reading, writing, arithmetic and other basic subjects. Warren did very poorly despite his high IQ test results. It was baffling to the testers because Warren had obvious intelligence, but just didn't seem to know how to use it effectively.

Lesley Warren refused to give clear, concise answers on some of the other tests and seemed to deliberately underperform on others. Warren clearly had a great deal of difficulty addressing, acknowledging and describing emotional events in his life. One female psychological evaluator later summed it up: "Lesley's poorly organized defenses helped us understand his behavior. He seemed to be able to control himself and to some extent his environment through passive defiance. However, as his anxiety increased, he had few other defensive resources. Lesley's honesty perplexed us about his behavior. The basic fear was one of rejection. He was not consciously aware of the dynamics underlying his behavior, and due to the hurting experiences, when he'd experienced emotions he made numerous attempts to avoid awareness of feelings."

The experts' recommendations were crystal clear: "Due to the nature and long-standing duration of Lesley's difficulties, therapy will, of necessity, be intensive and long term." Dr. Paul Kelly concluded that Warren was suffering from a dysthymic disorder—a long-standing, smoldering depression. It wasn't the sort of depression that comes and goes. It was ever-present. Dr. Kelly believed it had become a part of Lesley Warren's personality. He doubted if Warren realized it himself.

All the experts at Broughton agreed that Lesley Warren was on a classic one-way route to substance abuse. "The key is that if such people do not get proper treatment, then they will tend to gravitate toward substance abuse. They're not happy with life and [are] looking for something else or trying to treat themselves," said expert Dr. Bruce Welch. "Very often they'll go for alcohol or stimulants if they're not getting the right kind of medicine or right kind of treatment."

Yet, some doctors inside Broughton Park State Hospital believed that Warren's claim to be depressed at night was a breakthrough because it showed that he did have feelings after all. In the summer of 1982, Lesley Warren—already described by experts as a deeply disturbed fourteen-year-old loner—was released back into the care of his mother and her family. It was recommended that Warren move in with his grandparents and visit his mother and stepfather on weekends.

His grandfather gave him a run-down, cream-colored rust bucket Monte Carlo and it became his only lifeline. Lesley Warren was a good driver, even in his midteens. He'd often spend hours running errands for his relatives just because it gave him an excuse to cruise around Asheville admiring the pretty girls who seemed to be on every street corner.

It was around this time that at least two women in the Asheville area went missing. Whether Lesley Warren was connected with the disappearances will never be known. But in August 1982—a short time after his release from the hospital—Warren's behavior once again began deteriorating. He started disappearing from his grandparents' house for days on end. He hadn't even turned fifteen.

One night later that summer, Warren knocked on neighbor Betty Pressley's door; he was dressed only in shorts and a T-shirt, with a rifle under his arm. When Pressley answered, Warren claimed he had spotted a prowler on the grounds of his family's house.

Betty Pressley, thirty years old and just five feet tall, with brown, sun-streaked hair, later recalled: "He seemed very nervous and upset. Then my husband came to the door and Lesley said he had to go because he had to get back to work."

The Pressleys didn't think much about the incident until a few days later when Betty saw Lesley's grandmother at the grocery store and asked about the prowler. "She said there was no prowler and pointed out that Lesley was not working at the time," Betty Pressley later recalled.

By that summer of 1982, Lesley Warren had grown into a slim teenager of medium height with a mop of dark hair that tended to stick up and sometimes provoked cruel remarks from other kids. Warren attended the Enka Learning Center in Morganton, near Asheville. Teachers reported that he excelled in art and biology and his general behavior seemed to have drastically improved.

On September 15, 1982, Lesley Warren was transferred to the Enka High School. Experts assured school officials that the troubled teenager had completely recovered from his earlier problems. Enka High School and its recreation area were located just southwest of the picturesque Enka Lake, a couple of miles from Warren's home in Candler.

A few weeks after starting at Enka, on the day after his fifteenth birthday, Lesley Warren's mother found a marijuana pipe in his bedroom at home. When she confronted him with the discovery, he shrugged his shoulders and accepted full responsibility for the drugs. She later recalled that her son had readily, almost enthusiastically, admitted taking drugs.

Warren had been experimenting with drugs on a regular basis for at least one year. His mother soon learned to recognize the symptoms whenever Warren was under the influence. After just a few puffs on a cannabis joint, he would become even more introspective than he already was. "You just couldn't get any sense out of the boy," his mother later recalled.

In mid-September 1982, neighbor Betty Pressley discovered what Lesley Warren's true intentions had been when he'd called at her home earlier that summer. On this occasion, Warren turned up at the Pressley house wearing gym shorts and no shirt and said he'd locked himself out of his grandmother's home. Warren asked if he could wait at Betty's home until his family got back. Betty Pressley agreed and Warren sat down in the living room, where they chatted for a few minutes.

Warren asked his neighbor if she had a screwdriver, which he could use to get back into his grandparents' house. Pressley told him to go down and look in the basement. Warren soon found what he was looking for and left her house. A few minutes later, he returned, this time asking for a hammer. Once again Pressley sent him into the basement. A few minutes passed; then Warren hollered for Betty Pressley to come downstairs to help him. Seconds after getting down the stairs, Warren pulled a small revolver out of his pocket and pointed it at Betty's head. He told her to sit on the stone floor and then tied her up with a jump wire, leaving her hands in front of her.

Moments later, Pressley's cousin Sharon Carver walked into the house and appeared at the top of the basement steps. As she shouted for Pressley, Warren came into view. He aimed his revolver at Carver and pressed the trigger. She fell to the floor and tumbled down the stairs into the basement.

With Carver unconscious, Warren turned his attentions back to Betty Pressley and started dragging her up the basement stairs. He ordered her up the main stairway to a bedroom, where he pushed her onto a bed. The sheer terror on Betty Pressley's face did nothing to deter the teenage Warren. "His face showed no sign of emotion. It was weird. So cold," she later recalled.

With her hands tied up and Warren standing over her, Betty Pressley presumed the worst—her neighbor was about to rape and possibly even kill her. She shut her eyes just as Warren put the gun down on a bedside table and began moving toward her.

At that moment, Sharon Carver appeared in the bedroom doorway. Warren's shot had only grazed her. Warren turned to face her just as she smashed a fist into his face, preventing him from grabbing his revolver. Carver hit out so hard that Warren lost his balance and fell to the floor, sobbing. Carver quickly kicked the gun off the table and out of his reach.

Warren scrambled to the edge of the bed, still crying. Carver ordered him not to move while she removed the jump wire he'd used to tie up her cousin and then tied Warren up to make sure he could not escape. Then Carver called the Buncombe County sheriff and Lesley Warren was arrested for kidnapping.

Something bad was happening to him, but he did not have the education or the experience to know how to deal with it. Lesley Warren felt guilt-ridden by what he had done in one mad moment at his neighbor's house. He knew his lack of self-control might create even bigger problems in the future. But he did not know what to do or who to turn to.

Warren was immediately withdrawn from Enka High School, and on October 4, 1982, court-appointed doctors recommended he undergo intense and immediate psychotherapy treatment. Phyllis Warren never forgot how her son shook all the time following his arrest for the attempt to kidnap his neighbor.

Lesley Warren was refused bond and sent to Buncombe County Detention Center to be locked away until his trial. Warren, just fifteen years old, was extremely scared. But it wasn't the thought of a lengthy spell of incarceration that bothered him. He was more worried by the obviously uncontrollable nature of his behavior in relation to the Betty Pressley incident.

There was a time bomb inside him and it had started ticking. . . .

Three

Buncombe County Detention Center intern Louise Vaughn had the difficult task of checking on each of the juveniles who were being held in the lockup during the fall of 1982. One evening she walked into Lesley Warren's cell to find him hanging by the neck. She immediately called for help. Warren was resuscitated and regained consciousness.

Afterward, Lesley Warren was asked why he'd tried to kill himself. "I needed to die before I hurt someone real bad," he told one member of the detention center staff.

Little else is known about what happened that day, but Lesley Warren was undoubtedly fighting a battle with his inner demons, and his guilt about his criminal urges was sending him further and further into a dark, depressing abyss.

Warren was eventually given a court-ordered evaluation at the Dorothea Dix psychiatric hospital in Raleigh, the state capital. Counselors decided to send Lesley Warren back to Broughton Park State Hospital because they were concerned by his suicidal tendencies and remained convinced he had serious psychological problems. Afterward, he would be expected to serve time in a juvenile evaluation center.

When Phyllis Warren visited her son at Broughton just after he had been admitted, he told her he could not do any of the schoolwork being sent to him. He was "hanging in rags" at the time and virtually unable to speak properly. But within months, the staff at Broughton had convinced Warren he was more than capable of catching up with the eighth-grade work he had earlier failed. He also completed his ninth-grade workload.

Lesley Warren was quickly transferred to the juvenile evaluation center (JEC) in Swannanoa, near Asheville. Encouraged by his schoolwork at Broughton, he buckled down and managed to get his graduate equivalency diploma (GED). For the first and probably only time in his life, Lesley Warren bonded with an adult.

Twenty-nine-year-old JEC behavioral specialist Jayme Hurley worked daily inside Greenwood Cottage, the locked wing of a unit specializing in intensive supervision and counseling. Lesley Warren was one of at least ten troublesome students from around the state ordered to receive intense attention in custody at the unit.

JEC social worker Catherine Jenkins and head psychologist John Pavone conducted lengthy group counseling sessions with the locked unit's students over several years. Hurley, who often worked alongside Jenkins, was Lesley Warren's primary counselor, and she soon advocated that Warren be allowed to enter the JEC's regular program, which meant more freedom. But due to the serious nature of his previous offenses, Lesley Warren was only allowed to attend classes with the other, less serious offenders for a maximum of two hours a day.

The majority of JEC staff members considered Warren a serious threat to the safety of others.

Jenkins later recalled, "We were told that Lesley was not to be alone with any staff member, especially female staff members."

But Hurley believed this rule was unnecessary and she frequently told colleagues she trusted Warren and thought the male staff members did not like the teenager because he was so "obviously intelligent." Jenkins watched that interaction between Warren and Hurley on a daily basis. Eventually, Hurley got her way and Lesley Warren was allowed to go off campus with prerelease students.

Jenkins remembered Warren as an extremely quiet student at JEC. "He was a loner who rarely interacted with anyone his own age. He had an emotional 'flatness' that made me uneasy," she said. Jayme Hurley encouraged the awkward, shy Lesley Warren to confide in senior social workers, but Warren never really opened up to them properly. "Jayme was the only person he seemed to trust," recalled Jenkins.

On a number of occasions, other staff noticed how Lesley Warren would walk into Catherine Jenkins's office to speak to Hurley and they would then go out into the hall for a private conversation. "Jayme tried to encourage him to come in and talk in front of me. When he did, the subject was always very unconfidential—such as school. But it was Jayme who really showed Lesley respect and caring," Jenkins later recalled.

Hurley's patience and understanding were all the more remarkable because she had already spent many difficult years in the locked unit with juveniles, many of whom had been sentenced to long periods in custody. Hurley always made a special effort to keep in constant touch with all ten of the inhabitants of Greenwood Cottage.

"To many students, Jayme was the ultimate mother figure," recalled Jenkins. "She made a point of talking to them all about their past and what the future held for them." Hurley even taught the youths personal hygiene. She was not afraid to discipline them when it was needed, either.

"She worked with some of the most disturbed youths in the entire DYS system. And from time to time she would find a youth in IDP who she would 'take under her wing,'" recalled Jenkins. "There was a pattern to the kind of student she took extra time with—he typically would have a history of anger and aggressive behavior, he would be intelligent and he would like to read."

Jayme Hurley, an avid reader, encouraged the setting up of a library inside the locked unit. Her favorite novelist was Stephen King and she was very impressed when Lesley Warren said he had already read some of his books. In fact, King's novels had already had a deep, disturbing effect on the impressionable, troubled teenager.

In Hurley's mind, the fact that Lesley Warren read Stephen King made him an even more "special" student. One time she told Catherine Jenkins, "He'd already read Stephen King before he came here. Now that is impressive."

Jenkins later recalled, "[Jayme] was so excited that she had found a student who was intelligent enough to appreciate her favorite writer."

But the books of Stephen King were about to be blamed for an appalling tragedy at the JEC.

Jayme Hurley actively encouraged Lesley Warren and some of her other student inmates inside Greenwood Cottage to read Stephen King's horror

novel *The Shining*. It is the story of a writer who
moves his family to an isolated home in Colorado
and then gradually starts losing his sanity. His son
is the only other person who realizes what is happening. The son notices the phrase "Red Rum"
written on mirrors around the house. In the end,
"Red Rum" is revealed as M-U-R-D-E-R spelled back-
ward. Then the father tries to kill his wife and son
with an ax. The story of *The Shining* is still etched
in the minds of many of the staff at JEC to this day
because of a chilling incident that occurred some
months after Lesley Warren's incarceration.

Two of Warren's friends inside the cottage escaped from the JEC compound and broke into a
nearby house, where they stole guns and bomb-mak-
ing paraphernalia. Before leaving the property, they
daubed "Red Rum" on a mirror. Then the two teenagers hid out in a shed close to the JEC building in
Swannanoa. Within hours the property's owners—
an elderly couple—had stumbled upon the youths,
who then attacked the man with an ax. He died
from his appalling wounds several days later in the
hospital.

Social worker Catherine Jenkins later explained,
"Jayme had allowed those students to read *The Shining,* which was in the unit library. After the incident,
some other members of the staff implied that Jayme
was responsible to a degree."

Despite this chilling incident, Hurley continued
to advocate more freedom of choice for her students. She even pointed out that millions of people
had read Stephen King's novels without copying the
behavior of his characters. "Still, it was disturbing
to all of us, including Jayme," Jenkins later recalled.

Hurley continued to pour praise on her favorite
student, Lesley Warren, and acted out the role of

mother/big sister/mentor all rolled into one. There
were some occasions when her friend and coworker
Catherine Jenkins believed Hurley crossed the line
in her relationships with some of her students, including Warren. "Jayme sometimes lost her objec-
tivity with those students. Lesley was the last one
and I often talked to her about this," Jenkins later
explained. "She even acknowledged that it was
true."

But Hurley insisted to Jenkins: "I trust Lesley
more than a lot of people I know, including some
of the staff in this place." Another time Hurley told
Jenkins: "I trust Lesley with my life."

Jenkins stayed in touch with Hurley for many
years. She never forgot how Jayme would regularly
talk about Lesley Warren and how much she liked
him.

After being released from JEC in 1985, Lesley
Warren moved in with his uncle Carl Russell Warren, in Campobello, South Carolina, a two-hour
drive from Asheville and his dreaded family. Warren
told friends he believed he'd turn his life around if
he could stay away from Candler. Warren later recalled that his nephew was well behaved throughout
his stay and got on well with his own children and
treated him and his wife with the utmost respect.
"He seemed happy and content," Warren said.

Counselor Jayme Hurley's encouragement and
wise words also had a profound effect on Warren,
and he told family and friends he was determined
to stay out of trouble. In Campobello, part of Lesley
Warren's attempt at rehabilitation was to begin dating a pretty young blond schoolgirl named Tracey
Bradshaw. Warren even inquired about the possibility of joining the U.S. Army. He was pleasantly surprised to discover he was not obliged to declare any

of his problems with the police and incarceration because they had all occurred while he was a juvenile. It really seemed to Lesley Warren that fate was on his side and a new, exciting career in the U.S. Army beckoned. With a career plan in the pipeline, Lesley Warren, now eighteen, proposed to sixteen-year-old Tracey on the basis that he was about to enlist and he wanted her to be his wife and accompany him around the world.

Just before joining the army on January 28, 1986, Lesley Warren moved back into his mother's home in Candler. She'd insisted he spend his last few months of "freedom" back with his family. Warren hated staying there, but he tolerated it because he knew that it was only for a short period of time.

On April 10, 1986, Lesley Warren was told he would be sent to Fort Benning, Augusta, Georgia, to begin basic training within weeks. His mother believed her son was running away from something by joining the army, but she did not appreciate just how much Lesley Warren feared being sucked back into his old and dangerous habits. Warren believed that Tracey's presence in his life would help him quell the hatred and anger that sometimes made him feel like exploding in fury. Marrying seemed the best way to deal with those inner demons. Warren was so determined to enlist he didn't hesitate to lie on the most crucial part of his army questionnaire, the section concerning the subject of drugs.

"Have you ever used narcotics, LSD or other dangerous drugs?"

Warren ticked the "No" column.

"Have you ever been a supplier of narcotics, LSD or other dangerous drugs or marijuana?"

Warren once again ticked the "No" column.

"Has your use of drugs or alcoholic beverages

ever resulted in your loss of a job, arrest by police or treatment of alcoholism, or for drug abuse or suspension or expulsion from school?"

Warren once again ticked the "No" column.

But Lesley Warren showed a level of honesty when it came to the bottom line and he wrote in hand under a column headed "remarks": "Used marijuana once with a friend, and never again."

Lesley and Tracey married on May 9, 1986, in Campobello, South Carolina. He was already in the army and had just started basic training at Fort Benning as a radio operator in the range-control division. The couple both seemed young and shy to those who attended the wedding, but in Campobello a lot of young people married early because there wasn't a whole lot else to do.

The ceremony was well remembered by everyone who attended as being a very special day with Tracey in a long white wedding gown and her teenage husband dressed in full army uniform. However, the photos show a radiant Tracey with a glum groom, barely able to smile even as he is photographed holding Tracey's hand while they sign the register, sharing a plastic cup of champagne and even during their first lingering kiss as man and wife.

Tracey stayed at home in Campobello while her new husband completed his basic training at Fort Benning. At the end of 1986, Lesley Warren joined the Tenth Mountain Division, based at Fort Drum, in upstate New York.

In January 1987, the couple lived together on the base at Fort Drum. Within weeks they moved to an apartment block on Academy Street, in the nearby city of Watertown. They soon switched to another, better apartment in the same building.

Watertown (population 30,000) is best known for

its dairying and manufacturing, as well as its tourist business, with U.S. Interstate 81 carrying traffic up from the South. It had once been an important papermaking town, but for most of the century there had been little industry to keep its young people at home. On the shoreline of the nearby Black River, numerous abandoned mills stood derelict and shabby. Watertown had never truly recovered from the Great Depression of the 1930s. In some ways, it was a college town without the college.

Nearby Fort Drum, which had been a training area for the National Guard and the Army Reserve for most of this century, had just been rebuilt at a cost of many millions of dollars. Its army population had increased by about 35,000, including soldiers and their dependents, and provided a big financial boom to the area at that time.

During the Second World War, Fort Drum had played host to three U.S. Army divisions who served with distinction in Europe. But the arrival of the Tenth Mountain Division and the construction of world-class firing ranges and an upgraded maneuver area confirmed Fort Drum's reputation as one of the finest training installations in the country.

For Lesley Warren's young wife, Tracey, it was a difficult period of transition. The shy seventeen-year-old was just out of school and her husband had assured her they'd try for a family as soon as possible. Despite his own unhappy upbringing, Lesley Warren believed he could be a caring, loving parent.

On the same day Warren joined the army, a teenage Southerner named Mike Vineyard, who hailed from Kentucky, also signed up. Both youths were on the delayed entry program and they had initially encountered each other at basic and then at advanced training as infantrymen at Fort Benning. Both were awarded expert badges for rifle and hand grenade handling. They'd both been signed to A Company, First Battalion of the Twenty-second Infantry, at Fort Drum.

Their paths were about to cross. . . .

Four

Within weeks of moving to Watertown, Tracey Warren announced she was pregnant. In some ways, Lesley Warren was delighted, but there was a flip side: Tracey immediately lost her appetite for sex. That deeply frustrated Warren. Although he had hidden his urges from numerous psychiatric experts over the previous few years, all his problems since that attempt to kidnap his grandparents' neighbor were associated with his overactive sex drive. By marrying Tracey, he'd hoped his obsessive carnal curiosity might be quelled. Soon Tracey was slouching around the house in baggy pants and a T-shirt emblazoned with BABY ON BOARD across the front. The last thing she was interested in was sexual relations with her husband. As his wife's sex appeal plummeted, Warren knew that it would become more difficult to control his urges.

Tracey noticed that her husband had become resentful about her increased weight and the fact she was so excited by the impending birth of their child. It was around this time that Warren began withdrawing into his own private world of perverted fantasies. From the outside, he appeared completely normal; inside, his mind was a twisted twilight zone. His grasp on reality began to slip as his daydreams of domination and destruction became increasingly vivid. Soon the need to act out these demented fantasies would become overwhelming.

Lesley Warren began trawling for a catch outside his marriage. He sought women out as new sexual partners. He focused on certain locations and the types of women he felt most attracted to—many were similar in appearance to his wife, Tracey. It was almost as if he was trying to replace her as a sexual partner. Warren followed a number of women as they went about their daytime chores in shopping malls. Other times he cruised some of Watertown's most notorious lovers' lanes. A clock was ticking inside his brain and it was now only a matter of time before he went over the edge.

In May 1987, the story of the month was the AIDS epidemic sweeping the world. Lesley Warren had a blind hatred of homosexuals and insisted to his family and friends that AIDS was God's punishment. By the mid-1980s, one in thirty of all young and middle-aged men were estimated by medical experts to be already infected in the United States. That meant 1.5 million people had the disease and it was predicted that by 1991 AIDS would be second only to accidents as a cause of premature death among American males. Lesley Warren was stumped for an explanation as to why AIDS was also spreading steadily among heterosexuals.

Other nationwide news at the time included top Republican administration officials telling Congress that implementation of the U.S. plan to protect Kuwaiti oil tankers from Iranian attack would be delayed. It was clear that the introduction of a new policy would significantly expand U.S. military involvement in the Persian Gulf, especially in the wake of the Iraqi missile attack that killed thirty-seven sailors aboard the frigate USS *Stark,* in May 1987. A number of congressmen and analysts drew comparisons between the U.S. government's new Gulf policy and its commitment of marines to Beirut back in 1983.

At Fort Drum, many of Lesley Warren's fellow soldiers relished the prospect of going abroad to fight a war. Not many of them had much time for the shy, quietly spoken Southerner. "He didn't make friends real easily," remarked one soldier. "And he had a blank expression on his face much of the time. Made me think he was someone I wouldn't like to cross. Something dead in his eyes and he never laughed, never cried. It was like he didn't have any emotion inside him."

At the bottom of Lake Ontario, the Black River empties into a picturesque little port called Sackets Harbor, which is sheltered from the surges of the lake and the southwest winds that roll across the water and make it seem more like an ocean than a lake. The Oneida and Onondaga tribes of the Iroquois Nation knew the true value of this fertile land along the lake's shores. They hunted and fished in great numbers and so it was no surprise when the farmers of New England moved into the area after the American Revolution.

Land speculator Augustus Sacket purchased vast tracts and led the first influx of settlers to the region that surrounded the natural harbor on Black River Bay, on the edge of Lake Ontario. But it was the War of 1812 that put Sackets Harbor on the map after the U.S. Navy ship *Oneida* became the only vessel to oppose the British fleet stationed across the lake at Kingston, Ontario.

After the war, Sackets Harbor, with its commercial trade and shipbuilding, became the north country's most celebrated and prosperous village. And the building of a military post called Madison Barracks marked the beginning of a long and successful interaction between military service personnel and the village.

In 1977, Sackets Harbor was designated one of fourteen parks administered by the New York State Urban Cultural Park System. The New York State Seaway Trail, a 454-mile scenic tourism route from Lake Erie to the St. Lawrence River, passed through the village. For many, Sackets Harbor truly was a hidden treasure and it was a place Lesley Warren liked to prowl.

Fellow unit soldier Mike Vineyard was another shy Southerner with a young wife, but since the couple lived out in Sackets Harbor they didn't have much to do with the Warrens, apart from seeing them across a yard at the occasional cookout.

Vineyard later recalled: "He [Lesley Warren] didn't say much, but I sensed he was trouble, so we didn't mix." Just like Lesley and Tracey Warren, Mike and Patsy Vineyard had been thrown together as a couple back in their home state of Tennessee before Vineyard had enlisted. The Vineyards also both came from estranged families.

Patsy Diane Kiser Vineyard was a petite yet shapely 115-pound twenty-year-old brunette, standing five feet four inches, with hazel eyes. She turned heads wherever she went. Despite her young age, she had the air of someone who had seen a bit of life. Patsy

Vineyard's family had been so badly estranged at one stage during her childhood that she spent three of her high school years living with a family friend named Carlie A. Gentry.

At that time, Patsy attended the Horace Maynard High School in Maynardville, Tennessee, and then went to college at East Tennessee State in Johnson City. Patsy told friends she lived with the Gentrys because her natural family had been "stained by a divorce." It wasn't until both her parents had remarried that Patsy was reconciled with them.

Mike Vineyard had a similar background. He'd spent most of his later school years at Doyle High in Knoxville, Tennessee, with the Manis family, who were close friends of his estranged parents. Like Lesley Warren, he did not go to college. But, unlike his pretty young wife's, Mike Vineyard's family were never reconciled and whenever the couple went back South they stayed with Vineyard's "adopted" family, the Manises. Even the reception for the couple's wedding in October 1986 was held at the Manises' home in Knoxville.

"I know what makes them tick," Mary Manis later said of the Vineyards. All their family and friends prayed that Pasty and Mike Vineyard's marriage would be a long and happy one because they were "like two identical peas out of a troublesome pod."

One family friend later explained: "They had something special going because they both knew what it was like to see their [own] family ripped apart and they were determined to make sure the same thing did not happen to them."

The couple had moved to the Shipyard Apartments in Sackets Harbor, in February 1987, shortly after Mike Vineyard had been posted to Fort Drum. That week, Patsy, delighted by their new home, phoned her "adopted" mom, Carlie Gentry, and told her: "This is the happiest time of my life."

When Mother's Day, May 1987, came around, Patsy called her aunt Opal M. McCubbins in the Tennessee town of Seymour, near Knoxville, and told her she and Michael were planning to come home for Memorial Day. "She told me how they were fixing up the apartment, how happy she was, how she loved it, how pretty it was," McCubbins later recalled. "She sent some pictures down, said she went to the lake a lot. If she was unhappy, I would be the person she would tell."

On that same day, Patsy Vineyard also phoned her natural mother, Ora H. Kiser, in Knoxville, to see how she was. Mrs. Kiser later recalled that her daughter sounded happy and very settled in her new environment. John Caldwell, one of Michael Vineyard's oldest friends from Knoxville, was also at Fort Drum with him. He reckoned Patsy and Michael were "made for each other." Caldwell was engaged to be married and often went out with his fiancée and the Vineyards for dinner or a night at the movies.

Many neighbors in the Shipyard Apartments were intrigued by Patsy Vineyard's high-pitched Tennessee accent, and most could tell when she was at home because she noisily vacuumed the apartment every single day without fail. She was obsessive about keeping the place spotlessly clean. Shipyard Apartments landlady Phyllis M. Bezio said that if Patsy had "one little hair out of line, she wouldn't come out of her apartment."

Soon after arriving in Sackets Harbor, Patsy and Mike Vineyard became regular visitors at the local Presbyterian church. Congregation members and Shipyard residents Robert and Lydia Shockley saw

the Vineyards up to four or five times a week in the
months following their arrival in the area.

In early May 1987, Patsy Vineyard told Lydia
Shockley that since her husband was about to go
out in the field, she was thinking about traveling
home to Tennessee. "Mike will never know I've
gone," Patsy told Lydia, who got the distinct impression that her friend was feeling homesick.

Another Shipyard Apartments resident who knew
Patsy Vineyard reasonably well was an older lady
named Irene Busler. She taught Patsy how to bake
cakes and decorate them. Irene was like a mother
figure to young Patsy, who made a point of telling
her older friend whenever she was going anywhere.
She also told Busler she was afraid of the dark and
hated being alone when Mike was away in the field.
Patsy mentioned to Busler she might be pregnant
but said that she didn't feel "mentally ready" to
have kids. Patsy also told her she had a yeast infection. Irene Busler concluded that Patsy Vineyard was
the type of girl who loved to cook and clean her
home for her beloved husband, Michael.

A few days after Mother's Day, 1987, Patsy Vineyard visited Watertown to get her New York State
driver's license from the DMV. While lining up, a
young soldier started talking to her. He mentioned
he was "looking for a place to stay." Patsy Vineyard
told him that the Shipyard Apartments, where she
lived with her husband, might have some vacancies
and gave him her husband's name and phone number. He never got around to mentioning his own
name.

The following afternoon, that same soldier telephoned Patsy Vineyard while she was alone in her
apartment. He asked if he could come and take a
look at the Vineyards' place, for he had an interest

in renting a similar apartment on the same block.
Patsy Vineyard remained calm and polite but insisted the young soldier should call back when her
husband got home later that day. Patsy told her husband, Mike, about the stranger when he got back
from Fort Drum. Neither of them gave it much
thought when the young soldier didn't bother calling that evening.

A couple of days later, on May 12, Mike Vineyard
was sent on "Operation Phoenix," a ten-day strike
exercise in which more than two-thirds of his First
Battalion, Twenty-second Infantry, Tenth Mountain
Division, were to take part. Lesley Warren and his
friend Tom Walker were among the soldiers not involved in the exercise. Mike Vineyard's departure
left Patsy feeling lonely and just a little scared to be
on her own.

Angie Gautreaux, who lived above the Vineyards
and was married to Fort Benning platoon leader
Todd J. Gautreaux, described Patsy as "a nice lady"
who kept to herself and baked cookies for children.
Angie saw Patsy tanning herself on Wednesday, May
13, and the two talked about how good her tan was
and how nice her hair was. Patsy was also seen sunbathing by a couple of other neighbors at the Shipyard Apartments.

A few days after her husband went on Operation
Phoenix, Patsy Vineyard engaged neighbor and fellow churchgoer Robert Shockley in some small talk
while he was out front of the Shipyard complex trying to help Tom Walker fix his 1976 Chevy Caprice.
Patsy asked Shockley if he would like a cup of tea,
which he turned down.

The following day, Patsy Vineyard made one of
her regular five-minute walks to the nearby Presbyterian church. At that time, another of the Vine-

yards' neighbors noticed a man in his early twenties apparently watching Patsy from behind some bushes. The man seemed to be sweating profusely and the neighbor later recalled that it looked as if he was high on drugs. But she could not give a clear description of the man in the bushes.

During that same period, another of Patsy Vineyard's friends and neighbors noticed Patsy sunbathing in a two-piece swimsuit outside her apartment. Denise Walker, whose husband, Tom, was Lesley Warren's new friend from the same unit at Fort Drum, reckoned Patsy liked showing off her body, although Patsy's friends and relatives later refuted those claims.

One time Patsy mentioned to neighbor Irene Busler that she didn't really get on so well with neighbor Denise Walker because she thought Denise's husband, Tom, twenty-four, had a slight crush on her.

Patsy Vineyard had baby-sat for the Walkers' eight-month-old child. Tom Walker reckoned Patsy adored children and he and his wife wondered if she might have been pregnant in May 1987. Patsy had earlier admitted to the Walkers she wanted "at least two or three kids." Denise and Patsy had hung out a lot together in the spring of 1987, going on long walks. Earlier in the year, Tom Walker and Mike Vineyard had regularly driven to Fort Drum together.

By May 1987, Tom Walker was hanging out "a lot" with his new army buddy Lesley Warren. Walker even went out of his way to pick up Warren from his Watertown apartment en route to the army base each morning.

One night Patsy Vineyard told her husband that she thought Tom Walker was a creep because she

was certain she'd caught him spying on her while
she was sunbathing in front of the apartment block.
"Their curtains pulled back suddenly and I'm sure
he was up there watching me," she said.

During one lunchtime, Warren and Walker
walked out into the fields behind the Shipyard
Apartments to do some target practice with their
private collection of handguns. They returned about
an hour later and startled Patsy Vineyard sunbathing
in her swimsuit out in front of the apartments. She
was so upset by their presence she made a point of
telling a neighbor about the incident later that same
day. But she never elaborated on what had specifically happened. Minutes after the meeting with
Patsy Vineyard, Warren and Walker beat a hasty retreat to Walker's broken-down car, which Warren
was trying to help fix. Only later did Walker tell his
wife about the incident.

On May 15, Lesley Warren once again visited the
Shipyard Apartments with his friend Tom Walker.
This time Walker needed him to help fix a leaking
pipe in his Caprice. Warren repaired it within forty
minutes, but the car still didn't sound right, so
Walker went back to his apartment. Just before
nightfall, Warren said his good-byes and appeared
to head off back to his home in Watertown, according to Walker's later testimony.

Instead, Warren headed toward Patsy Vineyard's
apartment. He knocked on the door and is believed
to have told a startled Pasty Vineyard that her husband had been hurt in an accident while out on
Operation Phoenix. When she realized her car was
out of action, she had no choice but to go with
Warren to Fort Drum.

Not long afterward, Denise Walker thought she
heard a scream out in the parking lot of the Ship-

yard Apartments. She ran out into the warm night air; there was no sign of anyone, so she went back into her apartment. She didn't notice Patsy Vineyard's car parked nearby with a flat tire.

Less than an hour later, Lesley Warren waded into the shallow water near Sackets Harbor and dropped Patsy Vineyard's strangled, sexually assaulted corpse into the Black River. Warren even remembered to throw Patsy Vineyard's jeans into the river after he'd dropped her body into the water.

Warren later explained: "It was nighttime. There were no people around at the time. I don't think it was real secluded. It was a pretty popular area 'cause of fishing and swimming, and . . . there was some lighting out there. Some streetlights came on when it got dark. We'd just been down by the lake, a kind of sandy, grassy area. It was down below some old army barracks. It was a good fishing hole. A lot of people swam there."

Lesley Warren felt little remorse or regret about murdering Patsy Vineyard. His emotional void, which had been getting wider and wider since the day his father burned down the family home, was beyond repair. He later claimed he'd met and seduced Patsy Vineyard. He didn't want to admit he'd tricked her. Warren claimed he and Patsy Vineyard were both drunk when he killed her. "I'd been drinking, we both had, but not . . ." He never properly expanded on his claims. But as one investigator later said, "We knew his story was partially bullshit." Patsy Vineyard was not even a drinker and she would not have gone out at night without her husband.

At 7:00 P.M. on May 19, Mike Vineyard arrived back home from the ten-day training exercise. His wife was nowhere to be found. At 9:41 P.M., Vineyard called the New York State Police (NYSP) to report his wife, Patsy, missing. Vineyard told investigators there was no sign of a struggle. "She is an extremely tidy person," he said. "I don't understand what's happened to her."

He also told officers he was baffled as to why the bed was unmade and dirty dishes had been left in a drainer. "She always cleans up as she goes along." Some of the mail had not been opened and a number of overdue bills were in envelopes with checks made out but they hadn't been posted. It just didn't add up. Vineyard frantically called his wife's relatives in Tennessee just in case she had traveled down South, but that drew a blank.

Mike Vineyard concluded his wife must have left the Shipyard Apartments voluntarily. Vineyard based this assumption on the fact his wife did not normally wear her wedding ring around the house and— since he could not find the ring—he believed she'd taken the time to put it on before leaving the home.

The Vineyard investigation was headed up by the New York State Police, who had jurisdiction over the Sackets Harbor area. The military police at Fort Drum helped supply records, but they could not become directly involved. Within the base, they and the NYSP had joint jurisdiction. Patsy Vineyard had civilian status and she had disappeared off base.

Investigator Richard H. "Dick" Ladue of the NYSP, a former lifeguard on the lakes, had lived and worked in the Watertown area for more than fifteen years. In 1984, Ladue hung up his trooper's hat to go for promotion into the Criminal Investigations Division (CID) of the NYSP. Ladue was enjoying a quiet evening at home with his wife and kids in their home about twenty minutes from Sackets Harbor when he got a call from the sergeant at the NYSP Watertown substation. "Gotta complaint of a missing female—a soldier's wife—husband's just returned from the field, where he's been out on maneuvers," came the message.

As Ladue later recalled: "She'd just disappeared into thin air." Ladue had a gut feeling about the case from the start. "I decided that since it was a missing woman and it appeared to be a little suspicious, I should get down to the scene."

Ladue was especially concerned because "the soldier had come out of the field and everything was in its place in the residence. There was nothing amiss and yet his wife was not there. No clothing was missing or anything like that, so that made it even more suspicious. If a female takes off, she will at least take a bag and other items, but nothing like that was missing from the apartment."

As Ladue drove to Sackets Harbor, he wondered if the couple had been experiencing marital problems. Maybe when he'd gone out to the field, she got lonely and wanted companionship or whatever, he thought.

Investigator Ladue found Mike Vineyard in a calm but very concerned state, and he immediately took down the numbers of all Patsy's relatives and friends whom she might have gone to visit. The following morning Ladue and three other NYSP officers interviewed neighbors in the Shipyard Apartments to discover when she was last seen.

Ladue later recalled: "Nothing unusual came to light either from the neighbors or the family. That bothered me." By the following lunchtime, Ladue was so baffled by Patsy Vineyard's apparent disappearance that he launched an extensive search of the local woods and fields around the Shipyard

Apartments. The military police at Fort Drum even sent over dozens of volunteers to help with the search. The NYSP's canine Skete was called in, but the dog could find no trace of the missing woman. Police still hadn't pinpointed the exact time Patsy Vineyard left her home at the Shipyard Apartments.

Her disappearance could only be classified as a missing person case. "If she'd been said to be mental or suicidal, then obviously this would have taken on a different light, but we found nothing," Dick Ladue later explained. At first, suspicion fell on her husband Mike Vineyard, but because he was out in the field at the time and "certain other evidence," Vineyard was quickly eliminated as a suspect.

Investigator Ladue remained baffled by the case. Detectives were especially puzzled that Patsy had left her side of the bed swept back. "You could tell that only one person had been sleeping in her bed, but her bikini bathing suit was found on the floor, which was completely unlike her." All the Vineyards' bills were neatly placed in stampless envelopes all made out ready to be paid. "We could work out within a day or two from the dates on those checks when she left the house," recalled Ladue.

Investigators soon assumed that someone had gone to the apartment, "told her that something had happened to her husband and the car had a flat, and that's how he got her out of the house." Despite no clear indications of foul play, Patsy Vineyard's disappearance was considered highly suspicious because "she had no real reason to be gone."

Two days after Mike Vineyard reported his wife's disappearance, police confirmed from a neighbor that Patsy Vineyard was seen on the apartment complex four days after her husband had left on his military exercise. Down in her home state of Tennessee, Patsy Vineyard's family and friends continued to report no sightings of her. Investigators knew Patsy Vineyard had taken her purse with her when she left the house, but she had left most of her clothing behind as well as the family car.

Mike Vineyard believed a false report of injury to him must have prompted her to leave in a hurry. That would explain the state of the house. Vineyard reiterated to police that his wife was not on medication and had not been ill when he'd last seen her as he left for the field on May 12. The most ominous sign to Mike Vineyard was that his wife had apparently left the house without even taking her makeup bag with her.

"That's the key to her absence," her "adopted mom" Mrs. Manis told police a couple of days after Patsy's disappearance. "Patsy would not go anywhere without makeup; even when she came downstairs in the morning, she was made up. I know she would not, even if they had a big fight, she would never leave him and let him worry. Somehow, someway, someone has gotten hold of her." Mrs. Manis was convinced that Patsy and Michael were very much in love. She even said of Michael Vineyard: "I could not love him more if he were my own."

Neighbors of the couple at the Shipyard Apartments also recalled to investigators that the Vineyards had seemed a happy couple who enjoyed the perfect marriage. "They looked so in love. They kept to themselves, but they still managed to be real friendly," one resident told investigators.

Some neighbors told investigators that Patsy Vineyard spent hours tanning herself out in front of the apartment, usually bringing a blanket, a pillow and a radio. But there was no suggestion she used her curvaceous body to flirt with the complex's male residents.

"She was a very sweet Southern belle, nothing more, nothing less," Shipyard landlady Phyllis M. Bezio told police. She insisted Patsy could only have been kidnapped from the apartment complex at night because there were usually so many people in and around the building they would have seen something in the daylight.

Michael Vineyard's friend and fellow Shipyard resident John Caldwell echoed the feelings of many when he said, "We're thinking it's someone who knew all of us: Pat, Vineyard and myself."

Patsy Vineyard's apparent abduction from the Shipyard Apartments had a worrying effect on the other residents. With a top rent of $450, the complex had been built in 1986 and almost half of the apartments were occupied by military families. But following Patsy's disappearance, children were not allowed to play outside.

Resident Karen L. Stewart told reporters: "I've got a four-year-old and I don't even let him go very far because something may happen to him. What's happened makes you wonder if you can go outside at night. It really makes you wonder, being in a small village, if it's safe for anyone. What if the maniac was out taking someone's kid?"

One of the Vineyards' closest neighbors, Todd J. Gautreaux, said he and his wife "felt very unsafe" following Patsy Vineyards' disappearance. "At night when I come home, my wife checks through the peephole. She's very cautious." Louisiana native Gautreaux was even having second thoughts about staying in the area. "If there is an opportunity to move to the base, I will," he said.

Children on the complex were being more closely

supervised and whenever a soldier resident went out in the field—as more than 60 percent did—the wives stayed in constant touch with each other. Even a long overdue Neighborhood Watch was initiated.

Meanwhile, New York State Police stepped up their investigation, now even more convinced Patsy Vineyard had come to harm. Watertown NYSP substation's senior investigator Bob Cooke—a twenty-year vet of the force—took over the day-to-day running of the investigation.

Cooke, who was born in Miami Beach, Florida, had spent his own childhood years as a self-confessed "army brat" following his father to Germany, Okinawa and Camp (now Fort) Drum. He attended Watertown High School, but had graduated from the American High School in Munich, Germany. Then he'd signed up for a tour of duty in Vietnam, courtesy of the U.S. Marine Corps. On May 6, 1968, he became a state trooper and spent his first three years on road patrol.

Cooke saw undercover police work as his route into the Bureau of Criminal Investigation. One tricky assignment involved him frequenting the campuses of Syracuse University and Oswego State University College. Cooke found himself buying heroin and even had to "give the impression I was snorting, but I wasn't."

His next undercover assignment brought him statewide publicity as he exposed "psychological and physical abuse" by employees against forty handicapped patients at a special state-run school. Indictments eventually prompted the arrest of twenty-four employees. Other cases included narrowly missing death in an exchange of gunfire with some notorious local criminals and taking the deathbed statement of a retired state police investigator.

But nothing really prepared Bob Cooke for the long hours of footwork and false hope that centered around the Patsy Vineyard case. Cooke had already concluded that murders were becoming increasingly difficult to solve because more and more of them were being committed by complete strangers. As the investigator later explained, "People don't realize how much a murder investigation takes out of you. Your eating habits are terrible, and you're not getting much sleep. It's draining."

Bob Cooke and his team of investigators at the NYSP wondered if Patsy Vineyard's disappearance was linked to two other unsolved homicides that had occurred in the area. They still sought the slayer of Irene J. Izak, a young Pennsylvania student, murdered on Interstate 81 in 1968, and the killer of Vivien R. Lazore, a Hogansville woman, who torched her house to cover up the murder in 1983. There was a genuine fear that perhaps some sort of serial killer was involved in all three homicides. And if that was the case, then the murderer could have killed other women as well.

On May 23, 1987, Denise Walker told investigators Patsy had said she'd wanted an abortion, but then she had her period and realized it was all a false alarm. Walker also alleged to investigators that Patsy "liked to show herself off" while sunbathing. Denise Walker also insisted that Patsy had been "having sexual problems."

Tom Walker described Patsy as an outgoing type of person who liked to cook. He claimed she was a regular visitor to the Walkers' apartment and that the two couples would sometimes go to the local mall or the movies together. Walker told investigators that Patsy sometimes got depressed when Mike was out in the field and she regularly mentioned this to his wife, Denise.

However, Tom Walker had already slid into the frame as a possible suspect in the Vineyard case. Investigators had already established that Walker and his friend Lesley Warren were working twelve-hour shifts as part of their range-control assignment, so they were not out in the field on Operation Phoenix.

The following day, May 24, Mike Vineyard went public with his views about the disappearance of his pretty young wife. "The police won't say it, but I'm going to say it. Yes, my wife's been kidnapped. Period," Vineyard told local reporters. He was determined to expose his views to the local media. He was particularly baffled by the pile of checks, ready to mail, dated May 13, that for some inexplicable reason had not been sent. "I know my wife pretty good and it don't make sense," he told one local newspaper. "She wouldn't go to bed if there were any dirty dishes. That's the way she is. Nothing makes sense from the get go."

His outburst infuriated the police, who didn't feel they had sufficient evidence for such a conclusion. It damaged the relationship between Vineyard and investigators, refueling the theory that perhaps he *did* have something to do with his wife's disappearance.

The NYSP continued to insist publicly they were dealing with nothing more than a missing person case. As one investigator later explained: "We didn't want the killer thinking we were hunting him down. We wanted him to relax and then he might go and make a mistake."

Meanwhile, hospitals in the region had been alerted in case someone matching Patsy Vineyard's appearance was admitted, but there was no response to their appeal.

Senior Investigator Bob Cooke of the NYSP and colleague Wayne Corsa traveled down to Tennessee to check out the background of both Patsy and her husband, Mike. They soon discovered that Patsy's family "were so far out in the mountains that the local cops wouldn't show us the way out there because it was a big moonshine area, and all that shit," Cooke later explained.

During their inquiries, the NYSP detectives established that during her midteens Patsy Vineyard had been involved with a Tennessee mobster who'd become her sugar daddy. "This thing was getting more and more bizarre," Bob Cooke recalled.

Cooke's take on Patsy Vineyard was as follows: "She came from a very poor background but dressed to kill." The investigators were told that her so-called sugar daddy had been jailed for having underage sex with her. The investigators never fully established if Vineyard himself knew about his wife's relationship with the mobster.

Investigator Bob Cooke began wondering if Patsy Vineyard's disappearance was in some way connected to her former friendship. However, Cooke and Corsa found nothing concrete to back up that theory. The two NYSP investigators did manage to locate the store in Tennessee where Mike Vineyard had bought his wife two rings. Back in New York State, investigators established that Patsy had called a salesman who sold them their car to say there was something wrong with it on a number of occasions. She left the salesman in no doubt she was coming on to him.

Patsy Vineyard's disappearance was heavily publicized in the local newspapers and some hopeful leads came in to the NYSP's Watertown substation. A missing purse was found four miles out of Sackets Harbor on a back road, but it turned out not to belong to the young army wife. Other leads included callers reporting they had seen someone matching Patsy Vineyard's description. As Investigator Richard Ladue later admitted, "There were a lot of red herring leads that turned out to mean nothing."

In late May, a decomposed corpse was discovered in remote woods near the town of Malone, more than 100 miles northeast of Watertown. The death was described by NYSP as "suspicious" and the remains were taken to the Alice Hyde Hospital in Malone for an autopsy. Franklin County coroner Lawrence Spaulding told local newsmen that no identifying features, such as clothes, a wallet or a purse, were found with the corpse. Spaulding blamed a recent heat wave and excessive numbers of maggots for the extreme decomposition of the body.

Over in Watertown, Bob Cooke and Dick Ladue were wondering if perhaps it could be the remains of Patsy Vineyard. A few hours later, they were told it definitely was not their missing woman. The search would continue.

On June 3, a chilling incident occurred; many believe it involved Lesley Warren. The twenty-year-old wife of another Fort Drum soldier, who lived in a house on the east side of Watertown, received the first of four calls from a man at 10:30 A.M. The caller said her husband had been injured during training at Fort Drum. The caller then said he would come and get her and take her to the post.

The woman wisely declined the offer and instead telephoned her husband's unit, where she was reas-

sured nothing had happened. The same man called
back three more times. Some hours later, a man
wearing military duty apparel arrived at her front
door. She refused to open the door and the stranger
departed.

When the incident was reported to New York
State Police, investigators immediately wondered if
the same trick had been used to lure Patsy Vineyard
to her death. Captain Joseph F. Loszynski, Bureau
of Criminal Investigation at Oneida, New York, told
newsmen: "This is an avenue we have pursued. It is
a remote possibility. There is a lot of mystique in
the Vineyard case which has not exactly helped us,"
admitted Captain Loszynski.

Soon after Patsy Vineyard's disappearance, Lesley
Warren sank into a binge of drinking and drugging,
trying to dull his sense of guilt, emptiness and despair. But he knew it would only be a matter of time
before those inner compulsions rose to the surface
again. Like an addict who can't stop getting high—
even though he knows he will eventually suffer the
inevitable crash—Lesley Warren would soon be on
the prowl for his next "fix."

At the beginning of June, police, firemen and res-
cue-squad personnel and military volunteers once
again combed the fields around the Vineyards'
apartment. Up in the skies, state police conducted
an aerial search by helicopter. A family friend told
the local newspaper in Watertown that Patsy Vineyard was "a very dedicated wife, one of those old-
fashioned girls that likes to dote on her husband.
There is no reason to believe she left voluntarily."

Almost three weeks after Patsy Vineyard's disappearance, investigators were no closer to knowing

what had happened to her. Investigator Dick Ladue even admitted to newsmen: "There is not enough information available to allow us to make any assumption. We have tried to cover all the far-fetched possibilities, and have come up with nothing."

State police prepared a circular containing Patsy Vineyard's photograph, description and possible clothing. It was dispatched throughout New York, to Ontario Provincial Police and to all neighboring states. Investigators had concluded that when she disappeared she was wearing faded blue jeans, a blue blouse with a large round collar, a red bow tie and a dark blue V-necked pullover sweater. She had taken her checkbook and all her jewelry. Investigators also revealed for the first time that the lights of the locked apartment had been left on, indicating she had departed during the evening and intended to return. Patsy Vineyard, said investigators, was an immaculately turned-out Southern girl with an accent to match who had apparently disappeared into thin air.

Five

Black River Bay, Storrs Point, Hounsfield
June 5, 1987

A brisk west wind was blowing and waves were flowing from the direction of the distant flickering lights of Sackets Harbor. Brian Chopskie's tiny cottage was just off a dirt road alongside the shallow waters of Lake Ontario, a strip they call the Black River Bay, which is filled with bluffs and swamps.

At 9:30 P.M., Chopskie, from Syracuse, his father and two other friends decided to get some wood for the log-burning fire in his cottage, located just 300 yards from the lakeshore road. Stumbling through the low-lying trees overhanging the shoreline, Brian Chopskie caught sight of the silhouette of something big and bulky lying washed up on the narrow beach called Hess Shore. As he approached, a swarm of flies hovered above what was clearly the remains of a human being washed up by the strong currents from the direction of Sackets Harbor.

Just a few miles away, Investigator Dick Ladue was at a relative's house enjoying an evening barbecue. At 10:00 P.M., the sergeant at the NYSP Watertown station called to say a body had been found on the shoreline near Sackets Harbor. Ladue immediately made his apologies and headed directly to the crime scene.

An NYSP identification team were already inspecting and photographing the remains and surrounding area when Ladue arrived on the scene. He was soon joined by Senior Investigator Bob Cooke, Investigator William Elliott and Lieutenant Peter Burns along with numerous uniformed NYSP troopers.

Dr. Virgilio Alon, Jefferson County medical examiner, arrived shortly before the body was removed just after midnight by a Black River Valley invalid coach to be transported to the ME's lab in Syracuse as no coroner's van was available. A few minutes later, Trooper Thomas G. Flynn told a crowd of gathered newsmen: "We have a body. It's going to be a long night."

There were no immediate indications how the victim had died, but Dr. Alon was confident he would soon establish the facts. He'd taught students at the state police academy and had also worked in Miami where he'd had extensive experience of deaths in water. Dr. Alon had already instructed his staff in Syracuse to be on standby for the arrival of the body.

As Dick Ladue later explained, "At that time we still didn't know if it was a suicide, an accident or a homicide, so we had a completely open mind. Officially, we couldn't do anything until she was positively identified." But he and the other investigators were certain they'd recovered the remains of Patsy Vineyard. A few hours later, troopers visited Private Michael Vineyard's home at the Shipyard Apartments to ask him to come and identify her.

Meanwhile, a check of dental records was ordered by the medical examiner, who feared that the body was so badly decomposed it might be unrecogniz-

able. It was then decided that Mike Vineyard should
not have to face the trauma of actually viewing his
wife's remains. Investigators told him what clothes
were on the body and he immediately confirmed
they belonged to his wife, Patsy Vineyard.

On the day after the body was removed from the
lake shoreline, Lieutenant Peter Burns, NYSP zone
commander, refused to confirm the identity to local
newsmen and insisted: "We treat any body we find
as a crime scene."

Investigators did not want Patsy's killer to hear
about the discovery in case they uncovered vital
clues near the location where her body had been
found. In fact, for forty-eight hours state divers from
Watertown, North Syracuse and Pulaski spent all of
the daylight hours in shifts scouring the waters just
off the shoreline of Black River Bay.

The day after the discovery of the body, District
Attorney Gary W. Miles of Jefferson County told
newsmen he hoped the autopsy would "answer
some questions about the circumstances." He said:
"We don't have any answers yet. We haven't nar-
rowed our options at all. We've got a situation here,
like anything else, if somebody comes forward and
said they did this we don't want it to be details they
read in the paper."

An initial autopsy on Patsy Vineyard was carried
out by Dr. Alon and Dr. Erik Mitchell, the Onondaga
County medical examiner. They concluded that she
had died as a result of manual strangulation. But
both admitted there was no actual physical evidence
to support their prognosis. Unable to scientifically
prove the specific cause of death, investigators
found themselves under intense pressure to come
up with some clues as to how she died.

Patsy Vineyard's death was initially described as

"suspicious," a routine precaution until something concrete came up. But all the officers involved and the ME's staff had no doubt Patsy Vineyard had been murdered. Officially, however, her death could not actually be classified as a homicide.

Back at Sackets Harbor and the lake shoreline, a state police helicopter scoured the ground and water below for clues. Down below, uniformed troopers and detectives searched the land near where the body was found. These search operations continued for more than a week after the discovery of the badly decomposed body.

NYSP investigators from the Watertown substation advised Mike Vineyard not to answer any further questions from the media, as this was simply fueling the confused reports emerging about his wife's death. Vineyard remained convinced his wife had been kidnapped when she originally disappeared. What probably happened, Michael Vineyard once again told all who would listen, was that while he was on Operation Phoenix, someone in uniform came to the door and told Patsy he'd been injured and that she had to sign some papers or something. "Then they took her against her will. That's what I reckon," Vineyard said to one neighbor at the Ship-yard Apartments.

Mike Vineyard told investigators that everyone knew his battalion was on an exercise because there had been a write-up in the *Fort Drum Sentinel,* the on-base newspaper. This made it well known locally that some of the soldiers were away from home. But Vineyard was incorrect about the newspaper story. As *Sentinel* editor Michael E. Cast later explained, "Standard operating procedure, to use army termi-nology, is to wait until the operation is over with.

This was precisely because the army wanted to avoid the sort of scenario Vineyard had been suggesting."

Vineyard's insistence on airing these theories in public once again irritated investigators, who were starting to repeg him as a possible suspect. They felt he was throwing up red herrings and that might mean he had something to hide. Many of the Vineyards' neighbors found it hard to accept the young private's theories about his wife's fate. "There are too many nosy people around here," said the Shipyard landlady. "We look at all strange cars. Nothin' gets past us. I don't believe she was kidnapped."

Then Mike Vineyard remembered the strange incident that had occurred a few days before he went away on the Operation Phoenix exercise. Vineyard told detectives how his wife went to get her New York State driver's license and a young soldier approached her "looking for a place to stay." Vineyard recalled that his wife said she had told the soldier the Shipyard Apartments might have some vacancies and gave him her husband's name.

Vineyard said the soldier phoned one time when Patsy Vineyard was alone and asked if he could come out and take a look at the Vineyards' apartment. She told him to call back when her husband was at home. "He never came out, and I haven't heard from him or nothing," Vineyard told investigators. They concluded that this soldier was probably the man responsible for Patsy Vineyard's death. Either that or her husband had conjured up a story to take the scent away from his own involvement.

On June 9, detectives went to the CID office at Fort Drum to reinterview Mike and Patsy Vineyard's neighbor Tom Walker. Police still had some reservations about Walker, especially since they'd discovered he'd once been arrested for grand larceny and

burglary of a residence in which he stole $10,000
in cash and checks. He'd served probation and community service for his convictions, and while he
talked freely about those problems, detectives still
wondered about his true role in Patsy Vineyard's disappearance. Walker had not been on the Operation
Phoenix field trip with Mike Vineyard.

Tom Walker told investigators he and Lesley Warren had become close friends over the previous few
months and Walker said he'd even occasionally allowed Warren to stay over at his home on the Shipyard Apartments complex.

Denise Walker told investigators Patsy Vineyard
did not like the girlfriend of another army friend
of the couple's from down South. She said Patsy
Vineyard was jealous of this other woman. The Walkers also insisted they had regularly seen another soldier's car parked outside the Vineyards' apartment
when Mike Vineyard was away in the field. "Usually
it was there in the evening time from about six-thirty
P.M.," Denise Walker informed detectives. "But
sometimes we noticed it still there the next day."

Investigators didn't really know what to make of
Tom and Denise Walker. There was something
about them that just didn't add up. But when the
Walkers were asked if they'd take a police polygraph,
they both instantly agreed. "It was hardly the behavior of people involved in a serious crime," one detective later recalled. But investigators held back
from carrying out polygraphs until they had proved
there were inaccuracies in the Walkers' statement.

A few days after Patsy Vineyard's body was discovered, Lesley Warren phoned his wife, Tracey, from
Fort Drum and asked her to tape the local 6:00 P.M.

news on Channel 7. Later that same night Warren
arrived home at their Watertown apartment on
Academy Street and specifically asked Tracey what
had been on the news about the missing soldier's
wife from Sackets Harbor.

Warren then sat down and avidly watched the
tape of the local TV news. Afterward Warren asked
his wife to make sure she taped the following couple
of days of news broadcasts. On each of those local
news programs, there was an item about the Patsy
Vineyard case, which had become a popular talking
point among soldiers and their families. Tracey later
said she thought nothing of her husband's request
and insisted she paid little attention to the local TV
news bulletins.

Lesley Warren gave Tracey a seven-diamond cluster ring he said he'd bought off a man on the street
in Watertown the previous day. Then Warren and
his wife purchased an orange two-door Mercury Capri through an advertisement in a local newspaper.
A couple of hours after driving the car home to
their apartment, Lesley Warren gave his wife another ring, which he said he'd found while cleaning
out the trunk of the car. It was a fourteen-karat yellow gold band with a diamond sapphire pocket containing approximately four diamonds and seven
sapphires. It had a retail value of approximately
$300. Lesley Warren hadn't told Tracey he'd taken
the ring from Patsy Vineyard's corpse.

Lesley Warren informed his friends and family
about Tracey's pregnancy in the middle of June
1987. Then the couple posed for a photograph with
his mother-in-law, Diane Bradshaw, and her husband, Herschel Bradshaw, during a visit to Campobello, South Carolina.

In the photographs, Tracey Warren made a point

of showing off the two rings while a family friend snapped away with a camera. On the same trip, the apparently happy couple also posed for another photo taken outside Lesley Warren's mother's home on Curtis Creek Road in Candler. Once again, the rings were clear to see.

Sometime afterward, the sapphire and diamond ring was sold at a pawnshop on Public Square in Watertown. Both Tracey and Lesley Warren later insisted they couldn't remember how much she received for the ring. Tracey claimed she gave the other seven-diamond cluster ring back to her husband and she had no idea what he did with it.

Meanwhile, Lesley Warren was becoming increasingly depressed about Tracey's pregnancy. It was even affecting his behavior in the army, where he was becoming noticeably more distant from his colleagues. "Lesley was in a dreamworld most of the time. If you spoke to him, you had to repeat yourself two or three times before you got his attention. He just didn't seem to be on the same planet as the rest of us," one former army colleague Dan Collins recalled.

On June 20, investigators once again interviewed Lesley Warren's friend Tom Walker at the Shipyard Apartments. Walker remained extremely cooperative and insisted he would do anything in his power to help investigators. He again volunteered to take a polygraph to clear any suspicion of involvement in the disappearance of Patsy Vineyard. Walker said he had no fresh information that was relevant to the case, but told investigators he would continue to keep his ear to the ground at Fort Drum and pass on any useful leads to detectives.

Walker was calm throughout the interview and investigators later described him as behaving in a

thoroughly "straightforward" manner. Once again
Walker openly talked about how he had been arrested at the age of eighteen when he and his
younger brother burgled a house. And he told investigators more details about how he'd hung out
in the company of Lesley Warren while many of
their colleagues were away in the field on Operation
Phoenix.

NYSP detectives also spoke with more than two
dozen members of Mike Vineyard's A company. But
the only other soldier who came under any suspicion was Tom Walker's friend Lesley Warren. Some
investigators even speculated about whether they
had both kidnapped Patsy Vineyard and then killed
her. But there was no evidence to back up such a
theory.

Only Senior Investigator Bob Cooke of the NYSP
had his eye focused firmly on Lesley Warren. "There
was something about him that didn't gel right, but
he had an alibi for his movements and he didn't
come across as a bad person. He had this baby face
that looked so goddamned innocent," Cooke later
recalled. Warren's response to Cooke's questioning
had been short and sharp and to the point, but he
did admit meeting Patsy Vineyard at a picnic held
in the Shipyard complex.

Bob Cooke wrote the following note about Lesley
Warren and Tom Walker in his case file:

> Lesley Eugene Warren 10/15/67
> Academy St H2O (Watertown)
> Apt 206B
> married
> Tracey Warren 10/1/69
> Both at the company picnic
> Friend Tom Walker—has been to his apt.

Does a lot of fishing with him.
Has own car.
Walker now rides to and from work with Warren. Last few months.
1st time saw Patsy with Mike at picnic.
Never saw Patsy walking
Friends with Denise Walker
Saw her laying in the sun
Walker has 4/10 shotgun
Saw her when walking block

Toward the end of June 1987, NYSP put up a substantial reward for information that might help solve Patsy Vineyard's death. But her body had been in such poor condition that investigators could only establish she had died between May 12 and 21. Police refused to state the specific amount of the reward. Investigator Dick Ladue explained at the time, "The state police feel strongly enough and we need information, so this is one way to go about getting it. We're devoting a lot of time to this case."

Although reward offers usually contained a provision for the apprehension and conviction of a suspect, police were not even making this a qualification in the Patsy Vineyard case. Yet they had still not officially classified the case as a homicide, accidental death or even a possible suicide. Investigators were awaiting the results of lab tests that they hoped would provide additional clues in the case. The NYSP at Watertown remained desperate for clues.

Inside Fort Drum, Mike Vineyard's commanding officer raised enough cash for Vineyard to be able to afford the flight back to Tennessee for his wife's funeral.

On July 15, NYSP investigators decided to put a

whole new list of questions to Patsy Vineyard's husband, Mike, in a desperate attempt to squeeze more information out of him. Many points seemed almost irrelevant, but Senior Investigator Bob Cooke and his team believed that going over old ground might help turn up new clues. These were the questions given by investigators and the answers provided by Michael Vineyard:

Q. The tumblers in the sink. Would she have used a clean one every time or would she have used the same glass?

A. She would use the same glass, rinse it out and use it again.

Q. The tire on her car was flat. After you put air in it the last time, did you have to do it again?

A. I can't remember.

Q. Would Patsy have dated checks the date she made them out?

A. She would have dated checks the day she made them out.

Q. Did Patsy sleep in the nude? [Her clothes on the floor were daywear and officers speculated that Patsy Vineyard got out of bed as a result of offender contact, gathered up her clothes and left the house at night.]

A. She slept in the nude, but sometimes wore panties and nightgown.

Q. Would Patsy call anyone to check validity of call/notification of husband being injured, etc., or would she be easily susceptible to a con or ruse?

A. She would have gone without checking.

Q. Would Patsy, given her background, physically battle an attacker or would she tend to be easily dominated and become passive [not cooperative] as a survival reflex?

A. Patsy froze a couple of times when I got through sexually with her. Patsy was easily scared. If she was grabbed, she would freeze.

[Then came the most significant question of all.]

Q. What was Patsy's relationship with the Walkers and Warren, given their possible involvement? Were any suspicions ever discussed before? Do you [Mike] have any more information about Walker watching her sunbathe?

A. Regarding Walker watching her sunbathe, Patsy was not sure it was Walker. But the curtains were pulled back in his apartment while she was sunbathing.

Q. Any recollection of Walker or Warren's attitude regarding women, sex? Any comments they made about pornography, use of prostitutes, bar pickups, etc.

A. Denise Walker told Patsy that Tom Walker was not a good lovemaker.

Q. Did Patsy wear any jewelry in bed, including earrings?

A. She always took off all jewelry to go to bed.

Q. Are her shoes missing? What would you [Mike] guess that Patsy might put on in the middle of the night?

A. Don't know.

Q. More about Patsy's habit of making the bed. In your [Mike's] absence, would Patsy possibly leave the bed unmade on a Saturday?

A. Possibly she would leave it unmade. However, Patsy was in red shorts and a tank top, which had been lying on the floor next to the bed. She would have put them on the next day to wear around the house and she would have put her jewelry on.

Q. Did Patsy routinely see Walker? Did they have refreshments together? Would Patsy be comfortable chatting with Walker and friends while sunbathing?

A. She would not have felt comfortable but she would not have done anything. But she would not walk out in front of the house with just her bikini on.

Q. What were your [Mike's] impressions regarding Walker's and Warren's personalities? Their likes and dislikes, strengths and weaknesses? How would he [Mike] describe them as personalities to someone who didn't know them and wanted to identify them by observing their behavior in a group of people—not a physical description. What did he [Mike] like/dislike about Warren/Walker then and now?

A. I was never on range control. Mostly at headquarters.

In reality, NYSP had hit a brick wall with their investigation into the death of Patsy Vineyard. The ME still couldn't officially say she had been murdered, although there was little doubt. Few clues had emerged about what really happened the night of her disappearance from the Shipyard Apartments. "This is the most difficult case I have seen in my career," Bob Cooke told a press conference. "We can't even put a label on it," he added, referring to the options of murder, suicide or accidental drowning. "We're still calling it a suspicious death."

Bob Cooke and his colleagues also knew that de-

spite all the tests from the Vineyard autopsy, there
was still nothing conclusively indicating if she was
dead before she entered the water. The NYSP reward offer produced few helpful responses. Dick
Ladue and Wayne Corsa were sent back down to
Knoxville, Tennessee, to talk to Patsy Vineyard's family about her private life. They discovered some bizarre details, but nothing that could be connected
to her death.

At 12:54 P.M. on July 18, Denise Walker contacted
investigators to tell them that she'd just remembered that Lesley Warren had told Tom about how
he and some friends had gone to Texas on a drug
run and how one of the criminals had threatened
Lesley with a gun. Denise also claimed that Warren's
wife, Tracey, once told her that she had tried to kill
herself by overdosing with some pills when they
lived in Watertown.

Denise also said she believed Tracey thought she
[Denise] had been having an affair with Warren. As
if to counter the allegation, Denise then recalled
how Warren told her husband he had an affair with
one of the girls who lived upstairs from their own
apartment in Watertown. The girl was Mexican.
Denise also reckoned Lesley Warren had a relationship with another girl called Debbie. Denise even
claimed to remember Tracey having a ring with diamonds in it; the ring sounded like Patsy Vineyard's.

At the end of July, a Watertown woman called
Donna Medford rented a boat and went out on Lake
Ontario on the opposite side to Sackets Harbor. She
had sex with a man, who then choked her. She was
wearing jeans and sandals at the time. Twenty-two-
year-old blond Donna—whose eyes were so green
that she was known to friends as "Jade"—often
spent her evenings in the bars of Sackets Harbor.

The killing had Lesley Warren's name stamped all over it.

It wasn't until early September 1987 that Senior Investigator Bob Cooke made a small breakthrough. He interviewed a resident of the Shipyard complex who said he had seen a man watching Patsy Vineyard from behind some bushes near the church they both attended. The informant said that the man looked as if he was out of his head on drugs.

A few days later in September, Denise Walker revealed to investigators that another GI's wife had been harassed by a telephone caller during the month of April, just a few weeks before Patsy Vineyard's disappearance. She also repeated her earlier claims that Patsy Vineyard had frequently sunbathed in a two-piece swimsuit outside her apartment.

But even more significantly, Denise Walker claimed for the first time that on the probable night of Patsy Vineyard's disappearance she heard a scream out in the parking lot of the Shipyard Apartments. She said she immediately ran outside, but when she couldn't see any sign of anyone, she returned to her apartment.

On September 24, Mike Vineyard was reinterviewed by NYSP investigators. Vineyard said that his last phone call to his wife before she'd disappeared had lasted twenty minutes. He also provided police with a full description and value of his wife's missing jewelry, including confirmation that he'd bought Patsy's diamond ring with payments at a Knoxville jewelry store for $1, 200.

Vineyard also said that Patsy had other jewelry, including a pair of fourteen-karat gold earrings, a gold Seiko watch, a gold necklace with the initial P on it and a diamond cluster ring. He estimated the value of the items at around $500.

Vineyard said his wife would never have gone for
a late-night walk alone and he insisted to investigators she only ever went to the local store in daylight.
But he did admit his wife sometimes walked to the
historical battlefield area on the edge of Sackets
Harbor. Vineyard said the only people who might
have walked with her were Denise Walker or one
other neighbor. He also said that his wife would
never have gone for a swim in the lake and that she
did not drink alcohol.

The next day, September 25, at 10:30 A.M., two
NYSP investigators reinterviewed Lesley Warren at
company headquarters inside Fort Drum. Warren
told detectives that during late April and all of May
he had been assigned to range control while everyone else went out in the field. Warren told detectives each man had worked twelve-hour shifts on
range control and even volunteered the names of
other soldiers assigned with him. Warren also confirmed to investigators he had worked on Tom
Walker's car in the parking lot of the Shipyard complex. But he couldn't recall the exact date. Senior
Investigator Bob Cooke remained highly suspicious
of Lesley Warren, but he still couldn't shoot any
holes in Warren's story.

Later that same day, NYSP detectives decided it
was time to take up Tom Walker's offer to submit
to a polygraph test. Walker was understandably nervous when investigators showed up at his apartment
with their equipment. Walker went through a brief
pretest interview, during which he was told the nature of the questions he would be asked during the
test.

Two pneumotubes were placed on his upper and
lower chest. Next followed a blood pressure cuff before wires were linked to two of his fingertips to

measure his eventual perspiration during questioning. The theory behind polygraphs is that they measure the fear of detection in a subject. Experts claim that when a subject lies his or her body goes into what they call flight mode and that is picked up on the graph linked up to those wires.

When the administering officer began asking some of his ten carefully formulated questions to the subject, Walker's body went almost instantaneously into flight mode. Over the following hour and a half, Walker took at least three separate tests, during which he was asked the same set of questions. Between each test, the heavily perspiring man was given a breather so that his blood pressure did not get too high. The polygraph machine measured Walker's temperature, blood pressure, perspiration and breathing throughout the questioning. A straight line on the polygraph would tell the examiner if he was not answering truthfully.

The specific questions and responses of Walker to the polygraph have never been revealed, but undoubtedly Walker would have been asked if he was involved in the murder of Patsy Vineyard and her earlier disappearance. Information about Walker's polygraph test was kept out of the local media. While polygraphs are by no means conclusive, they are used regularly by corporations across the United States for prospective employees, and it is estimated they have a 95 percent success rate in relation to establishing whether a subject is lying or not.

During the test, Tom Walker confirmed that he and Lesley Warren had walked back to the Shipyard complex after doing some target practice with their guns in a field behind the block. As they walked back into the apartment complex, the two men had moved behind Patsy Vineyard while she was sunbathing. Walker admitted that Patsy Vineyard was wearing a skimpy two-piece bathing suit at the time. Walker also confirmed that he and Warren then walked over to his car to try and fix it. Walker admitted in the polygraph he never told anyone other than his wife about the incident.

Senior Investigator Bob Cooke was also troubled by the fact Tom Walker sent his wife home to her parents' house in Washington on a vacation just a few days before Patsy Vineyard's body was discovered in Black River Bay. Cooke already had Lesley Warren marked as a definite suspect in the Vineyard disappearance; despite the Walker polygraph, he still had no concrete evidence to link Warren to her death. NYSP investigators even interviewed four of Warren's other soldier colleagues who didn't go on Operation Phoenix to try and gather more information about Warren's background and attitudes, but nothing clearly pointed to him being the killer.

In November 1987, the NYSP reluctantly began winding down the Vineyard inquiry. They remained convinced she'd been murdered and that her killer was probably in her husband's unit at Fort Drum, but no real evidence had been forthcoming. As one investigator explained: "There comes a time with an inquiry like this that you have to put it on the back burner and hope that luck eventually prevails and someone comes into the frame."

Six

Mike Vineyard and Lesley Warren continued crossing paths during the fall of 1987 and through 1988. But Warren was so reserved most of the time that Vineyard only later recalled a quiet soldier attached to the mortar platoon. "He kept to himself," Vineyard later said. "I never associated with him. We never had words, but I still thought he was a troublemaker."

Mike Vineyard never explained why he had reservations about Lesley Warren. "He saw me every day for a year and never gave any sign of what happened," Vineyard later said. "If I knew then what I know now, it would've been different."

By the time Lesley and Tracey Warren's first child—a boy named Joshua—was born on January 20, 1988, Lesley was feeling increasingly isolated despite his marriage. He felt excluded from Tracey's life from the onset because she heaped so much love and attention on their baby. But Warren was determined to ensure his child did not have as miserable a life as he had suffered.

Lesley Warren wanted to resume sexual relations with his young wife almost immediately after the birth of Josh in order to quell the urges racing through his mind. In some ways, he did feel bad about the death of Patsy Vineyard, and those demons kept reappearing on the horizon. He began dropping bizarre clues about his involvement in the murder of Patsy Vineyard.

In early 1988, the Warrens visited the Asheville house of his stepbrother Eric Murray. "I think he was in some type of trouble," Eric later recalled. "At one point, Tracey asked to talk to me on my own. She wanted to know if Lesley had talked to me about something that had happened and him [Lesley] getting into trouble over a girl in Watertown. I told her that Lesley hadn't talked to me."

With the pressure mounting at home and inside the army, Lesley Warren wanted to escape. On February 21, six weeks after the birth of Josh, Warren went Absent Without Leave (AWOL) from Fort Drum, abandoning his wife and child in the process. For some reason, only known to himself, Warren stole a pair of his platoon sergeant's boots before he went AWOL. His bid for freedom lasted all of four days and he was picked up by military police on February 25.

At a court-martial in March 1988, Warren was convicted of larceny and unauthorized absence, confined to base for seventy-five days and ordered to pay a fine. He was also demoted one grade from specialist to private first class. On April 28, Lesley Warren was returned to his unit, which had by this time transferred to Fort Benjamin Harrison in Indiana. But he was no happier. Tracey was even more preoccupied with little Josh, and Warren's inner rage had not been quelled.

Less than a week after he arrived at Fort Benjamin Harrison, Warren was reported AWOL again. The army now labeled him a full-fledged deserter. That summer of 1988, Warren traveled to New York City where he tasted the bright lights and seedy corridors of the metropolis. Like a 1980s version of the naive country boy from the South played by Jon Voight in *Midnight Cowboy*, Warren found himself sleeping in $5-a-night flophouses surrounded by crackheads and prostitutes.

On June 17, the army issued him a dishonorable discharge in his absence and his deserter status was reluctantly confirmed on July 1.

In New York City, the few people Lesley Warren befriended led him down a one-way alley from which there was no real escape. Warren even smoked crack for the first time.

In August 1988, Lesley Warren met Mary, a Mexican migrant worker, with whom he had sex. He later said that he and Mary went to his room in a New York boardinghouse, watched movies together and then went to bed. Warren later claimed he woke up to find Mary dead beside him. He said he buried her body in a field. No evidence of Mary has ever been found. "It might have been a nightmare. We just don't know," one investigator later explained.

After weeks of desperate loneliness and nonstop drug use, Warren left New York City and headed for Philadelphia. He was arrested there on vagrancy charges and put in jail. Warren was once again court-martialed and immediately reduced in rank from a private first class to E-1, or buck private. As one former colleague later recalled: "The army did everything to try and give Lesley a second and third chance, but it was clear he couldn't cope with life in the service."

Shortly after Lesley Warren's arrest, Tracey returned home to Campobello, South Carolina, but the couple stayed in contact through letters. Lan-

guishing in prison awaiting his court-martial, Warren wrote to his wife asking about the Vineyard case.
Tracey Warren remained in touch with friends back
in Watertown and had heard from them how the
death of Patsy Vineyard had remained unsolved.

Tracey became so irritated by her husband's near
obsession with Patsy Vineyard that she wrote him a
letter asking him outright why the subject was so
important to him. She knew Warren had been
friendly with Tom and Denise Walker, who lived opposite the Vineyards in that apartment complex in
Sackets Harbor.

Warren's response was to write a bizarre letter
from prison referring to how Patsy Vineyard
"wanted it as bad as he [Mike Vineyard] did." Warren did not explain what he meant, but promised
to tell his wife everything once he got out of prison.

Lesley Warren was officially "separated" from the
army in September 1988. At his court-martial, he
was also ordered to forfeit $1,340 in wages.

Warren and his wife were reunited just a few days
after his release from military prison and moved together with baby Josh into an apartment at the
Spruce Pines complex in Landrum, South Carolina.
Tracey Warren almost immediately confronted her
husband about the Vineyard case. Warren shrugged
his shoulders and made the reply sound as obvious
as the battery sitting under the hood of his orange
Mercury parked in front of the apartment.

"Mike [Vineyard's husband] paid me to kill Patsy
'cause she was dying of somethin'," came Warren's
matter-of-fact response. Warren told his wife the killing was planned between the three of them so that
Patsy Vineyard "would not have to suffer any more
pain." He claimed he drove over to the Vineyards'
apartment one night, knocked on her door a pre-

arranged number of times and she came out and got in his car.

Warren claimed he and Patsy then went to the lakeside where she drank a cup of poison until she passed out. Then Lesley Warren took a deep breath and told his wife in a deadpan, emotionless tone: "That's when I killed her. I choked her."

Warren insisted to Tracey that Patsy's husband had promised to pay him for carrying out the killing. He never mentioned the specific type of poison Patsy Vineyard had drunk and Tracey Warren never thought to ask. But Lesley Warren did explain how he dropped Patsy Vineyard's body in the lake at the spot where he always went fishing with his friends Tom and Denise Walker.

Tracey later recalled: "I don't know how much Lesley was paid to kill Patsy, but Lesley told me he just put the money in with $5,000 we had borrowed for the car and some furniture."

The subject of Patsy Vineyard's death was never again discussed by Lesley Warren and his wife.

Around this time, Lesley Warren suffered one of his frequent memory losses, which later led many to surmise that he may have killed more women. Warren was working at South Carolina Elastic at the time. Warren was "doing a little bit of everything for them, running a forklift, fixing knitting machines. You name it."

Warren later recalled: "I remember going to work. It was on a Monday. I'd been there a while, four or five months. I remember waking up and going to work thinking it was the next morning and they was wanting to know where I'd been, why I'd been out for two days. I thought they were joking with me. I didn't think I'd slept that long, but there was dirty dishes and dirty towels at home. I'd been there about four or five months when it happened."

Lesley Warren's only real aim after being discharged from the U.S. Army was to get hold of cocaine and the other drugs that had taken him to a new narcotic-fueled high during his life on the run. Within weeks of being reunited with Tracey and Josh, Lesley Warren was regularly injecting cocaine. Often he'd take enough in one session to give the average person an overdose. Those who encountered him during this period found him even more emotionally detached and characterless than he'd been in his midteens.

"Lesley had nothin' to say about nothin'," his uncle Carl Russell Warren later said. "He looked so damaged I wondered how much longer he'd be in this world. The guy was shot to shit."

Warren's drug taking and inner turmoil had combined to ensure he got virtually no sleep from one week to the next. His life was racing totally out of synch with Tracey and baby son Josh. She had little choice but to accept her husband's late-night excursions from their home in a desperate search for more and more narcotics.

Sometimes Warren snatched a few hours' sleep in the middle of the day. That's when Tracey took little Josh out to the park or on a day trip to an amusement park or the county fairground. She was a single parent in everything but name.

Even when Warren was straight, he suffered from such a short fuse that most conversations with Tracey ended in ferocious shouting matches. Then Warren would seek out yet more cocaine to get himself in a better mood so he'd stop being so nasty to his young wife. Not surprisingly, the round-the-clock injections of cocaine interfered with his ability to think and achieve anything constructive, like getting a job, paying the bills or just being normal. The couple survived on occasional jobs, state handouts and money from Tracey's family.

Warren compounded all his problems even further by drinking vast quantities of alcohol. Soon, popping open a can of Bud for breakfast was as normal to Lesley Warren as buttering a slice of toast. In an attempt to cut down on the cocaine, Warren began smoking large amounts of cannabis, but all that did was make him hungry for the heavier drugs.

Lesley Warren often wandered the streets near his home in Landrum with three intoxicants poisoning his system—cocaine, marijuana and alcohol. These combined to significantly compromise Warren's ability to think clearly and make basic decisions. "He was an emotional mess and the mental sickness that had begun so many years earlier was being reactivated by the drugs rotting his system," one family member later explained.

The four-year-old who'd been regularly slapped and beaten by his father for no apparent reason was losing even more of his sense of reality as an adult. The world had long since turned into an evil, threatening place filled with people who only wanted to harm Lesley Eugene Warren—or sell him drugs. Nearly twenty-one, Warren remained emotionally a child. The so-called "normal" development of a child into a youth into an adult simply had not happened. He was a walking time bomb ticking down to his next appalling crime.

In the early fall of 1988, Lesley Warren split up from Tracey after yet another argument about his excessive drug use. Warren moved back to his dreaded hometown of Candler, North Carolina, and got himself a job as a cashier at the Pisgah Valley Market Store, just a mile from his mom's home.

Warren was trained for the job by twenty-seven-year-old Saundra Davis, who was so taken by the handsome ex-soldier that within a few days of meeting, the couple were dating. It was the beginning of a three-month relationship during which Warren made a series of bizarre claims to Saundra Davis about his marriage.

She later recalled: "One day Lesley told me that when he was still dating his wife, Tracey, he went home to meet her parents and discovered that her mother was someone he had been to bed with." Warren insisted that Tracey's mom hated him because of their alleged "affair." But, Saundra Davis later said, he seemed "kinda proud of it and all."

One day Saundra Davis asked Warren if he had a photo of his estranged wife, Tracey. Warren insisted he did not, but when he opened his wallet a few minutes later, Saundra immediately noticed photographs of at least four or five women, all of whom seemed to be in their twenties. "One was a pretty redhead, but all the rest were dark-haired," she later recalled. Saundra Davis confronted her new boyfriend about all the photos. Lesley Warren—master of the understatement and in the habit of making everything sound as plain as apple pie—told Saundra: "It's no big sweat. They're just a couple of the girls I used to date."

But there were other more disturbing aspects to Saundra Davis's relationship with Lesley Warren. Only a month after first dating, Warren made it clear he liked using handcuffs "and stuff like that." Saundra Davis said she refused to take part in his sex games. Warren's sex drive soon dipped and their rate of lovemaking dropped. Then Warren claimed he wanted to try and get back with Tracey. He told Davis he still desperately craved the sort of normality that Tracey represented. He believed it might be his only escape route from the life of drugs and depravation that seemed to be looming around every corner. Saundra Davis was relieved to end their relationship.

On December 18, 1988, while still working at the grocery store on the Pisgah Highway, Lesley Warren enrolled in a three-month trainee truck-driving course at the Alliance Truck Driving Center. He was determined to get himself a proper job and wage in an effort to win back Tracey.

In the period just before Christmas 1988, Lesley Warren appeared more settled than at any time since he'd first joined the U.S. Army. He was still taking drugs but not in the quantities he had been while still living with his wife. He insisted his job at the Pisgah Valley Market store on Highway 151 was just a stopgap until he got his truck-driving certificate the following spring.

One day a pretty brunette woman named Bronya Owenby walked into the store and the two struck up a conversation. She turned out to be the cousin of Warren's previous girlfriend, Saundra Davis. Warren made a point of telling Owenby he'd just persuaded Tracey to move from her mom's house in Campobello back to Candler.

Over the next few weeks, Warren and Tracey became regular visitors at Owenby's home. But after Christmas, Warren began turning up at the house alone while Bronya Owenby's live-in boyfriend was out at work. Warren never made any moves on her. As she later explained: "At that time, we were just good friends, you know, that was all there was to it."

Then in the spring of 1989, Owenby's boyfriend, Leslie Waddell, moved out of her trailer home after a disagreement. Owenby and a few friends then held a cookout up at a well-known beauty spot called Camp Laurel off Pisgah Highway. Warren knew it well because sometimes he'd slept there under the stars when he couldn't face going home as a youngster.

Bronya Owenby takes up the story: "We decided to go to the store to get some more beer. There was four of us in a small Ford pickup, a Ford Ranger. I was sitting on Warren's lap beside the door. And on the way down to the store, he just started rubbing my leg, and that's when we started dating, I guess."

Soon after that, Warren turned up at Owenby's trailer with some beer and, as she later explained, "we began talking even more than before." The following day, Warren brought Owenby a dozen red roses. She thanked him profusely for the gift, but tried to play it down. Warren seemed genuinely smitten with Bronya Owenby and continued to give her a red rose every time he appeared at her home on Bailey Road in Asheville. Warren made it plain to her that he hated his father and left her with the lasting impression that he really didn't care about anyone.

One time the couple were driving into Asheville when Warren pulled a .44-caliber pistol out from under his jacket and began taking potshots at passing houses. A couple of days later, Warren took Owenby fishing at a local lake and told her that he'd been interviewed by police about the death of a woman in upstate New York. But he refused to elaborate any further.

Warren bought a green Camaro and a motorcycle, which he drove at breakneck speeds through the streets of Candler. The first time Bronya Owenby got in the Camaro, Warren hit the gas pedal with such force that the car fishtailed onto the main road. A pair of silver-colored handcuffs jangled as they hung from the rearview mirror.

"Why you got those, Lesley?" she asked.

Warren gave one of his customary shrugs of the shoulders.

"Nothing special."

Then he quickly changed the subject.

What Warren did not tell either his wife or girlfriend at that time was that he'd gotten back into the habit of driving over to Camp Laurel where he could sleep alone under the stars. He carried a sleeping bag in the car just in case he got the urge to escape the pressures of his strange life.

As his relationship with Bronya Owenby developed, so did his heavy drinking. On one occasion, Owenby tried to stop Warren from leaving her home in Candler on his motorcycle because he was so drunk he couldn't stand up properly. She later recalled: "I took his helmet from him and then he told me if I didn't give him the helmet, he would rip my fuckin' head off. He was real scary." She let him go and watched as he careered off down the street on the motorcycle.

But Warren continued to be a regular visitor to Bronya Owenby's trailer, where the couple would sit and drink beer and talk. Some nights Warren made Owenby lethal Long Island Ice Teas with Bacardi Light, tequila, gin and triple sec. "I don't know what else was in it, but it was another kind of liquor," she later recalled.

Bronya Owenby began noticing that when Warren

got drunk his character changed. "When he drank heavy liquor, he just felt he could whoop everybody," she said.

Many of the women who encountered Lesley Warren at this time said he was a confident, skillful lover, so well endowed that they could not resist his charms once he had sweet-talked them into bed. "Lesley had no problems in bed. He knew how to satisfy a woman and he was, well, very big," one girlfriend later explained.

Lisa Annette Lawrence was nineteen years old when she and boyfriend Danny McClure first met Lesley Warren in January 1989 while he was still working at the Pisgah Valley Market Store. Warren was dating Bronya Owenby at the time, but that didn't stop him from taking Lisa out. Like with other girlfriends before Lawrence, Warren continued his habit of driving with them down country roads shooting at road signs with his loaded .44 Magnum.

Warren ditched Owenby and dated Lisa Lawrence just a handful of times before she broke off the relationship. "I got tired of him," she later recalled. "He was good some times and violent other times." Lawrence only saw Lesley Warren once again at a local convenience store after their short relationship had ended. He completely ignored her. "It was as if I didn't exist," she later recalled.

Lesley Warren then dated Lisa Lawrence's sister Michelle for about three or four weeks. They first had sex in her Ford Fiesta in a deserted parking lot on the side of a mountain called Waterfalls, a local beauty spot popular with courting couples just off Highway 151. Warren had been attracted to both sisters because they'd experienced the same sort of rejection at home that he'd suffered. Both Lisa and Michelle had been kicked out of their family home and that made them vulnerable to Warren's understanding nature. But after Michelle Lawrence finished their short relationship, Lesley Warren showed a darker side to his character.

"He came by my house one night wanting me to go out with him and I wouldn't," Michelle later explained. "I wouldn't even come out of the house and talk to him. He got mad and left."

Warren returned and tried to persuade his old flame Lisa to go on a date. She turned him down. "That's when he got really mad. We had to tell him to leave the property," Michelle Lawrence later recalled. "He acted kinda scary." She never elaborated on what exactly happened that night.

On March 10, 1989, Warren qualified as a driver at the Alliance Truck Driving Center. He planned to find himself a good job and earn a decent living. Following his success with women over the previous few months, he was looking forward to meeting more of them on long hauls on the highways and interstates. He'd been through a series of poorly paid jobs at the grocery store, a couple of factories and even a fast-food restaurant. Now he wanted to begin living life properly. Warren began applying for truck-driving jobs advertised in the local newspapers.

Just as Lesley Warren was trying to turn over a new leaf, Mike Vineyard was discharged from active duty with the U.S. Army. He'd become a broken man since the death of his beloved wife. But Vineyard decided to remain a member of the army reserves when he returned home to Kentucky.

In May 1989, two months after getting his full

truck-driving license, Lesley Warren got a job at the
AM-CAN haulage company situated between Interstate 85 and Highway 81 just north of the quiet town
of Anderson, North Carolina. Around seventy drivers worked a company fleet of forty trucks, and on
his first day on the job, Lesley Warren was told that
for reasons of convenience not every truck had a
separate key. Each of the three vehicle models—
Freightliner, International and Volvo—had keys that
fitted every one of them, which meant drivers had
just three keys for the entire fleet.

Warren quickly realized there was no security system to prevent anyone from taking the trucks out
on unauthorized trips. The vehicles were locked
when they were left in the yard, but each of the
drivers had their own key with them at all times.
Warren heard from other drivers that any of them
could come in, drive a truck out of the yard virtually
unnoticed and take it out on the open road. The
AM-CAN yard was so busy at the time the company
was "slip seating" trucks so that no driver ever drove
the same truck two trips in a row.

As one manager later admitted: "If I seen a driver
out in the yard at midnight getting in a truck, I
probably wouldn't even go up to him and ask any
questions, because I'd know he drove for us and
that he was probably going on a trip. I just wouldn't
have any reason to question him."

In the AM-CAN office was a notice board that
showed what truck was going out at what time. At
night and on weekends, the company had a large
metal box filled with all the paperwork about journey details. The box contained the driver's bills, the
truck number of the vehicle he was driving and the
trailer he was going to pull.

But as one company employee later explained:

"If you went in there and wanted to use a truck, you could look and see when that truck was scheduled out. If it wasn't scheduled out, then you could probably get it for yourself till the next day anyway." Drivers knew the only time a truck would be noticed missing was when the yard checks were carried out on weekdays at 7:00 A.M. and 7:00 P.M.

Lesley Warren decided that once he'd settled into his new job he'd take AM-CAN trucks on pleasure trips just like a lot of the other drivers. Warren intended to cruise the highways and byways until he found exactly what he was looking for. Warren was soon borrowing AM-CAN vehicles to take girlfriends on cross-country trips, which regularly ended in them having sex in the truck's sleeping compartment. Sometimes Warren took Tracey with him. On a couple of occasions, he also had his young son, Josh, along for the ride.

In the early summer of 1989, Lesley Warren and Tracey turned up at the Asheville home of his stepbrother Eric Murray while driving a white truck without a trailer hooked up to it. Warren boasted about his travels and how he was regularly making runs to Mexico and California. Out of Tracey's hearing, he told Eric about the wild women he'd encountered and then proudly took Eric for a ride in the massive truck. Eric Murray was impressed by the luxurious brown tweed interior complete with a cooler and sleeper bed in the back where Warren claimed he'd had sex with dozens of women.

Just after the visit, Warren split up yet again from Tracey and moved back to his mother's home in Candler.

Warren later claimed that at this time he killed a woman called "Ronnie," whom he'd picked up and taken to South Carolina while working for AM-CAN.

Warren said he could not recall exactly what happened because by this time he was suffering regular blackouts and memory loss. He claimed he next became aware of his surroundings when he was in his truck in Tennessee. The body of "Ronnie" was next to him in the truck. He said he later dumped her body in a forest.

Seven

On Saturday, August 26, 1989, Lesley Warren promised a friend named Jerry Rogers that he'd borrow one of the AM-CAN tractor-trailers to haul some trash for Rogers's father. Warren agreed to take Rogers and former girlfriend Bronya Owenby on a trip out to the AM-CAN depot in Anderson, South Carolina, to get a vehicle.

Warren, now driving a yellow 1970 Monte Carlo, and his two companions ripped through a dozen cans of Budweiser en route to the AM-CAN yard. "We was pretty lit up," Jerry Wayne Rogers later recalled. Warren once again boasted how he'd been on truck runs to California, New York, Nova Scotia, Canada, Florida and Virginia. He even mentioned one "hairy" trip to Mexico. Two hours later, Warren drove his car up in front of a couple of gas pumps alongside the AM-CAN store. He got out of his car and walked into the depot through the front gate while his two friends waited in the Monte Carlo. Just around the back was the depot office and a big garage containing many of the trucks. A few minutes later, Lesley Warren returned and drove his two friends to the back office. Before getting out, Warren told his friends, "I'm goin' off to find a truck that isn't leaving, that nobody is goin' to make a run in."

As he headed back toward the office, Warren stopped to see if anyone was around and then walked in to get a number for a truck they could take. Three minutes later, Warren, wearing a plain gray T-shirt with a single pocket, jeans and black high-top Reeboks, reappeared clutching a piece of paper with a number written on it. The threesome then drove around the trucks and found the vehicle Warren was going to take. Bronya Owenby later recalled: "It was a brand-new truck, brand-new; it looked like it had been spit-shined, because of, you know, all the chrome and everything." The truck was a gleaming white Freightliner with fairy lights illuminating the doorways and a chrome step up into the driver's cab. It even had a pull curtain dividing the sleeper from the cab. Warren started the truck up and then beckoned to Rogers to help him. The older man left Owenby in the Monte Carlo and hitched into the cab next to Warren, who then carefully drove the tractor round the back of the depot to find an empty trailer. He eventually found one with stripes on the side and Rogers jumped out to start hooking it up. Owenby later recalled seeing a man and a woman standing by the yard office talking. There were also other employees working on trucks in the garage plus drivers cleaning their trucks. But none of them seemed concerned by the activities of Lesley Warren.

A few moments later, Bronya Owenby watched from the Monte Carlo as Warren expertly backed the truck up to the trailer and hooked it up. Then he jumped out and got back in the driver's seat of the Monte Carlo, which he parked nearby.

All three then climbed into the Freightliner cab to start their journey back to Candler. Within minutes, Rogers was snoozing in the sleeper area behind the driver. Rogers woke up just as they got to the Winn-Dixie Grocery Store, near Candler, where Owenby got out and did some shopping.

Then Warren drove the tractor-trailer back up Highway 151 toward Bronya Owenby's home before dropping Jerry Rogers off at the Pisgah Valley Market Store, where Warren unhooked the trailer at a nearby dirt spot. Rogers joined some friends in another car.

Warren and Owenby then headed for her house in the vast Freightliner. The original plan was to haul some trash off for Jim Rogers, father of Jerry Rogers, the following day, Sunday, August 27. At Owenby's home, Warren helped her put away her groceries and then she called her cousin Saundra Davis, another of Warren's former girlfriends.

As Owenby later explained: "I called her so we could all go out in the truck and go riding on Patton Avenue." At around 7:30 P.M., the threesome set off in Warren's truck for nearby Patton Avenue, where they sat and drank beer. Then they rode around for a while just cruising the streets. At about 11.30 P.M., Saundra asked Warren to drive her home. She later explained, "I just wanted to go home. He wasn't acting right."

Bronya Owenby later explained: "Lesley had been real quiet that evening. He stayed in the sleeper a lot of the time. I thought it was pretty peculiar." Forty-five minutes later, Warren dropped Owenby and Davis off at Macaroon's house. He stayed in the truck and made no attempt to accompany them into the house. "Just get all the trash out the back, will ya?" asked Warren. The two women removed beer bottles, chip packets and cigarette butts. "Then he backed off and left without a word," Bronya Owenby later recalled.

Saundra Davis was so worried about Lesley Warren's behavior that evening she spent at least five minutes discussing it with Bronya Owenby before driving away. Bronya never saw Lesley Warren again.

But Saundra Davis spotted Warren a few minutes later as she was driving home. He was fiddling with something in the truck on a graded-off lay-by. She noticed he had attached the trailer back onto the truck. "I stopped and spoke with him," she later recalled. "I asked him if he was OK, and he still acted weird, so I just told him I'd see him, and I went on home."

At 3:00 A.M. that same night, Jerry Rogers's father, Jim, drove by the spot where Lesley Warren had been seen by Saundra Davis. The truck was gone. It was only when Jim Rogers asked Bronya Owenby if his trash was going to be picked up that he mentioned Warren's truck not being there. At 9:00 A.M. that morning, Owenby drove down to the place where Warren was supposed to be. He was nowhere to be seen.

On the night of August 26, 1989, forty-four-year-old Velma Faye Gray drove from her home in Travellers Rest, South Carolina, to Asheville to perform at a concert with her brother and the musical group they'd formed. They called themselves the Reflections of Greenville and had appeared all over the Carolinas during the previous few years.

Usually, Faye, who worked at the nearby Furman University, and her brother Gary traveled together, but that evening Faye planned to stay at a sister's house on the way home so she drove herself in her immaculately clean red Mazda RX7.

During the Reflections of Greenville's gig at the

Elks Club in Asheville, Faye Gray looked stunning in a long, flowing dress. The group finished their performance around 12.30 A.M. as the party was breaking up. Gray changed into some dark-colored shorts and a blouse belonging to her daughter Cindy, which she'd picked up by mistake. She was particularly embarrassed by the skimpy tank top.

After the show, Faye Gray spent at least an hour helping her brother and the other members of the group carry their equipment from the second-level venue to their trailer in the parking lot. It was almost 1.30 A.M. by the time they were ready to leave. At one point, Faye Gray became so concerned by the tight-fitting outfit she wore that she said to her brother: "I hope I don't have to stop anywhere. These don't fit so good."

Finally, with all the equipment loaded, Faye said her good-byes and drove off in her red Mazda about five minutes ahead of the others. The group usually drove in a convoy and would stop for food en route at a specific drive-in, near Hendersonville. But as it was late, they all decided to head straight back home.

Less than an hour later, Faye's brother George Jackson noticed his sister's distinctive red Mazda as he was traveling down I-64. He flashed his lights as he came alongside the car. "Then she dipped hers up and down," George later recalled. "And then just gradually drove on out of sight."

Shortly afterward, Faye Gray pulled off at an Arby's where she stopped for some food. Meanwhile, George Jackson continued down the I-26 before going onto 25 south, the usual route home. He presumed his sister would take the same road.

Student Katie Manchester was out with her friends Tammy Carpenter, Kevin Campbell and

Teddy Garrett on that same night of August 26. They'd just met up at Ryan's Steakhouse, in Greer, near Travellers Rest. As Tammy later recalled, "It was so crowded we decided not to go in."

The group drove back to Kevin Campbell's house, where they left all their cars except for Tammy's red 1987 Ford Escort GT after she volunteered to take the four friends shopping and then out for a drive. At around 11:00 P.M., they visited a nearby beauty spot called Paris Mountain. Thirty minutes later, the group headed off to eat at the Burger King in Travellers Rest. Then Tammy drove up to another local beauty spot called Bald Rock, at Caesar's Head. It was by now around 2 A.M.

At around 2:30 A.M., Tammy Carpenter drove her Escort onto Highway 276 before deciding to turn off onto the White Horse Road Extension toward home. She later recalled: "When we got to the stop sign, that's when we saw her car to the left."

All of them noticed the red Mazda RX7 slued in a ditch on the side of the road with a woman—later identified as Faye Gray—wearing a white tank top, dark shorts, no shoes, standing alongside it. The headlights shone in the direction of the I-25 to the south. The car engine seemed to be still running. Faye Gray, who had brownish hair with blond streaks, was crying as she stood by the side of the road. Katie Manchester and her friends cracked open their windows halfway and heard her saying, "I wrecked my car. I wrecked my car."

Tammy Carpenter later explained, "She kind of put her hands up to her head and looked directly at us and said, 'Please help. I've wrecked my car.' " They were about to stop and get out when Tammy and her friends heard a vehicle coming from the opposite direction. The group halted at the stop sign just past Faye Gray and looked around.

"I saw some kind of light," Carpenter later explained. "I thought it was a car coming, so I waited just a minute. Then as I pulled out and turned right, I saw this big eighteen-wheeler." As the group drove past the tractor-trailer, the headlights of Tammy's Escort caught a trucker in his midtwenties walking back in the direction of the auto wreck and the woman. The door of his high-sided vehicle was swinging open in the wind.

As Tammy Carpenter and her friends drove around the corner, they came closer to the white semitrailer, which had the company logo AM-CAN on the back doors that opened. They later recalled it also had a large gold-and-red-and-black stripe going down the back of the trailer. The white-nosed truck had a wing on top of it with another distinctive AM-CAN trucking company logo.

The group watched the woman. Then they saw the man again and looked back at her. He seemed calm and friendly.

"Guess he's goin' to help her out of her troubles. Let's go home," Tammy Carpenter said to her friends as they carried on round the next right-hand corner in the direction of Greenville.

"Right."

As Carpenter's friend Katie Manchester said afterward, "We just figured someone was there to help her." And Carpenter later explained: "We didn't know if there was anybody with her. We didn't know what had happened that night, and we thought that since he was a trucker, he could be trusted, and he would call for help. We just assumed he was going to take care of the lady." Minutes later, Tammy carpenter dropped off her friends at Campbell's home and thought nothing more of the incident.

Lesley Warren later claimed that Faye Gray asked him for a ride to call for help and he promised to drive her in the tractor-trailer to a Texaco gas station/convenience store just a mile down the road. Warren liked the look of Faye Gray. She was a well-developed, well-nourished white female weighing around 140 pounds and five feet six inches tall. He particularly liked the look of her curly brown hair with light streaks.

In the cab's passenger seat, she made light conversation about how she'd wrecked her car, and Lesley Warren nodded agreement with everything she said. Then the huge truck rolled to a halt just out of sight of the convenience store/gas station. Faye Gray thanked Warren for his help and had just opened the cab door when the devil inside him struck with such a force of energy that Faye Gray stood no chance. Warren pulled her back into the cab of the truck, grabbing her shorts so hard they ripped in half, and slammed the door shut behind her.

Then he struck out at her face, leaving a small superficial abrasion on the bridge of her nose. He punched her in the chest and abdomen as well as on the spine. In a flurry of more punches, he smashed his fist on her back. Later, injuries showed that Faye Gray did not give up without a fight. She tried to scratch Warren, but that made him even more angry.

"Then I just choked her. I mean, she was laying half in and half out of the sleeper," Warren later recalled.

He made no attempt to have sex with Faye Gray. Warren later insisted no sexual activity occurred and denied attempting to pull down Faye Gray's panties or bra. When asked why he did not have sexual relations, he told investigators: "I don't know."

Once Warren realized Faye Gray was definitely dead, he placed her body in the sleeper behind him and shut the curtain. Then he got out of the cab. "I smoked a cigarette. I remember I was shaking," he later recalled.

With her body sealed behind his driver's seat, he headed back toward the AM-CAN depot in Anderson. Less than an hour later, Warren carried Faye Gray's body to the trunk of his yellow Monte Carlo. Then he got back in the truck and parked it inside the company yard before returning to his car.

With Velma Faye Gray's body now in the trunk of his gas-guzzling auto, Lesley Warren headed south. First he took route 85 up to 26, then drove through Landrum and Campobello, his wife's hometown. As he later explained, "I rode around for a little while. I wasn't sure where to go or nothing."

He eventually found himself approaching a narrow bridge crossing a popular fishing center called Lake Bowen, just off the intersection of Interstate 26 and Highway 9, near a town called New Prospect. Initially, Warren drove across the bridge and then continued a few hundred yards before turning around and driving back onto the bridge. He stopped the Monte Carlo on the middle of the bridge and got out to see if any cars were around. Then he opened the trunk, grabbed some shoelaces and tied Faye Gray's hands behind her back, even though she was already dead.

"I was going to pull her legs up and her hands and put it like in between the arch and just tie it like that," Warren later explained. He planned to weigh down her body with some cinder blocks he thought were in the truck. Warren said: "I thought they [the cinder blocks] were in the back, but they weren't. I don't know. I don't remember taking them out. I guess my wife did. But there wasn't any. So I just put her in the lake."

Moments after he'd heard her body hit the water, he noticed a car approaching from the other side of the lake.

Dorothy Deck usually took Highway 9 en route to her job as a nurse at the Mary Black Hospital in Spartanburg, twenty miles from her North Carolina home. At just after five o'clock that morning, she'd set off for the 6:00 A.M. shift. Deck's route that day took her out across Lake Bowen on the narrow fish camp side of the waterway.

At 5:15 A.M., as she approached the narrow bridge that crossed the lake, Dorothy Deck noticed a light-colored 1970s Monte Carlo parked up in the middle of the bridge. The front hood of the car was up. The lights were on but not the emergency blinkers. Deck presumed the owner was having engine trouble. She cracked her window down just as Lesley Warren came into view—out of the shadows—standing by the front fender of the car. Deck stopped in the narrow lane in the opposite direction from the other car.

"Havin' trouble?" she asked Lesley Warren.

"Uh-uh," came Warren's noncommittal reply.

As he moved three steps nearer to her car, he added, "I think it's just runnin' hot. I'm lettin' it cool down."

Deck didn't like the way he was moving toward her vehicle.

"OK," she replied, winding up her window hurriedly. She drove off before he could get any closer. About a mile farther down the road, it struck

Dorothy Deck as strange that the man should park his car in the middle of such a narrow bridge to let the engine cool down. She said she thought to herself: "And he didn't even have his blinkers on. There was a parking area just next to the bridge at the fish camp. Why did he stop in the middle of the bridge?"

Only a few hours earlier, Scott Stroud had begun his Saturday evening at his brother Jerry Sims's house in Travellers Rest. He had dressed up in his favorite vanilla-colored jacket and a dark shirt with flowers on it over blue jeans and cowboy boots. From there he went to his uncle Ervin Blue's house and grabbed a quick beer before "we went ridin' around," as Stroud later recalled.

Stroud was a man with nothing to lose. He had a criminal record as long as his skinny, blue-veined arms. His conviction included grand larceny in 1985, providing false information to police in '85, a burglary, carrying a concealed weapon and another larceny in '85, a trespass plus another trespass in '85 and an '86 conviction for use of a vehicle without the owner's consent, for which he was indicted on grand larceny of an automobile charge.

Stroud and Blue headed out to a bar called the Silver Fox, where they stayed until midnight. From there the two men went to the Waffle House off Wade Hampton Boulevard, Travellers Rest, and had a meal. Then they rode around and bought more beer. Scott Stroud virtually wrecked his Honda Civic by running it into a post, but the car was still drivable, so nephew and uncle continued their night out.

Eventually, Scott Stroud—all six feet four inches

of him—headed back toward his uncle's house by turning off 25 and then making a left on the White Horse Road Extension. That's when he spotted Faye Gray's red Mazda. Stroud later recalled the car was sitting with the back axle completely in the ditch and the headlights facing 25. The lights were still on and the driver's door was open.

Stroud didn't stop. He drove slowly past the car and delivered his uncle back to his home. But he kept thinking about the Mazda because it seemed like there was no one around and maybe he could pop back and steal it. After dropping his uncle off, Stroud spent at least thirty minutes driving around the area thinking about whether he should take advantage of such a "golden" opportunity. "That's when I decided to go back to see if the car was there," he later recalled. At first, Stroud claimed he returned to the Mazda "to see if I could help, you know, anybody, you know, see if they was still there, so I went back and the car was there."

Stroud parked his semiwrecked Honda off on the side of the road, got out and shouted loudly to see if anyone was around. He later admitted, "Wasn't nobody around. So I got inside the car, and I was highly messed up on alcohol and stuff, but I remember, you know, everything."

Inside Faye Gray's red Mazda, Stroud tried to find any identification that might indicate who owned the vehicle. Stroud later claimed that when he couldn't find anything he got out and shut the driver's door behind him.

"I just left it," he later recalled. "I left the White Horse Road Extension and made a right and then I hit the 290, heading down toward Greer."

Stroud pulled up at a filling station run by Leonard Clark. By now it was 3:00 A.M. He told Clark his name was "Scott Smith" and that he'd wrecked a car about "six or eight miles down the road at the end of the 290."

"Can you call a wrecker?" Stroud asked the filling station owner. A truck turned up at the gas station within minutes being driven by a woman. Stroud dumped his Honda Civic, got in the truck and they headed back to where Faye Gray's Mazda had been abandoned. Stroud got the truck to tow the Mazda to his grandfather Harold Lollis's house on East Darby Road in Travellers Rest. He continued to insist his name was "Scott Smith." After unhooking the car, Stroud paid the lady truck driver $90 and she left.

Stroud later explained, "I didn't have a flashlight in my car or nothing to see how much body damage was done, but there was some body damage to the left front end. But I couldn't do nothing with it 'cause the steerin' wheel was locked."

Stroud left the vehicle in his grandfather's yard, picked up his Honda Civic and headed over to his brother's house. It was by now past 3.30 A.M. Rushing into his brother Jerry's bedroom, he shook him awake.

"Jerry," Stroud gasped. "I done stole me a car."

"Why d'you go and do somethin' stupid like that?"

"I don't know" was Scott Stroud's reply.

Stroud then headed back to his grandfather's house with his brother Jerry in his Datsun. Jerry, who was a mechanic, examined the car and then told Scott: "Well, what we're goin' to have to do is bust the ignition out to turn the ignition on and then we'll put a tire on it."

In the pitch dark of early morning, Scott Stroud and his brother put the spare tire from the Datsun onto the Mazda. Then they gave it a push until it jump-started. At that moment, the tire they'd just put on exploded. "The front end was so badly damaged that it kept busting all the tires we put on it," Stroud later recalled.

Stroud drove the Mazda to his brother's house with a blown tire. "It was hard to steer, but we got it there," he explained. Jerry then patched up the front end. They put yet another spare tire on it just as daylight was starting to peep over the horizon. The effect of all the "alcohol and stuff" on Scott Stroud was starting to subside as dawn broke. "That's when I realized what I'd just done," Stroud later recalled.

He told his brother: "You know, I gotta do somethin' with this car. I don't even know why I got the thing, to be truthful with you." Stroud was now in a panic. His brother told him to follow him in the car and they drove to a nearby field off Allen Road in neighboring Greenville County. Stroud dumped the vehicle. "So what we done, we just left it there, let the law find it. You know, just—just let them find it."

Eight

Early on the morning of August 27, 1989, fisher-
man David Henderson and his friend Larry Collins
turned up at Lake Bowen just as an early-morning
mist descended on the area. Collins and Henderson
rowed their small dinghy out into the middle of the
lake to a position where it was floating under the
Highway 9 bridge across the lake. The two fisher-
men watched the sun slowly rising to the west. After
less than thirty minutes, they spotted something
bulky floating in the water.

"At first, we didn't know what it was because it
was so foggy," David Henderson later explained.
"We couldn't see it real good. Then I eased on up
and I seen fingernails sticking up out of the water,
and I knew what it was then. She was positioned
facedown with her hands tied behind her back."

Moments later, Henderson and Collins saw another boater, a man they both knew, and "we hollered at him to go get the lake warden up there at
the Lake Bowen station." Henderson and Collins
stayed floating alongside the corpse as the sun
gradually burned off the mist, revealing the full horror of their grisly discovery.

Spartanburg County Sheriff's Department detective Carroll Amory was off duty that morning, but
he'd been allowed to take home his police cruiser

as part of a countywide plan to encourage officers to keep their eyes peeled at all times. As a result, Amory was in the habit of monitoring police calls on the squad-car radio at all times.

Amory was a twelve-year vet, married with two children. He immediately recognized a Code One alert on the airwaves indicating a possible homicide over at Lake Bowen. Since he was only about four miles away at the time, Amory decided to take a look at what was happening.

He turned out to be the first police officer on the scene and got in a boat belonging to the lake warden to row out to where the body was located 200 yards from the shore. As Amory pulled alongside the corpse drifting just beneath the surface, he leaned over the edge of the boat before turning to nod confirmation to the park staff standing anxiously on the shoreline. Just then the EMS and Rescue Squad rolled up in their emergency vehicles on the causeway above. Faye Gray's body already had fully fixed rigor mortis and her exterior was almost completely blanched, particularly about the face and upper chest.

At 7:00 A.M., Faye Gray's body was retrieved from the water using two boats and a litter bag from EMS. Amory later explained: "We covered the litter with sheets, then lowered it into the water and brought it under the victim, and once we had the victim in the litter, the sheets were rolled over her to protect any type of evidence that may have been on the body at that time."

The corpse was clothed in a white tank-type slip over a cotton shirt, which was pulled up above her breasts. Underneath, she wore an unsnapped, cream-colored brassiere pulled up beneath her shirt. She also had on a pair of shorts, which had been pulled down around her hips with her pubic hair barely visible. Beneath this was a pair of white bikini-style panties, which had been rolled up several times. Her hands had been hog-tied behind her back and each wrist contained three loops of the shoelaces.

The body was taken to the lake landing jetty before being loaded into an ambulance. Amory followed in his Q-car as the ambulance headed for the Spartanburg Regional Medical Center.

Pathologist Dr. John Wren was paged at 8:00 A.M. that morning about the body found floating in Lake Bowen. It was being transported to Spartanburg Hospital for an autopsy as soon as he could get there. Resident pathologist at the local medical university for one weekend a month, Wren also had worked a full three-month rotation of forensic autopsies at the Medical University of South Carolina from June 1979 until he arrived in Spartanburg. Wren also had a Ph.D. in chemical engineering and had testified in courts across South Carolina as an expert witness.

Wren, an anatomic and clinical pathologist, also had specialized training in forensic psychology. Pathology, the study of the disease process in the body, is divided into two main areas: anatomic and clinical. Anatomic deals mainly with tissues removed during surgery to determine the extent that a disease has spread. The most specialized branch of anatomic pathology is forensic pathology, which is concerned with the medical/legal investigations of death. The other branch is clinical pathology, which involves laboratory tests with body fluids.

Spartanburg officers Amory and his colleague Lieutenant Mike Ennis attended that initial autopsy. Dr. Wren knew he needed to quickly establish the history of the victim, but since she had not yet been identified, it was highly unlikely. Wren began an external inspection of the body in an effort to obtain any trace evidence that would show if she had been physically attacked. Faye Gray's body lay on the ME's slab exactly as it had been found in the lake. She had arrived in a body bag, which had already been removed. She was still clothed, although some of her garments were in disarray. Her hands remained tied behind her back.

Dr. Wren carefully cut off the laces binding Gray's hands after first photographing every detail. Then he gave one of the laces to his assistant coroner and the other to Lieutenant Mike Ennis. Wren then proceeded to routinely describe to his minicassette recorder each article of clothing before removing it from the body. He also looked for any other trace evidence on the outside of the corpse.

After everything had been documented and numerous photographs taken, the body was unclothed and any loose hairs removed from the surface of the body. Wren carefully placed them in a container for the South Carolina Law Enforcement Division (SLED) to examine. The shoelaces, hairs, clothes and other evidence were handed over to SLED for specific forensic examination.

Head and pubic hair samples were then taken, as well as oral, vaginal and rectal swabs for microscopic and chemical examination. Then Dr. Wren and his team washed the body completely before trying to determine exactly what injuries were present. Wren noted Faye Gray had suffered numerous injuries, including several contusions that were not visible externally in her scalp region. Her left eye had a contusion with another injury on the upper eyelid. Gray also had an abrasion on the bridge of her nose and she had a petechial hemorrhage in her scalp and within her conjunctiva, the lining inside the eyelid and along the eyeball. These were small hemorrhages just visible beneath the skin and were common in people struggling to get air. They were the direct result of increased pressure of the blood in the region of the body where they occurred.

Gray had a contusion along her right spine near the hip bone plus other abrasions on her back. There were also some other marks that seemed to have come from fingernails. She even had what appeared to be a cigarette burn on one of her breasts, but it could have been an old injury. Many more contusions were found on her legs, predominantly her upper thigh and the top portions of her feet.

Dr. Wren then carried out an internal examination of the body. First he made an incision to expose the soft tissues of the thorax and abdomen. She had contusions along her shoulders bilaterally at the top of her back. The only other significant finding from the internal examination was that she had an area of hemorrhage in the soft tissues of her neck and to the right of her jaw.

Wren concluded that Faye Gray's death had occurred probably between 2:00 and 4:00 that morning, but he could not be any more specific. Wren could tell which injuries occurred before death because of white blood cells that accumulated in the area around the injury. He concluded that her injuries were consistent with manual throttling, strangulation or a blow to the same area. "It would have to have been a rather small concentrated blow, not a large one," Dr. Wren later recalled. Ultimately, asphyxia was the cause of Faye Gray's death.

Wren later recalled: "She could have been manually strangled. Usually, the hyoid bone is broken, but this did not happen. She could have been smothered. She could have had a laryngospasm, which means that a person, if they're suddenly emerged in water, some people's larynx and the vocal cord will spasm and not open again, and the person will die from lack of oxygen.

"Usually, it means manual throttling," Dr. Wren later explained. "I might add that this only occurs in people as they get older. In children, it usually doesn't occur, because they don't struggle quite as much. Or then another cause could have been drowning, although this could be ruled out in this case because when a person drowns, they inhale a lot of water. They even swallow water. She hardly had any water in her stomach. Another reason why she couldn't have drowned was because when a person drowns in water, they usually have a lot of frothy fluid, which she didn't have in her body. Basically, there were five manners of death. Homicide, suicide, undetermined, natural and accidental."

Dr. Wren signed off his report by stating: "It's my opinion that this individual died as a result of asphyxia of multiple possible reasons but the most likely was laryngospasm and immersion in water."

At 11:00 that same morning, Faye Gray's brother George Jackson was awoken by a phone call from Faye's daughter Cindy asking him if he had any idea where her mother might be. They presumed Faye had stopped overnight in Hendersonville with her sister, but she'd never got there. They couldn't understand why Faye hadn't called.

Cindy then began calling up all the family and friends she knew in the area. Across town, Faye Gray's boyfriend, Lance Ledford, and a number of other anxious friends and relatives decided to go out and try to find her. George Jackson decided to drive back up the freeway and try to retrace his sister's footsteps. Initially, he and his wife rode up and down the route he knew his sister would have taken, to see if there was any evidence of an accident. "We thought maybe she might have run off the mountain or something," George Jackson later recalled.

It was only when Jackson passed the White Horse Extension Road looking for a sign of his sister's distinctive red car that he spotted what appeared to be an accident site. "It looked like a fresh spot on the road where maybe a car had slid off or whatever, right there close to Highway 25," he later recalled.

George Jackson noticed a small ravine where a car could have spun off the road and ended up in a ditch. There was a stop sign with a trench, but he couldn't see any sign of any vehicles beyond it. Jackson alerted his son and two other friends to the area and the group got down on their hands and knees to begin combing the grass. Eventually, they found a patch of red paint chips in an area alongside the road.

"With her car being red, we automatically assumed she'd probably had an accident," Jackson later explained. Jackson and his wife picked up as many of the paint chips as they could and dropped them in a plastic bag. He then alerted Greenville County Sheriff's Department on his cell phone. Law enforcement officers arrived within minutes at the scene and instructed Jackson, his family and friends to stay back while they examined the scene. The red paint chips were then carefully rebagged before being turned over to forensic investigators from SLED.

At about 5:00 P.M., Jackson drove to the home of Henderson County sheriff Larry Bellew, his first

cousin, who immediately took George and his wife
to the sheriff's department in Henderson. He made
some calls and filed a missing person report on the
regional Teletype. Within a matter of minutes,
neighboring Spartanburg County responded to the
Teletype. George could tell from the sheriff's response that something was wrong.

"I gotta prepare you. I think it's goin' to be bad,"
said the sheriff. He took a deep breath and carried
on: "We found a person in the lake, Lake Bowen,
and she fits the description of Faye."

George Jackson was asked if Faye had a hysterec-
tomy and he confirmed that his sister had. Jackson
and his wife then made the difficult journey to Spartanburg, and George identified his sister through
photos shown to him by sheriff's investigators. He
had no doubt it was Faye the moment he saw the
pictures.

That night Tammy Carpenter and her friend,
nineteen-year-old Katie Manchester, saw TV news reports about Faye Gray's crashed Mazda and realized
that the lady they saw on the highway the previous
night might have been harmed. She later explained:
"I saw on TV that a car, a red Mazda RX7, had
crashed, and they said that a lady's body had sur-
faced in Lake Bowen, and so I contacted the police."

On August 29, Detective Carroll Amory got an
anonymous phone call about Faye Gray's distinctive
red Mazda. The caller stated that Gray's vehicle
might be located around the Compton Bridge Road
area, about three miles from where her body was
found in Lake Bowen. Amory and a Spartanburg
police pilot immediately took off in the county sheriff's single-engined reconnaissance plane.

Amory knew the car had been originally wrecked

on Highway 25 in neighboring Greenville County so the tip-off made sense, but there was no sign of the Mazda when he flew over the area. Amory then instructed the pilot to begin flying back across Highway 11 and toward Highway 25 where the crash had taken place. Minutes later, Amory spotted what he thought to be the car sitting off the road in a woodland area. Amory immediately radioed his colleagues on the ground to notify them. For the following thirty minutes, Amory and the pilot circled above the car while they guided three Spartanburg County cruisers to the car's location, which turned out to be a few yards across the county line.

Officer on the ground Robbie Hendrix, a detective with the investigations division of the Spartanburg County Sheriff's Office, immediately called out the police forensic team, who took photographs and video footage. Then the Mazda was towed to Spartanburg County's Impound Yard.

Hapless car thief Scott Stroud was at his brother Jerry Sims's house when he saw the six o'clock news. "We was all sittin' there on the couch, all three of us, me, Jerry and his wife, Corina. It was Channel seven, the news came on, and the guy said, 'Today investigators found a very important clue to a woman's death,' and then they showed the car in the field."

Stroud later explained: "Me and my brother knowed that we put that car up there. And, boy, we just—we just—we just broke up. We didn't know what to do."

Stroud decided to wait until the 11:00 P.M. news to get more details about the investigation. "Then I thought the best thing to do was to go down to Greenville County Law Enforcement and tell them my involvement in stealing the car."

At midnight that August 30, Scott Stroud and his brother became prime suspects in the murder of Velma Faye Gray. The following morning, SLED investigators turned up at the Greenville Law Enforcement Center where detectives helped them take statements while other officers went to search Jerry Sims's house.

Spartanburg County investigators Amory and Ennis had no reason to believe that any other killings had been committed by the person who'd assaulted Faye Gray. But they knew from Katie Manchester and her friends that an AM-CAN truck had been seen in the area. The two detectives visited the AM-CAN depot in Anderson and spoke to staff, even though number one suspects Scott Stroud and his brother had been questioned just hours earlier.

Joe Kelley, operations manager at AM-CAN, was responsible for all the trucks that ran freight from state to state and into Canada. One of the first drivers he mentioned was Lesley Warren, who'd started working at the company in May that year and had left suddenly the previous day.

Kelley was immediately asked detailed questions about the circumstances behind the termination of Warren's job. "He just stopped coming to work," Kelley told investigators. He was also asked if he knew a man called Scott Stroud. Kelley said he did not, but went on to explain how AM-CAN operated as a company. When investigators went back to check to see if the truck Warren had used had any miles missing from the log, it did not.

Later that day, the first batch of witnesses were shown photos of truck drivers at AM-CAN, but they were not shown a picture of Lesley Warren because a copy of his driver's license could not be found by the company.

Among those interviewed by police were Katie
Manchester, Tammy Carpenter and their friends,
who'd driven past Faye Gray after she'd broken
down. They were shown numerous photos, including pictures of at least six truck drivers who worked
for AM-CAN. Katie Manchester pointed out a driver
named Honeycutt as being the man she had seen
the evening of Faye Gray's disappearance. Even
when Lesley Warren's photo was added to the set
shown to Katie Manchester, she failed to identify
him.

Katie's friend Tammy Carpenter was also shown
the same photographs. She picked out yet another
driver named Barry Beacham. Once again Lesley
Warren was overlooked.

Detective Carroll Amory was assigned the task of
specifically interviewing all the drivers from AM-
CAN who could have been out in trucks on the
night that Faye Gray disappeared. Among those ten
truck drivers was Lesley Warren. Amory contacted
him by phone and arranged an appointment for the
following day. "He was real cool when I phoned him
and gave off no indications whatsoever that he had
anything to hide," Amory later recalled.

When the detective arrived at Warren's home in
Candler the next day at 9:00 A.M., he found Warren
drinking a can of beer with a girlfriend. "It seemed
kinda early," Amory later recalled. "But he gave no
indication of any involvement. He came back with
straightforward answers to every question. The beer
they were both drinking was the only strange thing
about them."

Warren consumed at least six beers during the
seventy-five-minute interview. "I didn't know if he
was trying to hide something, but all he did was
drink beer," recalled Amory, who left Warren's

home that morning convinced he was not the killer of Faye Gray.

Detectives insisted on taking hair samples from one of Velma Faye Gray's former boyfriends, Bobby Dersch, also from Greenville County. The couple had enjoyed a nine-year relationship until shortly before her death. Investigators had been told that Dersch had a "violent" relationship with Faye Gray. Also, on the day of Gray's disappearance, Dersch had been frantically trying to find his former lover. Detectives established that at 4:00 A.M. before Faye Gray went to Asheville, she'd received a phone call from Dersch during which she'd told him to leave her alone.

It also emerged that at 2:30 on the afternoon before her concert in Asheville, Gray's boyfriend, Lance Ledford, had advised her to get a restraining order against Bobby Dersch.

Investigators felt that Faye Gray's former lover was their most likely suspect.

Nine

Two weeks after killing Velma Faye Gray, Lesley Warren called at Bronya Owenby's trailer and told her he'd gotten into trouble for taking a tractor-trailer and had been fired from his job at AM-CAN. He insisted to Owenby that he could still borrow a truck whenever he wanted.

Warren stayed a couple of days at his stepbrother Eric's trailer next door to Owenby's home. But he spent most of his time hanging out with Owenby. Then Warren disappeared again. Bronya Owenby later explained: "I was used to it. I wouldn't see him for a couple of weeks at a time. He'd just disappear."

Shortly after this, Warren began writing to Owenby. She recalled: "I got one letter in the mail, and the other times he would bring them to the house and tell me not to read them until he left, you know, until he was gone from the house."

On one occasion, Warren pulled up in her driveway and dropped something by the door. She was hiding because she couldn't face seeing him. After watching Warren drive away, Owenby opened the door to find a brown paper bag hanging on it. She later recalled: "Inside was a note saying that he was going to be gone for a while and that it had something to do with the law, and he didn't know when he would be back to see me again."

About three weeks later, Warren turned up once again at Bronya Owenby's house and she asked him what that note had meant. He wouldn't elaborate.

Over in Greenville, the nurse Dorothy Deck had finally heard about the discovery of Faye Gray's body in Lake Bowen and immediately called investigators to say she had driven over the bridge that morning and encountered a man behaving suspiciously. Deck was unable to pick out the man from the set of driver's licenses of AM-CAN employees picked up by police earlier.

Back at the Watertown substation of the New York State Police, the death of Patsy Vineyard in 1987 was still considered a sexual homicide, even though forensic evidence had never officially backed that conclusion. Officers remained convinced Vineyard's killer was probably an acquaintance familiar with her movements and also aware that her husband was away on a military training exercise at the time of her disappearance. Investigators believed that Vineyard's killer had preconceived and carefully planned her death and that he was confident his name would not surface as a suspect.

They had no idea that their killer had struck again.

A few weeks after losing his job at AM-CAN, Lesley Warren got work at a fence company in Asheville through Bronya Owenby's ex-boyfriend's father who owned the company. He was soon fired from there for using drugs. Bronya Owenby recalled: "He drove one of their trucks until he took a drug test, and they told him that he needed help."

Owenby wasn't surprised. She knew Warren was a heavy pot smoker and she'd seen him do cocaine

as well. She also knew that Warren was not averse
to stealing when he felt like it. He even boasted how
he'd stolen a saddle and spurs and a bridle from
the VFW Club on Leicester Highway. That was just
minutes after he'd been barred for abusive behavior.

But there was another side to Lesley Warren that
still appealed to Bronya Owenby. He gave her red
roses and splurged out on a silk teddy nightie. He
revealed later to Bronya that he had gotten it out
of the back of one of the trucks he was driving for
AM-CAN at the time.

Warren regularly drank in a number of local bars
near his Candler home, off the Leicester Highway.
His favorite place was the Nashville Club, a country-
rock and beer bar on Swenden Creek Road. Both
Warren and his stepbrother Danny were regular cus-
tomers. Warren seemed to have a good rapport with
Danny. As Bronya Owenby later explained: "They
were real close. Well, they lived together and they,
you know, went out drinking and everything together."

Warren told Bronya Owenby he didn't like most
of the other members of his family. "He hated his
real father, Doug Warren. He said he physically
abused him when he was little," Bronya Owenby
later recalled.

On December 13, 1989, a $3,000 reward was of-
fered by Faye Gray's family and friends for information about her death. The reward was eventually
increased to $5,000, but police remained no closer
to identifying the trucker who was the last person
to see Faye Gray alive.

In Candler, much of Lesley Warren's frustration
and anger came to the boil when he was drinking
heavily. Bronya Owenby explained: "He just got a
bad attitude and thought he could whoop every-

body. He didn't care who it was, you know. He'd probably shoot him . . . instead of look at [him]."

Owenby knew all about Warren's arsenal of weapons. He was always showing off his prized 9mm pistol, which he kept on him most of the time. She explained: "Another time I seen him with a mini fourteen, a kind of fold-up gun." After a fire burned down a trailer he was living in at that time, Warren told Owenby he had stolen some explosives when he was in the army. Warren's landlord later told Owenby the fire was started when Warren left an iron "plugged up laying on the bed." The incident undoubtedly had shades of Warren's unhappy childhood.

Throughout Lesley Warren's friendship with other women, he continued to visit his wife, Tracey, in Campobello, South Carolina. Warren told one girlfriend he wanted to keep in close contact with his son, Josh. Warren also said that he and Tracey fought all the time, including having physical fights involving fists.

"I know she hit him. I don't know if he ever hit her or not," one girlfriend later explained. But when she asked if Warren was the type of man who would let a woman hit him and not do anything about it, she replied: "No, I guess he'd hit back."

Warren repeatedly told his friends how much he hated the police and how his mother had him committed when he was sixteen to a mental hospital and that he had served time in a juvenile detention center. Bronya Owenby later recalled: "He said he used to escape with girls and go and let them catch him, and then he'd escape again."

Warren was rarely seen dressed in anything other than jeans, T-shirt and sneakers. He admitted to Owenby he'd been close to one woman counselor at JEC. "He said she took real good care of him when he was in there. She was nice to him and treated him like somebody." Warren said that he wanted Bronya Owenby to meet this woman counselor. He was full of admiration for the lady.

One day Owenby found herself being driven by Warren when he "just pulled the gun out from under the seat and started firing it out the window going up Pisgah Highway." He made little secret of his love for firearms.

But Owenby still only concluded that Warren had a "weird" personality when he got drunk at her house one night. Owenby was trying to get a troublesome male guest to leave when Warren got up and left the trailer. "He went out to his car and got his gun and ran this guy off the property," Owenby said. "He told him he was going to blow his brains out. And I think he would have done it, too," she explained.

But the most chilling incident of all occurred when Warren called at Bronya Owenby's home at 4:00 A.M. shortly after he told her he'd lost a job as a driver for UPS after just two days when he failed a drug test. "He had scratches all over him, all over his face, his forehead and his cheeks. Looked like they'd come from briars where he'd run through the woods. He was in a nasty mood. He had dirt all over him. He was wet, and it was raining. And he was on foot, not driving. He said he and his brother had been to steal some pot plants for somebody." Warren was breathing unevenly and was dressed in a drenched camouflage jacket and jeans with a black T-shirt.

"What happened to you?" Bronya Owenby asked.

"Got caught tryin' to steal some plants, and I stabbed the guy. I dunno if I killed him or not."

Bronya Owenby insisted Warren leave the house immediately. Warren stomped off in the rain and wind with no car in sight. The trailer home he shared at that time was miles away.

Around this time, Warren also drunkenly boasted to friends how easy it would be "to kill somebody and hide their body so nobody would ever find them." As Bronya Owenby later recalled: "He also talked about the army. Him and a friend would plot to rob this little store below our house, and I told them that if they did, I would call the law on them."

Warren finally split up with Bronya Owenby in February 1990. By then Warren struck her as being "crazy." She added: "It was the way he acted sometimes. He had a lot of problems."

Lesley Warren moved to a new trailer with ex-soldier halfbrother Danny Murray and his wife and son on a lot by Leicester Highway, on the outskirts of Asheville. Murray, twenty-nine, worked at a local plant hire store and had served in the army from 1980 through 1984. He and Warren talked a lot about their army days and he even got Warren a part-time job at the plant. Danny Murray looked a lot like his stepbrother Lesley, even though he was taller with reddish hair and heavyset. "But when they walked into bars together, there was no mistaking the fact they were brothers," their uncle later recalled.

Lesley Warren remained an avid Dean R. Koontz and Stephen King fan and read continually during his stay at Danny's place. Warren also bragged to Danny about his parachute jumps and jungle training while in the army. He claimed to have been thrown out of the army for selling acid (LSD). He never once mentioned the case of missing Patsy Vineyard. However, Warren did boast to Danny Murray that he'd been having a sexual relationship with one of his former counselors at the juvenile evaluation center—a woman called Jayme Hurley.

Murray got on so well with Warren that he wasn't even concerned when Warren proudly brandished his .44-caliber Magnum Ruger revolver at the supper table most nights. Often Warren would sit in front of the TV stroking the weapon menacingly.

Warren had even admitted to him that the South Carolina Police had interviewed him about a missing girl. He said the officers had taken photos of him and that he matched the description of the man they were looking for. He also admitted the main suspect was believed to have worked for AM-CAN trucking. "I reckon I know the man they're lookin' for," Warren told Murray as they chatted. But he never elaborated. Warren also informed his stepbrother he'd been fired from AM-CAN because he "took a truck to Bronya's house to haul off garbage and was caught and got fired."

Around this time one of Warren's neighbors, Misty Ferguson, introduced him to her sister Terry Quimby, who was staying at her Asheville trailer on a break from her home in High Point, near Greensboro, North Carolina. Warren and Terry got on very well and slept together during her visit. She later told her sister she "really liked" Warren.

Warren admitted to Misty Ferguson and her sister he'd lost his driving job at UPS because of something to do with a missing girl in Spartanburg, South Carolina. He admitted he'd been questioned about the woman but claimed he did not even know her name. As usual, Warren's favorite topic of conversation was his alleged exploits in the army. He even told Misty Ferguson and Terry Quimby he'd like to reenlist.

Warren made a point of telling everyone about his sizable collection of guns.

On one occasion, he even claimed he'd killed a man.

Warren also told Misty Ferguson and the Murrays that he'd taken and passed a sheriff's test in Buncombe County, but he said he didn't like the police, so he'd changed his mind about joining. Lesley Warren loved giving the impression he was a virtual superman capable of doing anything he wanted.

However, one drunken night the true dark side of Lesley Warren came to the surface. He admitted he preferred having sex with women when he was under the influence of alcohol and pot. His friends noticed he had a lot of difficulty holding his drink and was in the habit of grabbing any available liquor bottles by the neck and chugging them. "Lesley got real aggressive if he drank tequila. Tried to pick a fight with just about everyone," recalled Misty Ferguson.

Lesley Warren still had a fearsome reputation as a troublemaker in a number of bars and clubs near his trailer home. He'd shoot his mouth off about how much he hated his father and how he'd been beaten as a kid and how he'd like to kill his father "if I had the chance."

At the Mountain View Drive Club (off Biltmore Avenue), the Country Rock Club and his beloved Nashville Club, regulars noticed he'd acquired two sinister-looking tattoos: a black widow spider with a red spot in the middle of his left shoulder blade, and on his right shoulder blade, another spider in a huge web. There were times when Lesley Warren felt like a spider trapped in an evil web that was

spiraling out of control fueled by hard drugs and a
desire to cause murder and mayhem.

Lesley Warren and Danny Murray eventually fell
out when Warren stole a 35mm camera while they
were working together at the You Rent A Plant store.
But Danny Murray was more upset by Warren's blatant intravenous use of cocaine. Warren frequently
got "totally wired out and real tense," Murray later
recalled.

Warren also continued to regularly travel to Campobello to see Tracey and Josh. It was during one
such visit back in the summer of 1989 that Tracey
told Warren she was pregnant with their second
child. Warren managed to persuade Tracey to allow
him to rejoin her in Campobello. Within weeks of
arriving, both Warren and Tracey managed to get
jobs together in an elastics plant.

The couple split up yet again a couple of months
later. Soon afterward Tracey gave birth to a son they
named Matthew. Warren was back in the Asheville
area working as a day-shift plant worker at Lustar
Dyeing and Finishing. He kept to his promise of
always sending home a monthly check to pay for
food and clothing.

In January 1990, a New York State Police surveil-
lance helicopter spotted an even more fearsome killer than Lesley Warren sitting in a car parked on a
bridge above a frozen, half-naked female corpse.
The chopper crew tailed the car to the suburban
Rochester nursing home where Arthur Shawcross's
mistress, who faithfully adored him, worked.

The following day, Shawcross confessed to eleven
slayings. Classified as a "homicidal pedophile" when
he was earlier released from prison for the murders

of two children in 1972, the killer had switched targets so as not to be caught again. Shawcross found it almost as satisfying to choke a petite, unsuspecting woman in a compromising sexual position as he did snuffing out the life of a child.

Shawcross had been a troubled dropout from the town of Brownville, near Watertown. Other kids called him "Oddie" or "Crazyboy." But by 1990, that child had turned into a potbellied, forty-seven-year-old homicidal maniac. Shawcross's crimes became the north country's most lurid, disturbing nightmare and sent shock waves throughout the nation.

Like Warren, Arthur Shawcross seduced many women. He was married four times but admitted that when he felt frustrated he smashed a potted plant or a plate or a piece of furniture rather than take it out on his wife. Shortly after his arrest, he told psychiatrists he'd often go out and kill hookers on the nights he got "real upset." Arthur Shawcross seemed to have been marked from birth for a potentially violent life. While awaiting trial, he was found to have extra chromosomes in his cells, an anomaly associated with violent men. He was also found to have a metabolic disorder called pyroluria. He suffered from uncontrollable anger and mood swings.

In early 1990, New York State Police strongly suspected that Arthur Shawcross might have played a role in the disappearance of Patsy Vineyard. Shawcross had begun his killing spree around the same time in 1987. He was attending regular meetings with his parole officer after his early release following the killing of those two young children in Watertown.

Many of Shawcross's eleven women victims had

been prostitutes and drug addicts he picked up on the mean streets of Rochester, New York, at exactly the same time Lesley Warren was prowling the streets of Watertown and Sackets Harbor. Shawcross admitted that he returned to the bodies of two of his victims a few days after killing them and cut and sexually mutilated them. He also told investigators that he devoured their raw flesh.

Shawcross, like Lesley Warren, had long since crossed the thin line between fantasy and reality. He reckoned himself a Rambo-type figure and even boasted of raping, mutilating and killing Vietnamese women when, in fact, he had worked as a supply clerk on a large army base many miles from direct combat during the war in Southeast Asia.

Up at Watertown's NYSP's substation, Senior Investigator Bob Cooke approached the Shawcross task force to try and establish whether the notorious serial killer might be the man who murdered Patsy Vineyard. But there was little solid evidence linking them.

Back in the Carolinas, Lesley Warren had no idea that another, more bloodthirsty killer had smoke-screened his own evil deeds so conveniently.

Ten

Lesley Warren was proud of the pair of handcuffs hanging from the rearview mirror of the white 1968 Chevy van he bought in the spring of 1990. Whenever they jangled during a sharp turn, he chuckled at the sound they made. And he relished telling girls who noticed them that he liked to "be in control" of his women and how he never used a rubber during sex. Then he'd often veer off into a tirade of abuse directed toward "niggers" and "faggots."

But none of this disturbed his latest lady friend, Terry Quimby, who really believed she was falling in love with Lesley Warren. He'd even bought her a dog as a token of his love for her. When she returned to her home in High Point, North Carolina, after staying at her sister Misty Ferguson's trailer in Candler, she began writing regularly to Warren.

In his letters back to Terry Quimby, Warren made sexually explicit references to how another girlfriend of his "liked head." But Terry Quimby believed that Warren's frank admissions were further proof that he was falling in love with her. He even began regularly sending roses to her home in High Point.

But Lesley Warren continued to harbor evil thoughts and sexual obsessions toward other women. At the forefront of his mind in May 1990 was his onetime JEC counselor Jayme Hurley, who lived in the Asheville suburb of Swannanoa. During the Christmas holidays of 1989, Warren had even bumped into Jayme in Asheville and she'd given him her home phone number: "You call me anytime. I'll always be here," Hurley had told her former pupil.

At that time, Jayme Hurley was living a peaceful life in the quiet community close to the JEC building where she had formed such a close bond with Lesley Warren. The area was renowned for its pleasant blend of tastefully built modern developments and more mature neighborhoods, many in a rural setting of small, square plots featuring grazing pastures and colorful flower beds.

Hurley had quit the emotional roller-coaster ride of social services a few years earlier for a less demanding job in a local flower store. She told friends she preferred the quiet life away from the trials and tribulations of all those problem teenagers who came through her hands at JEC. By the late spring of 1990, she was living with her boyfriend, Chan Warner, in a pretty, detached cottage on Irving Street, a world away from the anguish and pain she encountered as a youth counselor.

Jayme Hurley told Catherine Jenkins, an old friend from her JEC days, that she often thought about Lesley Warren and what an impressive student he'd been. She said she'd bumped into Warren and told Jenkins he was "doing great." Jenkins was disturbed by Hurley's overtrusting nature at times and warned her friend to be careful about him.

"You know, I often wonder if I ever truly helped anyone at JEC—*truly* helped them," Jayme Hurley told her friend, totally ignoring Catherine's concern. "But Lesley made it all worthwhile because I know in my heart he is the one student I have truly helped. If anything ever happened to Lesley, if he got into any trouble again, that would really make me question my professional judgment."

Catherine Jenkins gently reprimanded her friend when she revealed she'd given Warren her home phone number. As Jenkins later explained: "Jayme spoke her mind and could easily stand up to anybody if she thought she was right. Underneath, however, she had a soft heart. If someone made a plea for help, she was there. If she had a fault, it was that she gave too much, which people then took advantage of."

During the last week of May 1990, Jayme Hurley was talking to a neighbor about her work at the JEC and made a strange comment that later struck her neighbor as being "kinda funny." Hurley told her friend: "One of these days, you are going to see more of those kids from the JEC on TV for robbing or kidnapping. Some of them were real scary."

On May 24, Lesley Warren dug out the scrap of paper with Jayme Hurley's phone number and called her at home. She was pleased to hear from him as she had always encouraged Warren to let her know his progress. Hurley's phone conversation with Warren lasted more than thirty minutes. Her neighbor later recalled that Hurley seemed far more nervous and edgy when she finally put down the receiver.

Warren later casually recalled: "Hadn't seen her in a while, and I told her I'd be stopping by, and she said that would be fine."

What Lesley Warren didn't realize was that Jayme Hurley had a few days earlier split acrimoniously from her boyfriend, who'd suddenly gone to live in Key Largo, Florida. In addition, Hurley had become dissatisfied with her job at the local flower store. It might have given her an escape from the emotional traumas of the JEC, but she worked long hours and was paid low wages. She wanted a "real" job once again, one with proper benefits and security, although she told friends she had no idea what she wanted to do next. Over the previous few months, Hurley had even worked freelance cleaning contracts for local businesses to raise more money. But just a few days before Warren called, she'd lost a big cleaning account and desperately needed to find more work to pay off all her bills. Jayme Hurley also wanted to move to a different house because of structural problems with the property, which she told friends her landlord had neglected.

On Thursday, May 24, at 8:00 P.M., shortly after calling Jayme Hurley, Lesley Warren dropped into Encores, one of his favorite bars in Asheville. He sat alone at the bar and drank three beers in fast succession. After finishing off his last bottle, he got up from the bar and decided it was time to visit his old JEC counselor.

Warren later made the following claims about what happened after he got to Hurley's house: "We talked for a while. I bought some cocaine. We started shooting it. We used it up. I can't really remember the time. Then we both left to go after some more."

Warren alleged Jayme Hurley accompanied him to a notorious apartment block called the Hillcrest, in downtown Asheville, where drugs were openly sold. Warren said he and Hurley bought more cocaine and then went to pick up a pack of needles from Eckerd's drugstore. "Then we went back to her house. We did a little more of the cocaine," he later claimed.

At 10:46 P.M., Jayme Hurley received a phone call from Catherine Jenkins. Jayme picked up the phone very quickly, on the second ring. She was in the bedroom while Lesley Warren was out on the couch in the living room. Jenkins was returning a call Hurley had made to her the previous Saturday. "Jayme was upset about her boyfriend moving out and going to Key Largo," explained Jenkins. The early part of the phone conversation centered around Jayme Hurley's departed boyfriend and all the unpaid bills he had left behind. The phone call would last fifty-seven minutes and the two women talked about a wide range of subjects, including books, music, mutual friends, money problems, their past experiences as counselors at JEC and plans they had to see each other in July.

When Catherine Jenkins asked Jayme Hurley if she would take her boyfriend back, she laughed and said, "Probably. But this time the rules would have to be different." About five minutes into the phone call, Hurley whispered something to her friend that was so quiet she could not hear what she was saying at first.

"What did you say, Jayme?" Jenkins asked.

"Lesley Warren is here," Hurley said.

"What's he doing there?" Jenkins replied.

"He's in some trouble and I told him he could sleep on the couch."

Catherine Jenkins told her friend she didn't think that was a good idea. "Are you OK?" she asked Hurley.

"Yeah, I'm fine," responded her friend in a quiet tone.

About three minutes further into the phone call, Jayme Hurley began whispering again. "I told him

I was tired and going to bed and that he could stay up as long as he wants."

Catherine Jenkins once again asked her friend if she was sure it was a good idea to have Lesley Warren staying at the house.

Hurley said, "Yeah."

The two old friends continued their phone conversation for another forty-five minutes. But about halfway through, Hurley interrupted her friend by saying, "Hold on a minute." Jenkins never heard Hurley put the phone down, but about five seconds later, she came back on the line.

"It's OK. It's just Lesley."

Jayme Hurley never mentioned him again during the conversation, but she did tell Jenkins she had decided that despite her current unhappiness with work she would never go back to being a counselor at the JEC in Swannanoa.

Catherine Jenkins then changed the subject by telling Hurley she had just started reading *It* by Stephen King. For years, Jenkins had avoided reading King books following the killing back in 1985. At about that time, two of Warren's fellow students at JEC had axed to death an old man in a direct copy of part of the plot of King's novel *The Shining*. But that evening, Jenkins explained the plot of *It* as far as she had read into the book. It is the story of a man who kidnaps people and then takes them into the river to kill them.

It is highly likely Jayme Hurley talked to Lesley Warren about the *It* plot after she finished her phone conversation with Catherine Jenkins.

On the phone that evening, the two women went back to talking about the danger they'd faced on a daily basis from some of the students and how working with so many aggressive people from such "crazy" backgrounds was a real strain. "I've never for one minute regretted my decision to leave there," Jayme Hurley told her friend, laughing. "I'm just not too sure about all the decisions I've made since then."

Hurley ended her phone conversation with Catherine Jenkins by yawning as she had done quite a few times through the phone call. Then Hurley told her friend how much she'd missed her since Catherine Jenkins had moved to Florida. Jenkins signed off by saying, "I love you, Jayme."

"I love you, too, Catherine," replied Hurley, putting the phone down.

Jenkins later explained: "Throughout the conversation, Jayme was relaxed, calm and in a good mood. She showed no hyperactivity or loss of memory. In fact, she showed no sign of being under the influence of alcohol or any other drug."

According to Lesley Warren, this is what happened next: "After she got off the phone, I went into her bedroom. We done a couple more shots of coke. She asked me to rub her back. Then it just kind of went from there. We had sex."

Warren said he remembered that Jayme Hurley had been wearing a bathrobe and a short halter-type, tank top. He claimed she had no underwear on. Warren insisted he had voluntary sex with Jayme Hurley for forty-five minutes. "After we was through, she was laying with her back to me. Then I just choked her to death."

That simple statement is all Lesley Warren would say about the actual murder.

Having killed Jayme Hurley with his bare hands, he sat on the bed. He later recalled: "I was trying to get myself together. I picked up the coke and the needles, tried to straighten up when I'd been there, spoons and all that.''

Then he wrapped Hurley's body in a sheet and carried her out to his van. ''I tied the sheet around her. I used one of her yellow tank tops to tie it,'' he said. Before Warren left the house, he turned off every light, including a pull chain that hung off the kitchen lamp in the ceiling. Warren had always been made to turn out all the lights by his mother, so it had come naturally to him.

At 7:50 A.M. the following day, Friday, May 25, Lesley Warren and his biological brother, Laron, turned up at their jobs at Lone Star Finishing in Asheville in Laron's 1977 Dodge Ram Charger. The two men finished work at 4:00 P.M. and stopped at an Exxon station for gas and then headed straight to Laron's house in Candler.

Warren and Laron sat around in the living room for a while before Lesley turned to his brother and said, ''Let's take a ride.'' They got in Warren's white 1968 Chevy van and headed off down Billy Cove Road in the direction of an area called Beaver Dam and then took a tunnel onto the long and winding McFee Road.

At no time did Lesley Warren tell his brother Laron where they were heading. Laron later claimed that during the drive he turned around to try and find a portable radio and noticed a body lying in the back of the van. All he could see was the shoulder, hair and one arm. She was lying facedown.

''What the hell is that doin' here, Lesley?'' Laron allegedly asked.

''It's Jayme Hurley. She OD'd on me.''

Laron pulled up a mattress cover that was lying

Victim Patsy Vineyard, 20, and her husband Mike.
(*Photo courtesy NY Bureau of Criminal Investigations*)

Vineyard was kidnapped from the Shipyard
Apartment complex in May 1987.

On June 5, 1987, Vineyard's body
washed onshore at Black River Bay.
(*Photo courtesy NY Bureau of Criminal Investigations*)

Victim Velma Faye Gray, 42.
(*Photo courtesy* Spartanburg Herald-Journal)

Gray was last seen standing next to her damaged car.
(*Photo courtesy* Spartanburg Herald-Journal)

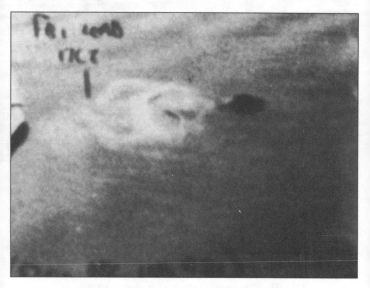

Gray's body was floating about 200 yards off shore.
(*Photo courtesy* NY Bureau of Criminal Investigations)

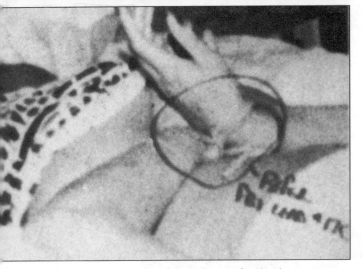

Gray's hands were tied with three loops of a shoelace.
(*Photo courtesy NY Bureau of Criminal Investigations*)

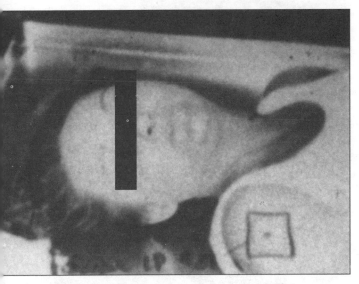

Gray had numerous injuries to her head and body.
(*Photo courtesy NY Bureau of Criminal Investigations*)

Victim Jayme Denise
Hurley, 37.
(*Photo courtesy Lee Hurley*)

Hurley was strangled in her Asheville, North Carolina, home.

Victim Katherine Johnson, 21.

Warren used an alias to rent a room with Johnson at the Town House Motel.

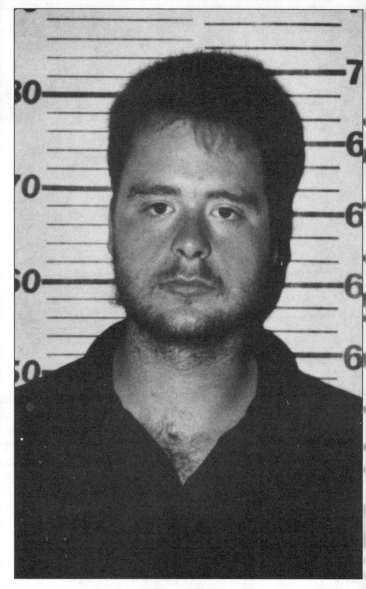

Leslie Eugene Warren, 22.
(*Photo courtesy Asheville Police Department*)

Warren was raised in this house on the outskirts of Asheville, North Carolina.

Warren was stationed at the U.S. Army base at Fort Drum in New York.

Warren was 18 when he married Tracey, 16.
(*Photo courtesy NY Bureau of Criminal Investigations*)

Wanted poster was issued when police realized
Warren was a suspect for several murders.
(Photo courtesy NY Bureau of Criminal Investigations)

Senior Investigator Bob Cooke and F.B.I. profiler
Ed Grant at "Warren Task Force" doorway
in the Asheville Police Department.
(*Photo courtesy NY Bureau of Criminal Investigations*)

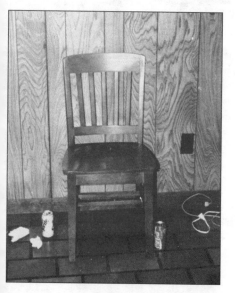

Wooden chair with
front legs sawed down
at an angle to keep
Warren uncomfortable
during interrogation.
(*Photo courtesy NY Bureau
of Criminal Investigations*)

Police pretended to have file drawers full of
evidence to trick Warren into confessing.
(*Photo courtesy NY Bureau of Criminal Investigations*)

Warren was walked past walls covered with enlargements
of fake fingerprints, photos, and maps.
(*Photo courtesy NY Bureau of Criminal Investigations*)

Investigator Richard H. Ladue.

Detective Carroll Amory.

Detective Mark McNeill.

Detective J.L. "Jerry" Grubb.

Patrolman Jeff Pate.

over the rest of the body and saw that she had brown to blond shoulder-length hair. "I didn't see no blood on her," he later recalled.

The corpse was dressed in a tan-colored bathrobe with the belt tied neatly around her waist. Laron noticed she was not wearing underwear, socks or shoes. "She had already started turning blue," Laron later explained.

Warren told his brother he was going to get rid of the body because "I don't need this kinda trouble." Laron said he refused to help Warren dispose of the body. "I don't want no part of this, Lesley."

Just then a local police cruiser came up close behind the van. Lesley Warren swallowed hard and told his brother to "shut the fuck up." For the next mile, they were shadowed by the county sheriff car, but then it turned right and drove off.

Warren continued driving and headed for the Pisgah Highway, northeast of Asheville. "We went all the way to above the waterfalls and stopped at about the third or fourth pullout," Laron later explained. "All the time, Lesley was asking me to help him and I kept saying no."

Warren then drove the van along a twisting, isolated country lane that led through the forest and up into the mountains behind Candler. At about 5:00 P.M., just as the surface of the road changed to gravel, Lesley Warren pulled up, got out and opened the side door of the vehicle. Then he once again pleaded for help from his brother. Laron refused and told Warren he wanted to go home. Warren ignored him and reached back into the van and grabbed Jayme Hurley's corpse by the ankles and began dragging her out of the van. With her body hanging half over the edge of the door frame, he stopped and picked up a short-handled shovel before grabbing the corpse around the waist and carrying her toward a bank at the side of the road.

Laron angrily told his brother he wanted to leave. Warren, who was by now forty feet down a steep embankment, yelled at Laron to go and come back later and pick him up. Laron reluctantly agreed. The last time he saw the body of Jayme Hurley was as Warren stumbled along with the corpse flopping over his arms in a sheet.

Lesley Warren struggled up the side of the mountain and kept falling over as the sheet covering Hurley's body snagged on the branches of overhanging trees. Eventually, he took off the sheet and carried her near-naked body over his shoulder. When he saw a break in the trees, he threw the corpse down on the ground with a thud and began digging a grave. After it got to eighteen inches in depth, he rolled her body into the hole and began shoveling the earth back over her. Then he threw back in the rocks and stones he'd dug out in the first place.

Sweating profusely, Warren ripped a piece of cloth off the sheet that had been wrapped around Hurley's body and hung it on a tree near the point where he'd dumped her so he could find it easily if he ever returned.

Warren later insisted that Laron did nothing other than drive him to the location. "Didn't help me get her out. Didn't help me carry her down or nothing," Warren said. But despite the coldness with which he described those events, Lesley Warren still had a conscience about the evil deed he had committed. "I'm sorry it happened," he later recalled. "We were real good friends and had been for a long time."

Laron Warren got home at about 5:30 P.M., ate

dinner with his wife, Missy, and their neighbor Pam
Davis and then headed back up the mountain about
an hour later. He eventually arrived at 6:45 P.M. at
the spot where he'd left his brother. He found an
exhausted, out-of-breath Lesley Warren sitting on a
wall. Laron noticed that he did not have the shovel
with him anymore. Warren's shirt was drenched in
sweat and his face, hands and arms were covered in
dirt. He immediately stood up and got into the van
alongside Laron.

"Gimme a cigarette. Mine are soaked," grunted
Warren, before adding, "You'd better not tell anyone what's happened."

On the way down the mountainside, Warren and
his brother stopped at their grandfather's house. Before going in, Warren took off his soiled shirt and
put on a Wilson Art jacket that was lying in the back
of the van. A few minutes later, they both returned
to Laron's house.

Later on that Friday evening, one of Jayme Hurley's best friends, Sara Burnette, called at Hurley's
house on Irving Street. She noticed the TV set was
flickering, but the house itself was bathed in total
darkness. The back door was slightly ajar.

As Burnette walked in, she immediately saw that
the couch was messed up and looked like someone
had been sleeping on it with a quilt and a screwed-
up pillow facing the direction of the TV set. But
Burnette saw no sign of a struggle. There were dirty
dishes in the sink. Maybe Jayme Hurley and her
guest had gone out for a late-night drink together?

That evening, May 25, one of Jayme Hurley's
neighbors on Irving Street, Joy Bagwell, also called
at the house. Upon walking through the open back
door, she noticed a T-shirt and underwear and a
pair of jeans lying on the floor at the foot of Jayme

Hurley's bed. "But there was nothing surprising in that as Jayme often left her clothes sprawled all over the place," Bagwell later recalled. "And she was always leaving her back door unlocked. She even left the keys in her red Monte Carlo parked in the driveway."

Bagwell noticed that the light in the kitchen had been turned off by the pull chain at the lightbulb rather than by the regular wall switch. Bagwell knew that something was wrong because Jayme Hurley was not tall enough to reach that pull chain. She also knew that Hurley would not leave the house for any length of time without asking her or someone else to feed her three beloved cats.

Eleven

The following day, Saturday, May 26, Lesley Warren, his wife, Tracey, and their two children, Joshua and baby Matthew, joined Warren's brother Laron and his wife, Missy, for a weekend outing at Lake Fontana. Just before they set off, Tracey insisted Lesley trash a filthy mattress cover in the back of the van. The group traveled in Lesley's van and Laron's Jeep to the lake. Within moments of getting in the van, Tracey noticed something else on the floor.

"What's that pocketbook, Lesley?" she asked.

"Didn't I tell you, honey? The van got stole a couple of days ago and whoever stole it left that pocketbook and the shoes and things that are in the back. I ain't had a chance to take them out yet."

Tracey examined the pocketbook. She later recalled: "It was big and black and had all that jungle stuff on it [camouflage] and had gold and bright colors on it and it had cantaloupes on it." She also noticed a burgundy-colored sheet with a flowery pattern all over it, which the group used to sit on the grass when they got to Lake Fontana.

But en route, a bizarre incident occurred. This later convinced Tracey Warren that something "weird" had been in the back of her husband's van. She explained: "We was just goin' down the road when the windshield shattered for no reason. It was spooky and I later reckoned it was connected to what had happened."

That Saturday morning, the Asheville Police Department were called by Jayme Hurley's worried father after he'd been contacted by the flower shop where his daughter worked when she had not shown up for work the previous day. Phone checks revealed that Jayme had spent almost an hour on the phone to her friend Catherine Jenkins in Florida. When she was contacted by investigating officer Sergeant Ted Lambert from the Asheville Police Department, she told the detective that a man called Lesley Warren had been staying at the house that night. She also mentioned his "troubled background" and how he had been staying at Hurley's house the night of her disappearance.

Two days later, on Memorial Day, Monday, May 28, forensic expert Sergeant Ross Robinson of Asheville PD's CID was called by his colleague Sergeant Ted Lambert to the Irving Street home of Jayme Hurley. Robinson immediately secured the scene by sealing the premises to prevent any disturbance of the scene. He then photographed the inside of Hurley's home and placed locks on the door.

Ross then began a painstaking search for fingerprints and trace evidence, collected pillowcases and bed linens and a lightbulb that appeared to have been unscrewed from one of the fixtures. Over the next few hours, he tested all wall surfaces for fingerprints and traces of blood. When he found a trace of fresh blood near the refrigerator, he advised Sergeant Lambert that in all probability Jayme Hurley had come to harm.

At 11:15 A.M. that same day, Sergeant Ted Lambert interviewed Hurley's good friend Sara Burnette at

Hurley's house. She told Lambert about Hurley's problems with her boyfriend, but that Hurley had cheered up over the previous few days because her boyfriend had been in contact and said he'd made a mistake by splitting up with her and wanted them to get back together. Sara Burnette described Jayme Hurley as quite a moody kind of person who thought she could save the world. "She's also a very trusting person," Burnette said.

Burnette said Jayme Hurley had used marijuana and cocaine on a "very limited basis" and that she did drink alcohol, but not every day. She described her as a fun-loving woman who often went to a local nightclub called Club 45 in Asheville. Burnette also reckoned Jayme Hurley "had a poor self-image of herself."

Ted Lambert then interviewed Jayme Hurley's next-door neighbor Joy Bagwell. She told Lambert she'd last seen Jayme at 6:30 on the night she disappeared. But they had only talked about her recently departed boyfriend, Chan Warner. Bagwell told Lambert that Hurley usually slept in her underwear and a T-shirt and sometimes even a nightgown. Going through the house with Lambert, Hurley's neighbor found that the only major items missing were a black jacket and the robe that Hurley regularly wore.

Bagwell also said that Hurley usually wore glasses rather than contact lenses because lenses gave her an eye infection. She noticed that Hurley's pocketbook was missing. It was more of a shoulder-type bag and featured pictures of wildlife on the outside. Jayme was a heavy smoker and a pack of cigarettes was still sitting on the nightstand. Jayme Hurley's glasses were then spotted lying on the sink in the bathroom. Bagwell and Lambert examined the telephone answering machine and discovered the tape was missing.

On the other side of Asheville that day Tracy and Lesley Warren had returned from their camping weekend at Lake Fontana. Tracey headed off to her home in Campobello, leaving her estranged husband at Laron and Missy's house in Candler.

Detective Sergeant Ted Lambert located Lesley Warren at his brother's house just a few minutes after his arrival, and Warren voluntarily drove his 1968 Chevy van to the Asheville Police Department for an interview, which was held at 5:00 P.M. on that Monday, May 28.

Lambert needed to urgently establish if Warren had been at Jayme Hurley's house and if he had any information that might help them trace the missing woman. Ted Lambert had Warren pegged as nothing more than a possible suspect at that time—not, as he later explained, "a primary suspect." Warren casually recalled to Lambert that he'd left Hurley's house while she was on the telephone to her friend Catherine Jenkins.

Lambert went through a number of other points with Warren and then asked him for consent to search the van he was driving at the time he had visited Hurley's house. Warren happily gave Lambert permission. "He was very cooperative," Lambert later recalled. Warren was then allowed to leave the building without any charges being made. His van remained in the police pound.

Meanwhile Tracey Warren had phoned Lesley's brother's house and Laron had come on the line. "He told me Lesley had been arrested. That he'd been taken down for questioning about a missing girl," Tracey later recalled. "Then Laron said he didn't know if I knew her, but it was Jayme Hurley. I knew who he meant when he said the name."

After his release from police custody, Lesley Warren drove back up to Candler and got drunk and stoned with neighbor Misty Ferguson, her boyfriend Royce Duckett and Warren's stepbrother Danny Murray. Warren openly admitted he'd been interviewed about the disappearance of Jayme Hurley and he told them he'd been at Hurley's home doing cocaine with her. One of the group later recalled: "It were almost as if he wanted us to tell the cops what he'd said."

Warren told the group that while the couple were doing cocaine, Hurley had died. He admitted quietly to Misty Ferguson he'd "freaked out" and then thrown her body in the river "near Alexander." Warren openly admitted to friends that he'd been doing cocaine since before he'd turned up at the Ferguson trailer that day.

Later that night, Lesley Warren went back to the Jayme Hurley burial site in the mountains. He parked his car and looked for the rag he'd deliberately left hanging on a tree as a marker. He walked around the area in the pitch dark for a few minutes to make sure nothing had been disturbed, then returned to his vehicle.

The following morning, Tuesday, May 29, Sergeant Ross Robinson carried out a careful examination of Warren's van. Inside, he found Jayme Hurley's pocketbook lying on the passenger side of the van on the floor. He also collected a flower-print sheet that was draped over an outboard motor and some blankets. Various particle samples were also taken and sent for testing at the State Bureau of Investigations, at Raleigh.

At 2:35 P.M. that day, Warren was pulled in for

another interview. This time he was the primary suspect and was advised of his rights. Warren replied that he understood them and Lambert began asking him detailed questions about the disappearance of Jayme Hurley. During that interrogation, Warren was asked about the pocketbook found in his van. Warren told Lambert and his CID colleagues it belonged to his wife and that they used it as a diaper bag for baby Matthew.

Warren insisted he'd arrived at Jayme Hurley's house at 8:30 P.M. after calling her on the phone earlier. He claimed he left Jayme Hurley's place at 10:30 P.M. and went straight to the Encores nightclub, where he stayed until closing time. He said he arrived home at 3:00 A.M. Warren repeated to investigators that Jayme Hurley was still on the telephone when he left her house.

Ted Lambert asked Lesley Warren if he'd taken anything from Jayme Hurley's house. He stated that he had not. He told investigators she had given him a book called *Dark Places* by Dean R. Koontz before her friend Katherine Jenkins had called. He also stated that Jayme Hurley had not at any time sat in his white Chevy van. He continued to claim the pocketbook found by detectives in his van belonged to his wife.

Warren was told the pocketbook had already been positively identified as belonging to Jayme Hurley. He did not reply for a few seconds, then admitted Hurley had given it to him "because it was torn and she didn't want it no more."

"We don't believe that, Lesley," Sergeant Lambert snapped back.

Warren again changed his tune. He knew he was in serious trouble, so he turned to Lambert and said, "I may need an attorney."

Lambert told Warren to wait in the office while he spoke to colleagues about whether to continue the interview. It was decided to carry on in case Jayme Hurley was still alive and he might help them find her.

Lambert took a long, deep breath and walked back into the interview room with two other investigators. Warren made no further requests for an attorney. As the conversation continued, Warren began revealing more and more details about his involvement in the case. As Ted Lambert later recalled, "It was just like a normal conversation. He was very cooperative. There may have been raised voices from time to time, but no direct hollering at him."

Captain John Annarino, a senior Asheville officer, joined the investigators. While he was alone with Warren, the suspect claimed to Annarino that a black man had come to the house after Hurley finished her phone call to Jenkins. Warren said that all three of them had been injecting cocaine and that Hurley had overdosed and died.

Warren lowered his voice. "This black guy said I had to help him get rid of her body." Warren said he was prepared to take the investigators to where he had dumped the contents of Hurley's pocketbook. Captain Amarino pulled his colleagues out of the interview room and told them to take Warren to the location.

Warren and at least six Asheville PD officers headed out to Beaver Dam Road, in Candler, where Warren said he'd thrown the items from the pocketbook. They quickly found it in a white plastic bag on the side of the road.

Warren then admitted there was no black man involved and that he and Hurley had shot cocaine alone. Then she overdosed and he put her body in his van and threw it into the French Broad River from the Pearson Bridge. Warren even recalled to Captain Annarino how the water had been very high and swift, and that when he threw her in the river, he saw the splash in the variable light. Warren was then escorted from the Asheville Police Department to the Pearson Bridge, where he pointed out where he said he dropped her into the water.

At 9.36 P.M. that evening, Warren returned to the police department building and was advised of his rights. He was then placed under arrest on a warrant for the outstanding misdemeanor of failure to produce a title for his vehicle, a car he was no longer in possession of. He was also arrested and charged with larceny of Jayme Hurley's pocketbook.

He was not charged with anything directly connected to the death or disappearance of Jayme Hurley.

A written statement was taken from Warren, which included the latest version of what he claimed happened the night of Jayme Hurley's disappearance. Warren was escorted to the Buncombe County Jail. Immediately after Warren's detention, Scott Jarvis, an Asheville attorney with thirty years' experience, was contacted by Warren's mother and hired to represent her son. He immediately visited Warren in Buncombe County Jail and began attempting to get a bail hearing set.

Detective Sergeant Ted Lambert and his colleagues mounted a frantic search for Jayme Hurley's body in the French Broad River between the Pearson Bridge and a waste-treatment plant. When that failed to turn up anything, investigators concentrated on land adjacent to the Warrens' family home in the Billy Cove area of Buncombe County.

Warren's mother, Phyllis, had at one time lived on Curtis Creek above the Pisgah Highway on a road that cut right through the forest up into the mountains. It was an obvious spot to dump a body. Officers combing the area found some yellow knotted binding-type material in a gully off the main track, but no sign of Jayme Hurley's body.

Lesley Warren was extremely careful not to talk about the case when he spoke to his wife, Tracey, from a Buncombe County Jail pay phone. "He didn't say much. Just that he couldn't talk," she later recalled.

The following Sunday, June 3, Tracey Warren, accompanied by Laron and his wife, Missy, visited Lesley Warren in jail. He was so worried his conversation might be monitored that he refused to talk about the accusations against him. He took the same attitude during all subsequent phone conversations from the jailhouse.

Warren's attorney, Scott Jarvis, knew it was highly likely that more serious charges relating to the death of Jayme Hurley would follow. "They [the DA's office] advised me that they had a strong suspicion," Jarvis later recalled, "that it involved a homicide, although they were not ready to file the charges at that point in time."

On June 6, Warren made a Buncombe County court appearance during which his bond was dropped to $25,000, even though the state announced in open court that the defendant was the primary suspect in the disappearance of Jayme Hurley. Warren was released from custody after his grandfather paid the bond plus a retainer to attorney Scott Jarvis. Shortly afterward, Lesley Warren dropped by Jarvis's offices in Asheville and told Jarvis that if anything more came up in relation to the disappearance of Jayme Hurley he wanted Jarvis to represent him.

Two hours later, Warren was reunited with Tracey at his mother and stepfather's apartment in Candler.

"So what's goin' on, Lesley?" Tracey asked her husband.

"I'll tell you later, Tracey. I promise."

Laron Warren later claimed that after Lesley Warren had been released from jail, Lesley told his brother: "No body. No crime."

Stepbrother Eric Murray recalled: "I went over to my stepmother's house to pick up my son. Police were still searching the French Broad River for this girl. Lesley said he used to screw her when he met her at some juvenile home. I think he said something about still screwing her since. He also said he was over at this girl's house. He said she'd OD'd and that he'd told police he'd thrown her in the river."

Later that morning, Lesley Warren took his wife and two small children for a walk up the side of the same mountain where he had buried Jayme Hurley's body. Lesley Warren was so detached from his emotions that he could easily cope with such an outing.

To get to the mountain, he drove up past Curtis Creek alongside the Pisgah Highway to where the road cut off and headed into the National Forest and the picnic area. Lesley Warren knew the area well from his early childhood. At the base of the mountain, he began pouring his heart out to his wife about Jayme Hurley.

"Tracey, I gotta tell you I been doin' cocaine a long time and I think I'm real addicted to it. You know me and that missin' woman, Jayme Hurley, we was shootin' up cocaine and I tried to stop her

'cause she was doin' so much, she took seventy cc
or something, and anyways she OD'd on it." He
spoke in short, sharp bursts as if desperate to get
the words out before he stopped saying them.

"I got real scared when she died and wiped my
fingerprints off everything in that house and then
took her up to the mountain and buried her up
there," he said, looking up beyond them. "I got this
shovel and dug a big hole and put her in it and
buried her with dirt and rocks and leaves and
bushes and stuff."

As the estranged couple stood on the side of the
mountain on what should have been a happy day
out, Lesley Warren turned to his wife and pointed
to the woods to where son Josh was playing just a
few yards ahead of them.

"We'd better not walk too far 'cause we might
walk over her."

Tracey took a deep breath but said nothing.

Warren even told his wife about the moments following Jayme Hurley's death. "I did her pulse and
stuff and then waited a little while and tried to do
CPR, but it was too late. I took her pulse again, still
wasn't nothing. That's when I decided to take her
up here. I picked her up and put her in the van.
Didn't know what else to do. I told the police she
OD'd on cocaine and that I'd had put her in the
river. Now the police will never find her in the river
'cause she ain't there."

Tracey Warren later recalled: "I just remember
there was like a little dogwood tree right there, like
kind of right in the middle and then this little hill
went down and it kind of leveled out. It was by a
mound of dirt and it sloped down one direction
and kind of went flat into another."

Warren explained to his wife how Jayme Hurley

had bled profusely after she died. "She bled so hard. When she OD'd her eyes rolled back and that's when she started bleeding out her nose and mouth and ears and stuff, and she started jerking real bad," Warren said.

It was only as Lesley Warren provided his wife with the gruesome details that he admitted the sheets and blankets in the van had been used to move the body. He also mentioned the pocketbook.

"I told the cops I threw all the stuff out of the pocketbook, the wallet and ID and stuff as I was goin' up the road. I took them out there and showed them where I threw it because I had nothin' to hide." He paused and then continued: "I'm scared, Tracey, 'cause if I'd told the cops that I'd buried her, then they'd have said I killed her and I really didn't, Tracey. I really didn't."

Tracey later recalled: "He seemed kinda scared and he was trying to be honest because he told me about a lot of stuff. Like cheatin' on me, the women and stuff, and the rest of it."

Warren even admitted to his wife he'd been back to the mountain since the killing to make sure Jayme Hurley's grave had not been discovered. He said he'd buried her because "I didn't want her bobbing to the surface, like she would have done in the water."

Warren told his wife: "I went back up there to see if she was still there and dogs hadn't dug her up or anythin' happened to her, or anythin', but she was still up there." He said there were rocks and leaves and bushes over the spot where Hurley was buried, so he knew where to find her. Warren never once voiced any concern for Jayme Hurley's family or what they were going through following her disappearance or even speculated on whether the police were going to accuse him of killing her.

Warren turned to his wife: "I'm not going to turn up in court."

Tracey Warren later recalled: "He was telling me bye, 'cause he just, I mean me knowing him the way I do, I know he was trying to say he's not going to be around for a while, so I knew right then he wasn't showing up for court because the police and people were trying to nail him for [the] kind of stuff he didn't do."

Warren went off into the bushes on the pretext he needed to empty his bladder. "I know he did some cocaine," Tracey later recalled. "I could tell."

On his return, Warren told his wife: "I'd like to try and get up here and get a place to live and go to court and see what happens, but I ain't gonna go." Then he snapped back to the Hurley killing: "I tried to tell her [Jayme Hurley] to slow down, she was doing too much and that was it," Warren added as if to reexplain his reasons for murdering another human being.

Tracey Warren asked her husband why he didn't simply tell the police the truth. Warren shrugged his shoulders and replied: "If I'd left her there in that house and called the police, they still would have thought I did it. You know what, Tracey? If I'd really thrown her in the river, it wouldn't have mattered 'cause the fish would have ate her or something. You know she would have deteriorated and you wouldn't have been able to tell, but by me burying her, you still ain't going to be able to tell and the cops will say I killed her."

Warren's words to his wife were as confused as his state of mind.

But Tracey still managed to respond: "They'll say she OD'd and they'd know she done it to herself, surely?"

"I know I was right to do it this way, Tracey," Warren said. "I know."

His face went paler and he seemed to be lost in his thoughts. "All I was thinkin' about was gettin' rid of her. I didn't know what else to do." At that moment, Tracey recalled, her husband looked like a frightened child caught with his hands in a cookie jar.

That evening Tracey and Warren and the children spent the night together at a friend's house. The following morning, Lesley Warren dropped his family home in Campobello and then headed back to Candler.

At 3:30 P.M. on June 7, Warren, his brother Laron and grandfather Eugene West turned up at the Asheville Police Department to obtain a release for Warren's 1968 Chevy van. Arrangements were made to allow him to pick up the van the following day at 5:00 P.M. Sergeant Ted Lambert was playing for time. He knew he had to find Jayme Hurley's body as quickly as possible or Warren would disappear.

Just before the group left the Asheville PD building, Ted Lambert asked Warren if he would consent to giving blood, hair and urine samples as part of the ongoing investigation into Hurley's disappearance. Warren surprised Lambert by immediately agreeing to the request. At 5.30 P.M., Lambert drove Warren to the St. Joseph Urgent Care Center in Asheville and the samples were taken.

Afterward Lambert told Warren: "Reckon we need to talk some more, Lesley."

" 'Fraid not, Mr. Lambert, sir, my wife's just come into town from South Carolina and I gotta see her."

"That's fine, Lesley," replied Lambert. "When would be a good time for you?

"How about tomorrow afternoon, about three?"

"That'd be fine by me, sir," said Warren.

Early next morning, Ted Lambert reluctantly abandoned the search for Jayme Hurley's body after ten fruitless days and thousands of man-hours. He feared Lesley Warren wouldn't return later that day for his white 1968 Chevy van. Lambert and his colleagues would just have to continue chasing down leads and try to establish more information about the last days and hours of Jayme Hurley's life.

As a result, Ted Lambert decided to drive down to the Spartanburg area of South Carolina where Tracey Warren lived with her family in Campobello. Lambert first visited the Spartanburg County Sheriff's Department to carry out some background checks on the family.

Ted Lambert was in the middle of a meeting with a senior officer when Detective Carroll Amory walked into the captain's office. Amory stopped in his tracks when he heard the name "Lesley Warren."

"What d'you say that name was?" asked Amory.

"Lesley Warren."

"Sounds real familiar to me. Think I gotta file on him. Hold tight here a minute," said Amory.

Amory returned to the captain's office a couple of minutes later with the Velma Faye Gray case file and pulled out a photo of Warren.

"Is this the guy?" asked Amory.

"Sure is."

As Carroll Amory later explained, "We only had

him linked through the trucking company, nothing else at that time. All we knew was that he was one of eighty employees of that trucking company. We didn't know another damn thing about him."

Amory sat down with Lambert and it rapidly dawned on them that Lesley Warren was most probably a habitual killer. "I'd like you to come back to Asheville and we'll get Lesley in for you to talk to," said Lambert.

Within hours Spartanburg investigator Carroll Amory was poring over the two case files and comparing notes. "We soon realized that Lesley was our man," Amory later recalled.

That day Lesley Warren's mother, Phyllis, phoned investigators at the Asheville PD to tell them that Scott Jarvis would be continuing to represent her son, and investigators should contact him rather than her son. Jarvis was also representing Warren in a small-claims action against a man who'd bought a motorcycle from him and then not paid the full amount of cash agreed.

Phyllis also mentioned that her son had been interviewed about another missing girl called Patsy Vineyard in upstate New York in 1987 when he'd been serving in the U.S. Army. "Now we've got three agencies interested in one person," one investigator later explained.

It was only after linking the Hurley death to at least two others that Ted Lambert and his colleagues asked for help from the FBI's Criminal Personality Profiling Program. It looked like they might have a serial killer on their hands. Once the Bureau agreed to accept the case, profiler Ed Grant arrived in Asheville to begin studying all the available information on the life and crimes of Lesley Eugene Warren. Such profiles are a form of highly educated guesswork, involving as much intuition as science, and they sometimes miss their mark.

The FBI has compiled a "Top Ten" list of the general characteristics of serial sex-murderers:

1. Over 90 percent of them are white males.

2. They tend to be intelligent, with IQs in the "bright normal" range.

3. In spite of their high IQs, they do poorly in school, have a hard time holding down jobs and often work as unskilled laborers.

4. They tend to come from markedly unstable families. Typically, they are abandoned as children by their fathers and raised by domineering mothers.

5. Their families often have criminal, psychiatric and alcoholic histories.

6. They hate their fathers. They hate their mothers.

7. They are commonly abused as children—psychologically, physically and sexually. Sometimes their abuser is a stranger. Sometimes it is a friend. Often it is a family member.

8. Many of them end up spending time in institutions as children and have records of early psychiatric problems.

9. They have a high rate of suicide attempts.

10. They are intensely interested from an early age in voyeurism, fetishism and sadomasochistic pornography.

Investigators would learn that Warren qualified for all ten of these characteristics, but at this time, they weren't even sure they had enough evidence to "go looking for Lesley Warren."

* * *

Just a few hours after being told about Warren's
link with the Patsy Vineyard case, NYSP senior investigator Bob Cooke received a phone call from
Sergeant Ted Lambert at Asheville PD. He asked
Cooke about the Patsy Vineyard case and said he
suspected she had been killed by Lesley Eugene
Warren. Cooke later recalled: "Ted Lambert said
he'd arrested Warren for possession of another missing person's purse or something, and he had been
dragging the river down there because Warren had
said he'd put her in the river."

Lambert told Cooke that Warren had claimed his
Asheville victim had died of an accidental drug overdose and he then "got scared and put her in the
river." Lambert told Bob Cooke he had spoken to
Warren's mother and she'd mentioned that police
up in Watertown, New York, had questioned her son
about a missing girl up there.

NYSP investigators immediately pulled the files on
the Vineyard case and found that Warren had been
a soldier in the same unit as Patsy Vineyard's husband, Mike. Senior Investigator Bob Cooke immediately recognized his name. Warren had not been
in the field at the time Patsy Vineyard went missing.
Ted Lambert also pointed out certain similarities between the Vineyard, Gray and Hurley cases. Vineyard's purse was never found and neither was Gray's.
Vineyard and Gray were found dead in water, and
Hurley had been supposedly thrown into a river, by
Warren's own admission. Cooke's colleague Wayne
Corsa then checked Warren's background out carefully and reconfirmed that he'd been at Fort Drum
when Patsy Vineyard disappeared. Warren and his
friend Tom Walker were two of just six members of

their unit who did not go in the field at the time of her disappearance.

Cooke and Corsa drove their black NYSP Pontiac Grand Prix down to Asheville, North Carolina, in thirteen hours. All they'd had time to pack were a couple of changes of underwear.

In Asheville, the two NYSP investigators checked into the Ramada Hotel and then met up with Ted Lambert at a nearby restaurant. The law enforcement agents discussed the various investigations. The following morning, Cooke and Corsa talked with the Spartanburg Sheriff's Department about the Velma Faye Gray killing, now also linked to Lesley Warren.

As Bob Cooke later pointed out: "Warren had been bailed out and was walking the streets. We all knew we had to move fast."

All three forces—Spartanburg, Asheville and Watertown—agreed to set up a task force to gather evidence against Warren. But, as Bob Cooke later explained, "all we had at that point was a suspect. Spartanburg had a body. Asheville did not. But Spartanburg had a link because Warren was working for the trucking outfit that drove right up the 81 highway and one of his trucks was seen that night. They also had people who'd stopped by this lady's accident on the side of the highway and saw a guy in a truck stop to give her assistance."

Spartanburg investigators told Cooke one of the things that confused them was that they couldn't find a truck at AM-CAN with the right mileage on it. Investigators were not fully aware of just how easily Warren could have taken any AM-CAN truck and used it for weekend trips to pick up girls, friends or relatives.

The first morning the NYSP investigators arrived

in Asheville was spent going over each case in order to produce a detailed synopsis of each killing. As Bob Cooke later recalled: "Warren fitted all of them like a glove." Arresting Warren became the task force's number one priority, but first of all, they needed to interview as many of Warren's family and friends as possible in order to gather sufficient evidence to make an arrest.

The FBI's serial killer profiler Ed Grant even assured Ted Lambert and his fellow investigators they would not find the body of Jayme Hurley in the water as Warren had claimed. They were convinced Warren had buried her in a shallow grave. Bob Cooke of the NYSP recalled: "They said it would be on a paved road, off in a gully, and they're telling us all this and we've just wasted our time dragging the river."

NYSP investigators Cooke and Corsa spent two weeks in Asheville and called up two more NYSP investigators as well as an ID expert to track down and locate at least half a dozen cars Warren had owned over the previous four years. Copies of Lesley Warren's work sheets when he was a truck driver at AM-CAN were examined in a bid to line up his work movements with any other reported homicides in the areas where he visited.

Bob Cooke and the other investigators realized that one of the most important leads was that the killer of Velma Faye Gray was seen by a nurse going to work at 5:30 A.M. This time Dorothy Deck picked Warren's 1976 Monte Carlo out from a lineup of vehicle photos. The pieces of the jigsaw were finally starting to fall into place.

Twelve

On June 30, 1990, Lesley Warren turned up at the home of his stepbrother Eric Murray where he showed off a stainless-steel .44-caliber Magnum Ruger pistol, which he said he'd purchased with money given to him by his wife, Tracey.

Warren, Murray and Murray's wife, Carla, sat drinking beer together for at least three hours. Warren even produced a ten-inch-long "Japanese-type" knife. Stroking it menacingly, Warren said the police "were trying to pin something on me."

Later that same evening, Warren's former girlfriends Lisa and Michelle Lawrence were sitting on a wall outside a store on the Pisgah Highway when Warren drove by in a car. He stopped and spoke to the girls. "He asked how we were doing," Michelle later recalled. "He was drinking a beer and said he was on probation."

Right in the middle of a calm and polite conversation, Lesley Warren pulled out his prized .44-caliber Magnum pistol with a long barrel and showed it to Michelle. Warren even allowed her to take two shots at some trees on the side of the road. The girls noticed Warren's eyes seemed very glazed. Moments later, Warren drove another 100 yards up the highway to a gas station, got out and went to a public phone booth where he made a number of calls. Lisa and Michelle left shortly afterward.

One of the calls made by Lesley Warren was to his mother. "You gotta come get me, Mom," Warren slurred. "I got a real bad headache." He then told her where he was. Phyllis was so worried by her son's call that she immediately got in her car. She didn't even know where Warren was living at the time, but she recognized from the tone of his voice that he was on the verge of "doing something real bad."

However, within moments of her arriving at the gas station, Warren injected himself with a "hot-shot"—a liquified form of cocaine, typically laced with heroin—in front of his shocked mother. She stormed off in tears.

In the early hours of the next morning, July 1, 1990, Lesley Warren turned up at his sister-in-law Missy's home on Billy Cove Road, Candler. Warren was wearing a white open shirt over a tight black jean shirt with blue jeans and white Converse sneakers with laces tucked in, not tied. He gave Missy Warren a letter to give to Tracey. She noticed the shirt he was wearing had blood on the left-sleeve cuff and possibly the right. "When I asked him about it, Lesley told me he had a nosebleed," Missy later recalled.

Warren asked for a bundle of letters from Tracey, which he'd left at Missy's home for safekeeping. Missy told Warren it was too late to start trying to dig them out, but Warren barged past her and found them in a cabinet in the living room. When he asked if he could sleep over, they had an argument. At 3:00 A.M., Warren stormed out of the trailer. An hour later, a nearby trailer belonging to Missy Warren's friend Pam Davis was broken into by a man. Nothing was stolen, but an intruder match-

ing Lesley Warren's description was seen running
away from the scene.

A few hours later, Missy picked up a shirt that
Warren had left behind on the sitting room floor
and noticed it contained a minicassette from a telephone answering machine. What Missy Warren
didn't realize was that it had come from Jayme Hurley's house.

In Asheville the joint investigation between the
Asheville Police Department, the Spartanburg
County Sheriff's Office and the New York State Police Department was continuing to gather evidence
against Lesley Warren. It was hoped that within days
a warrant for murder could be issued. Police were
convinced Lesley Warren was a serial killer.

On July 5, investigators visited Warren's brother
Laron, who told them about a strip of cloth he'd
spotted on the road next to the forest some miles
from his house. On inspection it appeared to have
hair and fibers on it plus some blood. Laron Warren
claimed he had only seen it the previous day when
he had been up the gravel road to check the reser-
voir that provided water for his home.

Laron, accompanied by four police investigators,
then drove farther up the twisting and turning
gravel road to a cabin that had been used as a summer house by the Warren family. In the cabin, investigators found a pocketknife and pieces of nylon
string. All the items were immediately bagged and
given to Sergeant Ross Robinson of the Asheville
PD for forensic examination.

Laron Warren also showed the detectives a spot
on the bank by the side of the road where it appeared that something had been dragged northside
of the gravel road. Senior investigator Bob Cooke
of the NYSP volunteered to climb to the top of the

steep bank where the trail ended, but he couldn't find any further evidence. The investigators took numerous photos of the area for later reference because they remained convinced that Jayme Hurley was buried somewhere in the vicinity.

At Tracey Warren's home in Campobello, a white long-sleeve shirt belonging to Lesley Warren was recovered by investigators, who then showed it to Warren's sister-in-law Missy Warren. She positively identified the shirt as the one worn by Lesley Warren when he appeared at their house at 3:00 A.M. on July 1. Missy stated it was the same shirt she had seen blood on.

NYSP investigators uncovered a case they suspected could be connected to Lesley Warren. On January 27, 1987, Beverly Sherman, a seventeen-year-old African American prostitute from Watertown, died from a .38-caliber gunshot wound to the head and possibly had her throat cut. Sherman's badly decomposed body wasn't found until April that year in a wooded area where hookers often took their "johns" for sex.

Another murder victim in Asheville was also linked to Warren. Twenty-three-year-old Pamela Michelle Murray had been abducted from a shopping mall on February 14 ,1987. She had earlier left her grandmother's house at 12:25 P.M. Pamela's body was discovered less than an hour later on nearby Azalea Road. She had been shot through the head after apparently trying to escape from her kidnapper.

On July 9, a meeting was held at the Asheville Police Department attended by Spartanburg County's Sheriff Bill Coffey, Lieutenant Daniel Swad, Detective Sergeant Gary Williams and Detective Robbie Hendrix plus Asheville's Ted Lambert and

NYSP's Bob Cooke and Wayne Corsa. The investigators realized they still needed more concrete evidence against Warren in order to make any murder charges stick—and that meant finding another body.

Just a few hours later, Laron Warren and his wife, Missy, were brought in for a new interview at the Asheville PD building. The couple now said they were "fed up" with Lesley Warren and specifically made a reference to Warren having stolen a ring from Missy that had belonged to her recently deceased mother. They told investigators they'd reported the theft to the Buncombe County Sheriff's Department and, as a result, a warrant was issued for the arrest of Warren for larceny.

Laron and Missy insisted they'd tried to help Lesley Warren on numerous occasions, but that he was deeply ungrateful to them. They also confirmed that Warren's marriage to Tracey was an "on-again/off-again" relationship, but that Tracey would stick by her husband no matter what. Laron insisted he knew no reason why his mother, Phyllis, had told investigators about Lesley Warren's "link" to the upstate New York missing woman case.

The following day, July 10, investigators tried to locate Warren's army buddy Tom Walker, who'd moved with his family to Ridgeland, North Carolina. In New York State, Investigator Maynard Cosnett, SP Oneida Auto Theft, traced the 1980 Mercury Capri believed to have been owned by Lesley Warren when he lived in Watertown in 1987. Cosnett quickly tracked it to a new owner in Spartanburg, South Carolina.

Lesley Warren went to the county courthouse in Spartanburg for a reason completely unconnected to his killing spree. He told staff he'd lost his ID and that he needed a copy of his birth certificate. Warren called himself "Bryan Allen Collins." Warren later explained: "I told them I needed another form to get an ID and they filled out the form saying, you know, that was my social security number and I took it back over to the Highway Patrol Department."

The name "Bryan Allen Collins" belonged to Warren's brother-in-law. He didn't know Warren was using his name. "I mean, it was . . . it wasn't hard to do," Warren later explained. "I just went in there and told them I'd lost my license. They took my picture and give it to me."

On July 11, Senior Investigator Bob Cooke of the NYSP and his colleague Wayne Corsa checked Asheville pawnshop records to try and locate any of Patsy Vineyard's jewelry, but they found nothing. Over in Spartanburg, similar checks were carried out by two local investigators.

On the same day, Warren's mother, Phyllis Murray, was brought in for further questioning at the Asheville Police Department. Murray described to investigators years of problems raising her son Lesley. Murray repeated to investigators that while Warren was stationed in the army in New York, he called her on the phone and told her about a friend's wife who was missing. She said she became suspicious after realizing her son had been interviewed about three separate deaths of women. Phyllis Murray told investigators that a few weeks later Warren called her back and told her that the missing girl had been found dead in a river. Warren also later told his mother that a black man who "walked the railroad tracks" had been responsible for the girl's death.

Warren's mother gave investigators photographs of her son and his wife, Tracey. One of those pictures showed Tracey Warren wearing what appeared to be Patsy Vineyard's ring. The photo had been taken just one week after Patsy Vineyard's death. Officers established from Phyllis that Lesley and Tracey Warren had driven to North Carolina with army buddy Tom Walker over the dates of May 21, 22 and 23, 1987, just a few days after Patsy Vineyard had been killed.

On July 12, Captain Loszynski of the NYSP sent three more investigators down to North Carolina to assist in the investigation. "We were in a battle against time because we knew that Lesley would make a run for it sooner rather than later if we didn't get enough evidence to warrant his arrest for murder," one investigator later explained.

The police also feared it was only a matter of time before Warren killed again, although some detectives privately admitted they needed him to strike again in order to nail him for his previous homicides. "It was a bad time for all the investigators," one detective later explained. "Warren was like a time bomb waiting to explode."

Also on July 12, NYSP investigators Cooke and Wayne Corsa accompanied Asheville PD Sergeant Ted Lambert to help officers carry out a new search of the Billy Cove Road area of Candler, near where Laron had already dropped hints about the fate of Jayme Hurley. But nothing more was found.

Cooke and Corsa then headed to Ridegland, South Carolina, to interview Tom Walker and his wife, Denise. Walker downplayed his close relationship with Warren while they were both in the army. He told the investigators he had "reestablished his relationship with God," which meant that hanging

around with Warren tarnished that image. Walker
adamantly denied any knowledge of Warren's involvement in the death of Patsy Vineyard.

During his interview with Cooke and Corsa, Tom
Walker also said he could not remember driving to
North Carolina with the Warrens in May 1987. His
wife, Denise, specifically recalled her husband visiting his parents' home in Whittier, North Carolina,
during the same trip. She also remembered telling
her husband about Patsy Vineyard's disappearance
during a phone call to his parents' residence.

Lesley Warren spent the night of July 11, in the
Spartanburg area and met up with his wife, Tracey,
early the following day. Later that morning, she
dropped him outside a local motorcycle dealership
where he asked to test-drive a gleaming black
Kawasaki Vulcan 750. The salesman refused to allow
Warren to take the motorcycle out on the open
road, but eventually he let him take it for a spin in
the parking lot. Seconds later, he watched in despair
as a smiling Lesley Warren expertly drove off toward
the exit onto the highway.

Warren later recalled: "I was just looking at them
[motorcycles]. I was looking to buy one. I was trying
to get a bank loan at the time. They wouldn't let
me drive it except around the parking lot. So I
drove it around the parking lot a couple of times
and drove off with it." A few minutes later, Warren
swapped the bike's tags with another motorcycle
parked near Spartanburg's main hospital.

At 2:30 P.M. that afternoon, Warren turned up at
his stepbrother Eric's place of work in Asheville riding the gleaming black Kawasaki motorcycle. Eric
immediately noticed that Warren had changed his

hairstyle so it was sticking up and had been dyed yellow. "It looked kinda funny and [like] something he had done himself."

Warren told Eric he had spent the previous few days camping out and that he'd call him later that night. Nothing about Warren ever surprised Eric. As he later recalled: "I would describe Lesley as a nervous kind of person on the edge." Then he added grimly, "He's also mean and a thief."

Later that same Thursday afternoon, July 12, Lesley Warren turned up at Misty Ferguson's trailer riding the black Kawasaki 750 and even joked that he wanted to paint it another color. Warren said he was planning to travel to Canada and get himself a truck-driving job.

Thirteen

The good citizens of High Point, North Carolina, population 76,000, thought they had won the war against crime—that is, until Lesley Warren drove into the city on his stolen black Kawasaki motorcycle. Fittingly, it was Friday, July 13, 1990. After years of problems with gangs moving in from the big surrounding cities and servicing a known drug supply route between Los Angeles and High Point, the federal, state and local law enforcement agencies reckoned they had turned the corner.

Around 4:00 P.M. that Friday, Lesley Warren swung off the High Point exit from Interstate 85. He was so unfamiliar with the city he bought a street map at the first service station he passed. Warren was looking for Terry Quimby, whom he'd befriended back in Candler when she'd stayed with her sister Misty Ferguson.

Warren got himself a room at the Town House Motel, just off Main Street, and took a shower following his long journey. As he later explained: "I just knew she'd [Terry] be at work that evening at the Ramada Hotel, so I waited till around six after the bar opened and went up and met her."

Lesley Warren stayed at the bar Tradewinds most of the evening. "I got pretty drunk, I guess," he later explained. "Don't remember much else of that night." In fact, Warren flashed a lot of big bills and downed a tankful of tequila. He got so drunk he became involved in an incident that might have altered the course of his criminal habits if fate had not played a cruel role.

At midnight Warren tumbled drunkenly into the Ramada parking lot to pick up his stolen Kawasaki. He could barely stand up. When he tried to flick down his bike stand, both machine and man fell over. Warren attempted to stagger over to the exit payment booth occupied by a middle-aged brunette attendant named Monette McKinney. She immediately noticed his arms were bleeding and gave him some paper towels. She said, "Now, you don't need to be driving, do you?"

Warren replied: "No, I don't want any trouble. How much will it be to park overnight? I'm only two blocks from my room at the motel. I can walk there."

"It's only five dollars," she replied.

Warren passed over a $5 bill and began trying to push his motorcycle back to where it had been originally parked. But he fell into a parked car owned by one of the Ramada hotel guests. Warren struggled back to his feet once again, left the bike leaning against the car and began stumbling up the ramp to the second level of the parking lot. McKinney called the police and told them that although Warren had been polite, he was extremely drunk and needed help to move the bike.

Patrolman Jeff Pate from the High Point PD happened to be around the corner in his cruiser and got to the scene within two minutes. He spotted Warren lying on the sidewalk just outside the parking lot. Warren sat upright when he saw the patrolman approach and immediately told him he didn't want to ride the bike and didn't want any trouble.

When Warren was asked for his license, he was too drunk to get it out of his pocket. Officer Pate removed it from his back pocket. It identified him as Bryan Allen Collins and gave a Longview Road, Spartanburg, South Carolina, address. The officer pushed the bike back to its original position in the parking space.

Officer Jeff Pate offered to take the man they knew as Bryan Collins back to his hotel room. A few minutes later, his black-and-white Caprice deposited Lesley Warren at the Town House Motel.

The following morning, July 14, Ramada Hotel parking lot attendant Ellen Holmes was working when Lesley Warren approached her as she sat in her glass booth by the exit. Warren told Holmes he thought he'd hit a car on the upper deck of the parking lot the previous night.

Holmes told Warren she'd found a note when she came into work that morning informing her that someone on a motorcycle had hit a car. Warren asked for the name of the car owner who'd written the note. Warren also wanted to know who had taken him back to his motel the previous evening.

Holmes laughed and said: "Man, you must have been in bad shape if you don't know who put you in bed." She told Warren she understood the police had been called to check the car he'd hit and they'd taken him home. Warren continued to insist he wanted to get in touch with the lady owner of the car he'd hit. Ellen Holmes told him to go to the Ramada Hotel reception for the information.

That same day, the Warren task force reviewed the entire Vineyard case file and began to put together a new profile of Lesley Warren. Meanwhile,

Spartanburg detective Carroll Amory interviewed Warren's onetime girlfriend Bronya Owenby, who placed Warren in possession of an AM-CAN tractor-trailer on or around the date of the Velma Faye Gray homicide.

Owenby, speaking from her home in Candler, explained to investigators how Warren regularly went to the AM-CAN yard and took a truck without permission. This explained to detectives why Warren was driving around in an AM-CAN truck when he was not working at the time. Owenby also told investigators about numerous other incidents involving Warren and concluded: "I think he's crazy."

That night, Lesley Warren didn't leave his motel room until around midnight, after Terry Quimby and a friend got off work at the Ramada. He later explained: "They stopped by and picked me up and we went and had a beer. But then Terry ran me back to the motel room because I wasn't feeling real well." Warren claimed the vast amount of tequila he'd drunk the previous night had made him feel "real sick."

Terry Quimby had no doubts about Lesley Warren. "I thought he was a nice guy," she later recalled. "He was a lot of fun. He'd make you laugh."

Warren was now well aware he was on the lam from the Asheville PD investigation into the death of Jayme Hurley. He told everyone he met in High Point he was "just passin' through."

Early the next morning, Sunday, July 15, NYSP investigators Cooke and Corsa traveled to Knoxville, Tennessee, to interview Patsy Vineyard's husband, Mike, who was living back at his former home after leaving the army. Armed with a number of questions formulated by a specialist FBI profiler, Vineyard was asked various details. Vineyard told investigators he remembered Warren from the army, but stayed away from him because he considered him a trouble-maker.

In High Point, Lesley Warren checked out of the Town House Motel and rode his motorcycle over to Terry Quimby's house with plans to stay the week. The couple had sex that morning in her home despite the fact there were other adults present.

On Sunday afternoon, Warren and Quimby attended a picnic for Ramada Hotel employees at a High Point park. They were accompanied by her two brothers, her sister and her two children. Warren drove his motorcycle with Terry's brother Freddy on the back. Warren played in a softball game at the park. As he later explained: "They also had the stupidest hat contest or something like that." For some reason, Warren did not eat anything and quickly got drunk on an empty stomach.

"I drunk a lot of beer. Uh, everybody kind of, well, the picnic was breaking up and they was, most people decided to go out and have a few more drinks," explained Warren. Just as the party of people including Warren were about to take off for a bar called Applebee's, he was introduced to Katherine "Kat" Johnson, one of Terry's Ramada Hotel friends, who worked part-time on the weekends in the hotel restaurant. Kat immediately agreed to join the group at Applebee's.

Kat Johnson, a graduate of Central High School in High Point, was a student at the nearby University of North Carolina at Chapel Hill and had a reputation among her friends as being "a sweet girl who loved animals and dreamed of being a veterinarian." She drove a 1984 Renault and lived with her family in a spacious detached house on Kensington Drive, one of High Point's most sought-after areas.

An American flag flew outside the Johnsons' red-brick house at all times.

On the way to Applebee's that afternoon, Warren drove his stolen Kawasaki with Terry's brother Freddy on the back. Warren told Freddy he would "have her [Kat Johnson] by the end of the night." He paused and added, "Just you watch and see."

The group stayed at the bar for at least two hours. "Everybody was drinking pretty heavy," Warren later recalled. "Beer, margaritas, lots of different things. Can't exactly remember what the specials were. Can't even remember offhand how much I had. I mean, I kept drinking through the rest of the day. We both did [he and Kat]."

At Applebee's, Warren got into an intense conversation with Kat Johnson, but he later claimed he couldn't specifically recall what they were talking about. She asked to ride back with Warren on his motorcycle when they left Applebee's.

Warren later insisted he did not use any cocaine the night he met Kat Johnson. But he did have a couple of hits of a marijuana reefer at the hotel cookout and when the group went to the bar. "I'd took a hit or two off one, but nothing, you know, maybe one or two hits off one, but that was it."

Warren later backtracked and claimed he took no drugs whatsoever on the night he met Kat Johnson. "Just beer and liquor from a bar that we'd went to earlier, but nothing stronger than beer."

Warren also later insisted he tried to dissuade Johnson from joining him on the bike, but she was insistent, so they headed over to Terry Quimby's house. En route, Warren stopped at a grocery store and bought a crate of beer. They also dropped round at Quimby's sister's house and got something to eat. Terry Quimby drove Johnson's car back to her sister's house.

An hour later, Warren drove his bike to Terry's house with her sister Robin on the back while Kat Johnson drove her car over to Terry's place. Warren never recalled exactly what time they arrived back at Terry Quimby's house, but he did say, "It wouldn't have been too late. It had just started to get dark, I guess."

The group consumed much beer. Kat Johnson kept asking Warren to take her on another ride on the back of his motorcycle. At first, he tried to ignore her, but it was clear to everyone else present that she had a big crush on Lesley Warren and wouldn't take no for an answer.

Warren noticed that Terry was getting very tired and kept falling asleep on the couch in the living room of her house. He and Kat drank some more beer. "We sat on the porch and talked," Warren later recalled.

More than an hour after arriving at the house, Johnson once again asked Warren if he would take her for a ride on his motorcycle. Warren later said, "Kat wanted to take another ride, so we did. We rode around for a couple of hours."

Johnson was dressed in jeans and a black-and-white-striped shirt. She hung on the back of Warren's stolen Kawasaki Vulcan, swigging from a bottle of beer as he careered around the country lanes and side streets just outside High Point. Sometimes Warren got lost because he was so unfamiliar with High Point. "A couple of times," he later explained, "I didn't know where I was at. I just rode around until I recognized one of the roads."

Eventually, Warren stopped and paid cash for some gas for his motorcycle at an Exxon station. All he could later recall about it was that it wasn't far from High Point's Main Street. "And it wasn't far from Terry's," Warren said.

Warren used the bathroom at the gas station. When he got back on the motorcycle, "we sat there and talked a little while. Started making out a little. Uh, I guess that went on for fifteen or twenty minutes."

Then, Warren claimed, he suggested to Johnson that they get a motel room together. "She said that . . . would be fine." To this day, Warren claims he cannot remember which motel they checked into that evening. "I'm not real sure whether it was the Town House or there's another one right down below it."

Warren claimed that using his fake driver's license in the name of Bryan Collins, he checked into a motel with Kat Johnson. "We went upstairs. I remember it was an upstairs room. Had sex, I remember. Spent a few hours in the room," Warren later said.

He claimed the couple had intended to stay all night at the hotel. "She [Kat] was supposed to leave for school early in the morning. She had an early class. She was going to leave from there and take a shower."

But Johnson's car was still back at Quimby's house, so Warren offered to ride his bike back to get the car. He claims that she gave him the keys and he went and collected the vehicle. Less than twenty minutes later, Warren returned to Kat Johnson in the motel room, where they drank some more beer. Then Johnson drove them both to the nearest convenience store to get another twelve-pack. Warren said they were either Budweiser or Bud Dry. "They're the only ones I ever drink."

By now it was around 2:00 A.M. With Kat Johnson at the wheel of her own car, Warren claims they then started driving around the area once again. At one stage, they went down a street called Westchester, and she told him she lived nearby at Kensington Drive. They passed a shopping mall shrouded in darkness. Then Warren later alleged that Kat Johnson took a sharp left-hand turn off the main road and headed along a deserted side road.

"We ended up in, like, a soccer field. I remember seeing the—the nets, you know; it had picnic benches and stuff, too. Up toward the front. There was a building. I remember seeing a building and the soccer nets. It was a brick building."

Warren claimed Johnson drove her car past the building and "pulled on down in the soccer field." He recalled: "Looked like somebody had pulled in there before. She knew where it was at."

It was a very different sort of park from where Warren had first met Kat Johnson just a few hours earlier. As he later explained: "Had a fence around it. A chain-link, plus a wood split-rail fence." He continued his story: "So, uh, we was drinking beer down there. I don't think we drunk too much. Had sex, intercourse, a couple of times."

Warren stated that sex took place on bare grass. He "couldn't remember" if he took her clothes off or if she did it herself. But he did recall taking off his own clothes and the precise location in the park. "Where the car was parked, there was a bank that kind of went up, about, maybe fifteen or twenty feet from the car, I think. Over toward the edge, it was just bank. No fence." Warren also claimed Kat had no panties. "I remember 'cause I know she didn't have any on to start with. I was messing with her on the motorcycle and, uh, she never had any on, no."

Warren went on to describe what happened next as they lay on the deserted bank by the soccer field. "Uh, I'm not real sure what time it was. I remember just laying on the grass. She was, like, had her head on my shoulder, kind of laying on her side."

He claimed they talked about seeing each other some more and Kat said she'd be around the following Friday. "I wanted to see her again and she wanted to see me." Warren continued: "She was rubbing my chest. Then I choked her and I know I did. I think I used my hands. I'm not sure if I used anything else."

Warren had no recollection of whether he was on top of her or if she was lying still with her head against his shoulder. But he insisted he didn't kill her during sex but "a bit after." Many years later, he admitted he was facing her as he killed her. "I think I straddled her. I was sittin' on her. She was lying down on her back."

A deadpan Lesley Warren later talked calmly and clearly to investigators about that night:

Investigator: "Did she scratch you or anything?"

Warren: "No."

Investigator: "Did she fight?"

Warren: "No. Not really."

Investigator: "Did she hit you with her hand or anything?"

Warren: "No."

Investigator: "Did she make any noise? Did she struggle?"

Warren: "Not much at all."

Investigator: "When you say, 'Not much at all . . . ' "

Warren: "Well."

Investigator: "Does that mean she struggled a little bit or . . . ?"

Warren: "Little bit."

Investigator: "Shivered or . . . ?"

Warren: "More than just shivered."

Investigator: "Did she try to get up from her lying position?"

Warren: "Uh, yeah, she did."

Investigator: "Was she able to get up at all?"

Warren: "No."

Investigator: "And why was she not able to get up from that lying position?"

Warren: "I guess I was on top of her."

Investigator: "Do you remember a piece of clothing or anything around her neck?"

Warren: "No."

Investigator: "Do you recall if she was wearing a bra that night?"

Warren: "Yeah. I believe she was."

Back on that dark, deserted soccer pitch, Warren lay next to the naked corpse of his latest victim and wondered why he had snuffed the life out of another woman. Why? He hadn't even been thinking about murder when he killed Kat Johnson. "That's just it," he later recalled. "There wasn't nothing. I mean, none of them, none of them, made me mad or done anything that would have caused me to do that."

Warren later said he'd tried over and over again to work out what it was about Kat Johnson that put him in the mood to murder her as he had done at least three other women. "I just don't know. I've thought about it a lot. Why? With any of them, why? But I don't, I can't put it, put it into words. I don't know."

Warren admitted he lost count of the number of beers he consumed the night he met Kat Johnson. "It was more than a six-pack, 'cause there was nothin' left the next . . . well, there was still some in the car the next morning, but I'd bought another case earlier, after we left the cookout. They'd had a keg there and when we left the cookout the keg was empty."

However, Warren did recall that shortly after killing her, he started Johnson's car and drove it to just twenty feet from where her body lay. Then he dragged Johnson's body with his hands across the grass while the body lay on its back. He picked her up in a fireman's carry and lifted her the rest of the way to her own car.

The weather, Warren later recalled, was "nice. I believe it had rained just a little bit earlier. It was clear." He calmly picked up all her clothes and put them in the car. "I was trying to hide them," he later admitted. "I didn't want to go to jail."

When later asked by investigators what he would have gone to jail for, Warren said: "Murder."

Then Lesley Warren went back to the spot where they had made love and he'd choked her to death, and fell asleep.

Warren later claimed that the next thing he recalled was backing Kat Johnson's car against the wall in a sloped area of the parking lot of the Ramada Hotel. He still to this day does not know why he reversed the car into the parking spot.

There did not seem to be anyone on duty in the parking lot kiosk when he drove in through the front entrance. "There was no gate there or nothing. When I walked out, I went out the same way, so I don't know if there was or not."

Warren has also never been able to explain why

he took Kat Johnson's body in her car to the Ramada Hotel parking lot. "It was almost as if he wanted to be caught," one investigator later said.

Terry Quimby later recalled how Warren had told her two different stories about the events of the previous night.

In the first version, Warren said he'd left Kat Johnson sleeping in his room at the Town House Motel on South Main Street. He even said he'd arranged for a desk clerk to give her a wake-up call so she could get to college on time.

In the other version, Warren claimed Kat Johnson had left the hotel for Chapel Hill early that morning before he had even awoken.

It was daybreak as Lesley Warren stumbled in a daze along the sidewalk toward Terry Quimby's house. Then he crept into the house and fell asleep on the couch in the living room. Warren later admitted to High Point investigators Grubb and McNeill that the only reason he hadn't killed Terry Quimby was "because she had kids. Guess that kinda saved her life," he said casually during their initial interview after the discovery of Kat Johnson's body.

On Monday morning, July 16, Sergeant Ted Lambert of the Asheville Police interviewed Betty Pressley, the neighbor assaulted by Lesley Warren in 1982 when he was a schoolboy. She recalled how Warren had tried to gain entry into her house three weeks before the assault that he later committed.

Tracey Warren's mother, Diane Bradshaw, was also interviewed that same day at the Spartanburg County Sheriff's Department. She recalled to investigators how she had been shown a letter by her daughter in 1988 that had been written by Lesley

Warren. At the time, Warren was in custody in Philadelphia due to his going AWOL. Bradshaw remembered that in the letter Warren had begged forgiveness from Tracey and even stated in the letter: "She wanted it as much as I did," and "The husband wanted me to do it."

Bradshaw told investigators she'd asked her daughter whom Warren was referring to and Tracey told her it was about the dead girl [Patsy Vineyard] in New York. Bradshaw told detectives that the only way to save her daughter was to convince her of the atrocities committed by Lesley Warren. Bradshaw then agreed to bring Tracey Warren to the Spartanburg County Sheriff's Department the following day, July 17.

That Monday evening, July 16, Lesley Warren was talking to some of Terry Quimby's friends at her house when he asked one of them if he looked like a killer. A few minutes later, he admitted to another of Quimby's friends that he'd "done one thing, and now they're trying to pin everything on me."

Over in Spartanburg, Lesley Warren's yellow 1976 Monte Carlo had been picked up by a Spartanburg County–owned rollback wrecker in Asheville. It was taken to Columbia to be expertly examined in the South Carolina Law Enforcement Division (SLED) lab to find out if it could be directly linked to the murder of Velma Faye Gray.

Warren already knew the police had impounded his orange two-door 1980 Mercury, which he'd left outside Misty Ferguson's home a few days before he left for High Point. Warren was aware that the car had a bullet hole in the back. He'd always claimed the damage had been caused when he'd shot at a man who was trying to steal the car.

Lesley Warren's propensity for firearms meant

that over the previous few years he'd owned an assortment of weapons including a cheap .22 (make unknown), a 9mm automatic Beretta, a 9mm Taurus automatic, a .38-caliber Smith & Wesson and a Smith & Wesson .357.

But now his huge .44-caliber Magnum Ruger was his pride and joy, and he told friends he wouldn't hesitate to use it if necessary. "If it's a matter of life or death, I know which I'd choose," Warren told one associate.

At SLED's Trace Evidence Lab at Columbia's Forensic Science Building, scientist John Barron examined the yellow Monte Carlo used in the killing of Velma Faye Gray. Barron had a B.S. degree in microbiology from Clemson University and had been employed for eighteen years by SLED. His department specialized in analyzing hairs, fibers, paints, gunshot residue and any other microscopic and trace-type evidence. Barron had earlier helped process the crime scene, but now he had the prized possession—Warren's car. The vehicle was minutely checked for trace evidence by visually going through it removing all hairs and fibers. Then it was carefully vacuumed to make sure nothing had been missed.

A specialized hair comparison was made using a comparison light microscope, which uses a strong light source that illuminates through the hair and enables scientists to compare the internal structures of the hair. Barron later explained: "When hair is examined with the naked eye, it just appears to be a solid color, but when we look at it under a strong light microscope, there are many different characteristics that are present. The comparison microscope enables us to look at hair from one source and compare it with hair from another source. It is not an exact fingerprint type of analysis, but it is very good as far as narrowing down, if you will, the class or group of individuals that could have contributed to the hair."

After examining the hairs from Velma Faye Gray and hairs in the 1976 Monte Carlo, John Barron found one of Gray's hairs in the rear floor passenger side of the car. Barron could tell the hair had been forcibly removed—pulled out before it was ready to fall out. "We could tell that microscopically because the tissue that the hair was embedded in was still connected to the root of the hair," Barron later explained. He also recognized some evidence of bleaching of the hair, which was consistent with Gray's hairstyle.

Upon close examination of Gray's clothing, John Barron found in the pubic combings hair that did not originate from the victim. Barron recovered hairs from the same person in the rear passenger-side seat of the Monte Carlo (examined on July 13). Bingo!

Also from the victim's shirt, Barron found two more of the same types of hairs. Two identical ones were then found on the floor of the Monte Carlo. But the final clincher was when Barron traced a black dog hair on Gray's shirt. Inside Warren's Monte Carlo, he found numerous black dog hairs, as well as old dog food.

The evidence was overwhelming. But in Asheville, Sergeant Ted Lambert knew he still needed to find the body of Jayme Hurley if he was going to ensure the arrest and conviction of Lesley Warren. For that reason, he put most of his hopes and expectations on Warren's wife, Tracey. Lambert believed she was the key because Warren must have told her what he'd done.

Fourteen

At 3.55 P.M. on July 17, 1990, investigators Ted Lambert and Bob Cooke briefly interviewed Tracey Warren at the county sheriff's office in Spartanburg. They pressed her for cooperation, but she insisted they return the next day to her mother's home on Park Street in Campobello.

Even then Tracey Warren spent the first few minutes talking about her love for her husband and their two children, Joshua and Matthew Warren. The investigators all agreed that Warren's wife was not easy to deal with. "She gave us a real tough time," Bob Cooke later recalled.

Tracey Warren's first reference to her husband's situation came when she confirmed to Cooke that Warren's army buddy Tom Walker had made two trips with the couple from Watertown to North Carolina just after the disappearance of Patsy Vineyard.

Cooke and his colleague Wayne Corsa produced the photo that showed Patsy Vineyard's very expensive engagement ring clearly on the finger of Tracey Warren in the summer of 1987.

Tracey insisted the ring had been given to her by her husband less than two weeks before the photo had been taken "sometime" in the summer of 1987 at Warren's mother's home. Tracey also told detectives that both rings had eventually been sold at the Square Lion pawnshop in Watertown.

It later emerged that the shop owner was murdered shortly after Warren's visit by a suspected hit man. Officers eventually interviewed the pawnbroker's wife and daughter, who checked through their records until they found a slip with Warren's name on it.

As Senior Investigator Bob Cooke of the NYSP later recalled: "It was all about souvenirs. Leslie must have really got his rocks off knowing his wife was wearing his victim's ring." Cooke assumed that Tracey Warren got sucked into her husband's life without realizing who he really was. "You gotta remember she was just sixteen or seventeen and very naive when they married."

Tracey Warren went on to fully cooperate with investigators, who spent many hours with her trying to build up an accurate picture of Lesley Warren. "The wives or girlfriends of serial killers are often in denial about their men. She took quite some time to break down, but eventually she helped us," recalled Bob Cooke. "You should have heard the stories he'd told her. What a con artist Leslie Warren was. He told her he found the ring in a car they had bought and she believed him."

Tracey Warren told investigators about her husband's explanation for the death of Patsy Vineyard. She recalled how her husband had told her he'd gone to Patsy Vineyard's apartment and that she came to the door after he rapped with a "secret" knock so that she would know it was him.

"You know what he told her?" Bob Cooke recalled many years later. "He told her that Patsy was dying of cancer and that her husband did not want to see her suffer, so he'd hired Lesley to kill her for him. Tracey believed him. This guy was something else—a complete Walter Mitty."

Warren's background still surprised investigators because they couldn't understand how he'd managed to enlist in the U.S. Army. "He should never have been allowed in there," Bob Cooke said years later. But Lesley Warren's juvenile records had been sealed. Investigators believed that if Warren's troubled background as a teenager had been known earlier, lives could have been saved.

The investigators asked Tracey Warren where her husband was. She volunteered that she'd dropped Lesley Warren at the motorcycle dealership in Spartanburg, where he test-drove a motorcycle and never returned it. Tracey also admitted she helped Warren obtain a fictitious driver's license in South Carolina on July 11, 1990, under the name of "Bryan Allen Collins." But she insisted she had no idea where her husband had gone.

Bob Cooke then asked Tracey if Warren had ever mentioned Jayme Hurley's name when they went to Fontana Lake on the weekend of May 26, 1990. Tracey recalled how on the way, Warren had driven her through a black neighborhood with apartments "across a bridge or something." She said her husband had stopped and spoken to a man called Stanley. Tracey said she didn't know if her husband bought cocaine. "I didn't see it on him, but he must have had some because when we got camping he snuck off and done it, 'cause I could tell in his arms when he came back."

Tracey Warren insisted she never once asked her husband's brother Laron or Missy about the death of Jayme Hurley. She then mentioned her husband's confession to his involvement in Hurley's death as the couple walked up Pisgah Mountain, the area where he'd buried Jayme Hurley.

Tracey recalled the dogwood tree just by the spot where he said he'd buried Hurley. She said she knew the area well because when she'd lived with Warren in Asheville they'd frequently gone up to the same spot.

"We used to go up there and just go and talk and just get out of the house. We had a dog then and we'd let it run wild," Tracey explained. Then returning to that last visit with her husband, she added, "Josh was running around right there at the edge of the spot, playing with the trees and chasing a spider. There was a big area in front and the back and on this side, but we always kept them right here on this side of us. And Matthew was asleep in his crib."

As Tracey spoke to investigators, she made it clear she thought she had been happily married to a "sweet, kindhearted, shy man" called Lesley Warren. Sometimes Tracey Warren seemed lost in romantic images of a happy, safe family out on a day trip to the mountains.

Sergeant Ted Lambert snapped Tracey Warren out of her nostalgia trip by asking: Had she seen any blood in her husband's van? Tracey hesitated: "No. Beside going to the lake I—I mean, I didn't pay no attention. I wasn't looking for it. As far as I know it wasn't there."

Tracey then told Lambert how the window of the van got broken while they were on that weekend in Lake Fontana just two days after Warren had killed Jayme Hurley. Tracey even admitted knowing that her husband had taken $40 out of Hurley's pocketbook.

The interview with Tracey Warren was finally terminated at 4:21 P.M.

Just before leaving, Tracey Warren agreed she would call the Spartanburg County Sheriff's Department if her husband contacted her, and gave permission for a trap-and-trace phone device to be placed on her mother phone. Tracey was staying with her mom.

At 8:30 P.M., investigators drove Tracey Warren to her own home on Longview Drive in Spartanburg. They wanted to examine some clothing belonging to Warren, which they then took away. Other officers visited Laron and Missy Warren's home again and took away a telephone bill that Warren had left behind.

Also that evening, the Spartanburg Police received an anonymous phone call telling them precisely where they would find the body of Jayme Hurley.

Investigators later issued a dramatic nationwide news release about suspected serial killer Lesley Warren. It read:

BE ON THE LOOKOUT FOR SUBJECT LESLEY EUGENE WARREN W/M 5'11" 194 LBS. DOB 15 OCTOBER 1967 SSN — — —. SUBJECT POSSESSES A NC DRIVERS LICENSE IN THE NAME OF LESLEY EUGENE WARREN RT1 BOX ___, PISGAH HWY, CANDLER, NC. SUBJECT WARREN ALSO POSSESSES A SC DRIVERS LICENSE IN THE NAME OF BRYAN ALLEN COLLINS W/M 5'11" 160 LBS. OF ___ PARK STREET, CAMPOBELLO, SC 29322. SUBJECT WARREN MAY USE SSN — — —. THIS SC DRIVERS LICENSE WILL REFLECT WARREN'S PICTURE

ON THE FACE OF THE CARD. THE LICENSE ALSO SHOWS DOB OF 080167 AND ISSUE A DATE OF 071190. SUBJECT WARREN HAS A SPIKE HAIRCUT AND GOATEE. WARREN HAS RECENTLY DYED HIS HAIR AND GOATEE AN ORANGE-BLOND BLEACHED COLOR. SUBJECT MAY BE OPERATING A BLACK KAWASAKI MOTORCYCLE OR A YAMAHA MOTORCYCLE, COLOR UNKNOWN. WARREN MAY HAVE A SLEEPING BAG ON HIS POSSESSION AND A TENT. SUBJECT IS KNOWN TO FREQUENT CAMPSITES. . . .

SPARTANBURG COUNTY SHERIFF'S OFFICE, SPARTANBURG, SC, HOLDS WARRANTS. . . .

SPARTANBURG COUNTY ARREST WARRANT _____ FOR MURDER AND ARREST WARRANT _____ FOR KIDNAPPING . . . SUBJECT SHOULD BE CONSIDERED ARMED AND DANGEROUS AND SHOULD BE APPROACHED WITH EXTREME CAUTION. . . . WARREN MAY HAVE ON HIS PERSON A .44 MAGNUM RUGER REDHAWK OR A 9MM SEMIAUTOMATIC. . . . ANY CONTACT WITH WARREN NOTIFY SPARTANBURG COUNTY SHERIFF'S OFFICE AT — — — OR TTY. . . . SUBJECT WARREN IS NCIC FOR MURDER AND KIDNAPPING. OPR/147 AUT/SHERIFF BILL COFFEY JUL 17, 1990.

On the next morning, Laron Warren took Sergeant Ted Lambert and other investigators to the body located on Pisgah Mountain, near the Blue Ridge Parkway. Laron explained how Warren had removed Hurley's body from his Chevy and taken it up the hillside, marking the location with the knotted shirt that Laron showed to investigators the previous week.

Investigators had already acknowledged that FBI profiler Ed Grant had accurately predicted that Hurley's body would not be found in water, but would be more than likely partially buried and in close proximity to a roadway in a remote area.

At 6:45 P.M. on Wednesday, July 18, Laron Warren led detectives to the body of a woman believed to be Jayme Hurley in a remote area of the Pisgah National Forest in Candler. Officers from the Buncombe County Sheriff's Department, the State Bureau of Investigation and the Asheville Police Department were immediately informed. The crime scene was secured and half a dozen uniformed officers were ordered to stay on site through the night so that everything would remain untouched until the next morning.

Heavy rain fell that night and into the morning. But investigators had bigger problems than the weather; dozens of poisonous snakes were slivering around the patch of woodland where the body was found. At least six snakes were killed by officers protecting the crime scene through the night.

A misty dawn crept over the Pisgah Mountains as Dr. John Butts, Buncombe County chief medical examiner, and his colleague Dr. Owl-Smith arrived to begin examining the remains of Jayme Hurley. They met with Buncombe County Sheriff's Department officers plus investigators from Asheville PD. The two examiners were then led 250 feet down a forty-degree slope to an area already covered by a plastic tarp. Butts lifted up the plastic sheeting to look at the decomposed human flesh for a few moments.

The body of Jayme Hurley was lying perpendicular to the slope and was covered by a considerable amount of dirt and loose rock at a depth of about six inches. Hurley was on her back with her feet pointing in a southerly direction. The legs were together, the doctors later noted. "The left arm was folded across the body in the groin region over the right arm, which was folded across on the right side."

Butts and Owl-Smith noticed that there was virtually no evidence of plants around or on the remains, suggesting the corpse had not been there for long. Dozens of small bugs and maggots covered the body and the smell of decomposition was overpowering. Butts and Owl-Smith carefully cleared all the earth around the remains so that a shallow trench would be dug on the downslope of the body. A sheet was then placed in the trench alongside the remains and the body was gently rolled onto the sheet, which was then used to pick up the remains and place them inside a black plastic disaster pouch. At 3:00 P.M., the corpse was carefully carried across the mud and grass by ME personnel to the roadway above where it was to be transported to Dr. Butts's lab in Chapel Hill for the autopsy.

Captain Dean Crisp of the Buncombe County Sheriff's Department would only tell newsmen that "foul play is suspected, but at this point in the investigation authorities are concentrating on identifying the body."

In High Point, Lesley Warren accompanied Terry Quimby to the local magistrate's office; she went there to swear out a warrant on a personal matter. She later said he showed no hesitation in walking into the law offices; she had no idea then that he had killed her friend Kat Johnson just four days earlier.

The following morning, Dr. Butts performed an autopsy on Jayme Hurley's body on behalf of Buncombe County at the medical examiner's building in Chapel Hill. His report completely contradicted Warren's later claims that Hurley had taken cocaine with him.

Butts's report stated:

These are the somewhat decomposed remains of a white female recovered from Buncombe County by myself on 7-19-90. The remains are received within the plastic body bag they were placed in at the time of recovery and are lying on a white sheet the body was lifted out of the grave site with. The remains are those of a white female. She is unclothed. There is a state of severe decomposition affecting the head and trunk; arms and legs show a lesser degree of decomposition, though there is a loss of the epidermal surfaces and dehydration and some saponification. Adherent dirt and rocks are noted scattered over the body with occasional tree and plant root material. The head and hair are matted with dirt and markedly softened especially on the left side. There is some reddish discoloration of the left side of the neck and back of the neck. No obvious defects are noted. The nasal skin is absent. A gold metal chain is present around the neck, unfastened. No jewelry is noted on the fingers. Examination of the body surfaces reveals no obvious penetrating injuries.

CAUSE OF DEATH: Strangulation.

But Dr. Butts warned investigators it could be at least a week before the results of all tests were known.

Sergeant Ted Lambert gave Butts Hurley's dental records, which had been obtained that afternoon from the office of Dr. Dale Deines. A rough comparison was immediately made between the dental records and X-ray bitewings taken from the body on site. Butts and Owl-Smith noted definite similarities.

In High Point that same day, Thursday, July 19, Ramada Hotel parking attendant Monette McKinney saw Lesley Warren for a third time. As he walked down the ramp from the second level, close to the parking lot wall, Warren looked directly at McKinney but said nothing. Warren later said that he had been considering killing the middle-aged brunette woman, but the arrival of another hotel guest forced him to drop his plans.

After many hours of Interviewing Warren's relatives and girlfriends, Senior Investigator Bob Cooke of the NYSP concluded that the suspected serial killer was "the type of guy who could walk into a bar, and if there's one hundred guys and five girls in that bar, he's gonna walk out with one of those girls. Don't ask me why. It wasn't just looks, but he had charm, real charm."

However, Bob Cooke also discovered something even more unique about Lesley Warren; it was something that undoubtedly contributed to his ability to seduce countless women. "One of the things we found out from these girlfriends was that this guy was well equipped, OK?" Bob Cooke laughed apprehensively. "Some of the girls said they didn't want to date him again because he hurt them. Some of them were so worn out they couldn't handle it." Bob Cooke pointed out, "All these girls experienced normal sex with Lesley. There was no hint of the sick-and-twisted stuff."

On July 19, Asheville investigators showed Missy Warren a white long-sleeve shirt that had been recovered from Tracey Warren's home in Spartanburg earlier that day. Missy Warren positively identified the shirt as the one worn by Lesley Warren when he appeared at their house at 3:00 A.M. the previous Friday. Missy also stated she had seen blood on it.

In a statement to the police, Missy Warren told how Warren had woken her up at their trailer home and demanded letters from his wife as well as leaving behind Jayme Hurley's telephone answering machine minicassette. The deposition secured from Missy Warren by the investigators was later handed over to Asheville Police for possible use as evidence. Laron Warren told the same investigators that he'd thrown away the answering machine tape.

At 5:10 P.M. on July 19, Missy Warren authorized the Asheville Police Department to place a telephone trace and/or trap on her telephone, which was listed in her name. The scruffy scrap of paper that Missy Warren signed giving investigators permission stated that the tap would last "for a length of time as determined necessary by them [the police] to complete their investigation in the death of Jayme Hurley."

On the same day, Senior Investigator Bob Cooke and his colleague Wayne Corsa flew to Hilton Head, South Carolina, to reinterview Tom Walker at his workplace. Cooke and Corsa suspected Walker might be withholding information about the Patsy Vineyard killing. However, both investigators were quickly satisfied that this was not the case.

At 12:51 P.M., Warren's mother, Phyllis Murray, was phoned and asked certain additional questions by investigators growing increasingly anxious that the suspected serial killer would strike again if they did not catch him very quickly.

As one investigator later explained: "The family were, I guess, being loyal to Lesley. I suppose you'd call it being protective. We couldn't get much from there."

Meanwhile, Lesley Warren went back to the Ramada Hotel bar Tradewinds virtually every night. He even made a point of leaving his motorcycle on a meter outside so as not to alert the parking lot staff following his drinking problems the previous week.

The fact that Kat Johnson's body lay crumpled in the trunk of her own car parked just a few yards away did not seem to concern Lesley Warren.

On Thursday, July 19, Warren was once again back at the Ramada, but this time he had problems with Terry Quimby's husband, who'd been in the bar drinking with them and then discovered that Warren was staying at his wife's house. Warren later explained: "He was pretty drunk and I drove there to make sure she got home OK. To give her a ride. They were going to call the police 'cause we was goin' to fight in the road out there. I was just—I was just trying to get him to go."

But the evening passed without the police having to be called. Lesley Warren continued to prowl the streets unhindered.

Fifteen

On July 20, 1990, the Warren task force distributed a Wanted poster on the fax machines of law
enforcement agencies across the nation. It featured
a recent photo of Warren and read:

    WANTED
    BY
    SPARTANBURG COUNTY SHERIFF'S OF-
FICE
    SERIAL MURDER
    SUSPECT
    Outstanding Murder Warrant _____
    Outstanding Kidnapping Warrant _____

Spartanburg County Sheriff Bill Coffey,
Asheville Police Chief Jerry Beavers and New
York State Police Lieutenant Ed Grant an-
nounced today that their agencies have identi-
fied a suspect in three related murder cases.
Suspected *serial* killer 22-year-old Lesley Eugene
Warren of Route —, Box —, Pisgah Highway,
Candler, NC, is being sought in connection
with the murder of three women from New
York, North Carolina, and South Carolina.

On Tuesday, July 17, the Spartanburg County
Sheriff's Office signed warrants against Warren

charging him with kidnapping and murder in the death of 42-year-old Velma Faye Gray of . . . Alta Vista Circle, Travellers Rest, SC, on August 27, 1989.

Warrants are pending against Warren by Asheville Police in connection with the disappearance and death of 39-year-old Jayme Denise Hurley of . . . Irving Street, Asheville, NC. Hurley disappeared May 24, 1990. Her body was recovered yesterday off Highway 151 in the Candler area of North Carolina.

New York State Police investigators and the Jefferson County, New York, District Attorney's Office are concluding their investigation into the death of 20-year-old Patsy Diane Vineyard of Sackets Harbor, New York. Vineyard, the apparent victim of a sexual homicide, was reported missing from the residence in May of 1987 and her remains were recovered in Lake Ontario one month later. Lesley Eugene Warren has been identified as the killer in the New York investigation.

Warren was last seen in Spartanburg County on July 12, 1990. He is described as a white male, five feet 11 inches tall, weighing 194 pounds. He has a "punk" hair style, long in the back and short in the front, and a goatee, both of which were recently dyed an orange-blond color. He is a former truck driver, construction worker and factory worker.

The release was signed by Coffey, Beavers and Grant.

Besides the information earlier issued, the Spartanburg County Sheriff Department warned: "Warren is a former truck driver and has traveled extensively from South Carolina to Nova Scotia, Canada, on Routes I-77 and I-81. He is possibly headed to the Canadian border."

At about 12:00 midday on July 20, investigators Cooke, Weidman, Jung, Emory, Hendrix and Lambert arrived at Asheville Police Department to coordinate the search for Lesley Warren. They had little to go on other than the fact that Warren held two driver's licenses, one of which was in the name of his brother-in-law Bryan Collins. But they were about to get the biggest break in the entire case.

On July 21, at approximately 2:00 P.M., Tracey Warren took a phone call from her husband. Warren was still in High Point, North Carolina, although he told his wife he was in Tennessee.

"I wrecked my motorcycle in Charlotte, Tracey," Warren said. "I broke my arm. It's in a cast. I need some money, please."

When the location of the trace was read out, Asheville Police investigator Stan Weidman immediately recalled that Warren's Candler neighbor Misty Ferguson had a sister living in High Point. Two investigators headed at high speed to Misty Ferguson's trailer.

They needed to know more from Misty about her sister's relationship with Lesley Warren. At the trailer park, twenty-seven-year-old Royce Duckett told investigators Misty was at the local Laundromat and she'd been planning to call her sister anyhow. The two officers immediately took Duckett over to the Laundromat on the Leicester Highway. At 2:30 P.M., as the Asheville cruiser entered the parking lot, Duckett spotted Ferguson on a public phone just outside the store.

The two officers and Duckett approached Misty and identified themselves. Without getting off her phone call, Ferguson told investigators that Lesley Warren was staying at Terry Quimby's house. Then she went back to her phone call. The investigators immediately radioed Asheville PD and relayed the information to Sergeant Ted Lambert, who contacted the High Point Police Department after getting further information on outstanding warrants and also faxed them the NCIC entry on Warren.

The first time High Point Police Department detectives J.L. "Jerry" Grubb and Mark McNeill heard the name "Lesley Warren" was as they walked back into their office after lunch at the local Arby's. Officers in Asheville were on the line saying they'd traced a call to the house of a Terry Quimby. Grubb and McNeill were immediately warned that Warren was a suspected serial killer and probably riding a stolen Kawasaki Vulcan motorcycle.

Grubb later explained: "The way we work in High Point is that Asheville had warrants, but Warren was in High Point, Guilford County, so they had to call us to go get him. We had to get a fugitive-from-justice warrant and serve it on him. Then we'd send him back to Asheville."

Minutes later, Mark McNeill was driving his unmarked High Point PD Granada with Jerry Grubb on his tail in his burgundy Ford LTD. They were heading for Terry Quimby's place with a posse of other uniformed officers and a SWAT team.

At approximately 2:20 P.M., the officers found Quimby's detached wood-grain house without much trouble, but they immediately noticed it was located next to a kindergarten. A few youngsters were even playing in the yard as they rolled past before parking their vehicles in the driveway of a neighboring house. They presumed Warren was in Quimby's house because the stolen 1988 black Kawasaki with the South Carolina license plate was parked up front. They'd also been informed that Terry Quimby had kids, which meant they would have to try and take Warren with the minimum amount of violence.

Grubb takes up the story: "When we saw the bike there, we got the street blocked off by uniform and checked to make sure it was the right motorcycle. Then we got people out of the houses nearby for their own safety. We went next door to the nursery [kindergarten] and told them to get the kids inside. Then we moved toward the house."

Quietly, half a dozen officers took up positions in the front yard near the motorcycle. The two detectives then used a cell phone to call the house to see if Warren was in. Terry Quimby picked up the phone and told them he was in and that they should come up to the front door. "It seemed he was expectin' us," Grubb later recalled.

McNeill approached the front door. Lesley Warren appeared in the doorway, then walked out with Terry Quimby standing directly behind him. McNeill immediately ordered Warren not to move and flung him against the wall of the house and searched him. In his back pocket was the fake driver's license in the name of Bryan Collins. He offered no resistance.

"Are you Lesley Eugene Warren?" McNeill asked.

"Sure am" was the quiet response.

"This your picture on the license?"

"Yup."

As McNeill later explained: "There wasn't a whole

lot else to talk about except to secure the scene and make sure he did not have any weapons."

Detective Grubb added: "We served the warrant and said the officers investigating the case would like to talk to him."

"That's fine by me, sir," responded Warren. "I'd be more than happy to talk to them. Tell 'em to come on up."

Warren had with him $87.58 when he was arrested. He also had a carry-on bag containing a pair of Nike trainers, a fringe vest, a pair of rubber boots, a raincoat, a pair of suspenders and a pair of cord pants.

Lesley Warren was then thoroughly searched and High Point police removed the contents of his pockets, including a set of Renault car keys.

"Who do these belong to?" he was asked.

"They're mine," he answered.

Warren was handcuffed and went in a van belonging to the High Point patrol transport detective division. At 2:45 P.M., as the pickup team traveled back to High Point police headquarters on Leonard Avenue, Grubb called Warren task force investigators in Asheville to tell them their man was in custody. A collective cheer went up throughout the CID.

"If you can just hold him till we get there, that'd be just dandy," Ted Lambert asked Detective Grubb.

In Spartanburg, Detective Carroll Amory was told the news of Warren's arrest. He was ordered to go home and rest that afternoon because he'd have a long night ahead of him.

"I lay down for a couple of hours, got up, took a shower, got dressed and went back to Asheville," Amory later recalled.

At High Point PD, Detectives Grubb and McNeill sat Lesley Warren in their office and attached one of his cuffs to a desk leg. He seemed calm and happy to make conversation. "Most of what he talked about was anything but what he was charged with," Grubb later explained.

Asheville police officers Captain Lee Carter and Detective Don Babb were immediately dispatched to pick up Warren. They drove out on Interstate 40 East, then took 77 and 85 into High Point. On the outskirts of High Point, the two officers stopped at a garage and gassed up their vehicle in preparation for the return trip. They also grabbed a soda and a pack of crackers before heading for the High Point police station on Leonard Avenue. Warren was escorted in cuffs and ankle chains to the officers' Asheville PD van, which took the same route back to Asheville. They only stopped once at a drive-in to get food for Warren.

Babb and Carter spent much of the two-and-a-half-hour drive discussing Babb's recent trip to Walt Disney World in Florida. Lesley Warren did not join in the discussion.

It was only after Warren's dramatic arrest that Terry Quimby began to worry about what may have happened to Kat Johnson. Her parents had been out of town on vacation since before Warren had met her. Terry presumed Kat had returned to college in Chapel Hill on Monday morning and she hadn't been expecting to see her at the Ramada until that Friday evening. But now she wondered about whether Warren might have harmed her.

On July 20, task force investigators began at 6:15 P.M. circulating photocopies of Warren's South Carolina license plate in case any other police departments recollected encounters with the suspected serial killer. By 9:20 P.M., Asheville PD had also distributed copies of Warren's false South Carolina driver's license in the name of his brother-in-law Bryan Allen Collins.

At 9:26 P.M., Warren arrived at the Asheville Police Department's gray ten-story building and was led straight to the Warren "task force office" set up with the FBI, who'd been coordinating with local police throughout the hunt for Warren.

Present were Asheville PD's Ted Lambert, Don Babb, Captain R.L. Carter, Officer Bud Webb and Jan Phillips from the Asheville Police Victim Assistance Department. From Spartanburg were Carroll Amory and Mike Ennis. Then there was NYSP's Stan Weidman, Stan Young, Bob Cooke, Wayne Corsa and Ed Grant. Officer David Caldwell represented SLED. Each of the investigators was ordered to "look busy" when Warren was escorted through the "task force office."

Amory later recalled: "We had been told to stand in certain spots and be doin' certain things as Warren was brought in. But they wanted me to make sure I was one of the first people that he saw. When he walked in, he looked me straight in the eye and he was cuffed, and as soon as he saw me, his eyes went straight to the floor."

"Lesley, how ya doin'?" Amory asked Warren.

His eyes stayed on the floor and he did not say a word.

At least a dozen people were in the Warren "task force office," busy working the phones and inspecting documents as Lesley Warren was brought through shackled and handcuffed. Empty pizza boxes lay on desks. On the walls were photos of Warren's victims. Blowup shots of fingerprints that could have belonged to anyone were strewn about, as were maps showing the locations where bodies had been found. Filing cabinets were tagged with the victims' names.

It was all a complete facade, a movie set that would have put a Hollywood art director in line for an Oscar. The intention was to convince Warren that the so-called task force already had all the evidence in place. The reality was they desperately needed a full confession if they were going to make most of the charges stick.

Bob Cooke later recalled: "The filing cabinets with all his victims' names; the maps where bodies were found; even the front door had 'Warren Task Force' written on it. We had crime scene photos blown up of the girl thrown off the bridge. Pictures of a Chevy van blown up. All agencies names were spread everywhere: FBI, DEA, etc. It was all bullshit, but he didn't know that. We'd even been out to garbage cans and stuff to find things like the pizza boxes. We even found a photo of a dead animal and had it blown up. But it had no connection whatsoever with the killings. Even a photo of his military ID card was blown up."

Bob Cooke explained: "What you do is you only give him three minutes max in the staged area because you don't want him to spend too long looking at everything. It's all about shock value. Then you immediately get him out and take him to a room and leave him to stew."

All the agencies agreed that Sergeant Ted Lambert would initially discuss each case with Warren since he had effectively coordinated the manhunt. Lambert had Warren's shackles and handcuffs removed prior to going into the interview room. He didn't want him to feel restricted in any way. In the corner of the room stood a video camera on a tripod. Lambert switched it on.

The plain wooden chair that Warren was told to sit in had its front legs sawed down at an angle so that he would find it difficult to sit back comfortably. This would make him more likely to confess, according to the FBI. "You don't give a serial killer suspect a chair with arms on it," Bob Cooke later explained.

The interview room also contained one desk and two chairs for investigators, plus two fans and one air cleaner, which was designed to remove smoke from cigarettes in the room. Warren, dressed in a light blue button-type shirt with blue jeans and a pack of Camels hanging out of his top pocket, looked unfazed.

A stenographer was also installed in the interview room and every spoken word was to be typed into another office where it was instantly transcribed. A laser printer then printed out five copies of each full page. A tape recorder was also running throughout.

Initially, Ted Lambert made a point of referring to all the activity Warren had just witnessed in the "task force office."

"You know, we found Jayme," Lambert said, referring to Warren's most recent known victim.

"I heard," Warren replied in a flat, toneless voice.

"The only thing that can help you, Lesley, is the truth," said Ted Lambert.

He advised Warren of his rights by getting Warren to sign a rights waiver form plus a verbal acknowledgment that he understood those rights. Lambert read through each of the rights on the form one by one. When he'd finished reading it and Warren had acknowledged his understanding, Lambert signed it. Lambert later insisted he'd asked Warren specifically when he signed the form if he wanted an attorney. Warren replied that he understood.

Ted Lambert offered Warren a Coke, which he then got for him. Warren was also asked if he needed to use the bathroom. He declined.

Warren was asked why he felt the need to change his name.

> Warren: "I was going to try to hide."
> Lambert: "And why did you need to hide?"
> Warren: " 'Cause I knew the police were looking for me."
> Lambert: "And what were they looking for you about?"
> Warren: "In reference to several deaths."
> Lambert: "OK. And, uh, would that be the ones you're here on?"
> Warren: "Yes."
> Lambert: "The only thing that can help you, Lesley, is the truth."

Lambert began discussing the homicides that Warren was suspected of committing. He made a point of asking Warren to start talking about whichever killing he felt most comfortable discussing. Warren quickly indicated his involvement in the Jayme Hurley case. Warren admitted he'd had sex with Hurley after she'd finished her phone call to her friend Catherine Jenkins. Then he choked her to death before loading her body into his van and driving home. He said when he got off work on the Friday after the killing, he drove to the base of the mountain before finding a burial site. Warren told Lambert that he took a shovel and dug a shallow hole, laid the body of Hurley on her back, covered her up as she was naked at the time and then took his shovel back to his brother Laron's house.

After a brief discussion about all three of the

homicides he was known to have committed, Ted Lambert asked Warren if he thought there were some more. "Yup" was Warren's reply. "There is."

Then he told Lambert he'd choked Kat Johnson and left her in High Point. He explained how he'd met Johnson. Warren even revealed that the set of keys found in his pocket that afternoon belonged to her car, but he couldn't remember what make it was.

"It would be gray or silver—I can't remember. It would be like a Renault or a Volvo body style. Four-door," Warren told Lambert.

Lambert emerged from the interview room to say that Warren had admitted to the murders of Patsy Vineyard, Velma Faye Gray, Jayme Hurley and Katherine "Kat" Johnson. Lambert told the other investigators that Kat's homicide had occurred on the previous Sunday evening, July 15, 1990.

Bob Cooke summed up that first interview session: "Ted is a great interviewer. He has that Southern accent, drawl and basically within twenty minutes Lesley rolled over, which for a serial killer is a fairly unusual thing to do."

Sergeant Ted Lambert later said that at one stage, Lesley Warren told him that he may have killed as many as eight people.

At 10:30 P.M., Detective Jerry Grubb got a phone call at home from his High Point PD division captain Steve Campbell.

"You might want to go down there and see them in Asheville 'cause they think we've got one of his bodies up here."

As Grubb later recalled: "Up until that time, we'd had a great afternoon; then it kinda rained."

At 11:00 P.M., Lesley Warren was given another Coke because one investigator had put a cigarette out in the first one by mistake. Then Warren put his own cigarette butt in another Coke, so yet another one had to be brought to him.

As the police report later explained: "The reason for the confusion on the Coke cans is that all the cans were sitting beside Lesley; he was drinking one and using the other as an ashtray."

At 12:09 A.M., Warren agreed to make a full statement about the murder of Kat Johnson to Ted Lambert as High Point investigators were not expected to begin their interview with Warren until early the next morning. After telling how he met Kat Johnson, Warren explained what led up to her murder: "We stopped in a church parking lot. Messed around a little bit, made out. I suggested we get a motel room."

Warren then outlined how he choked the life out of Johnson. Afterward Lambert asked him: "Anything you'd like to add to it? Anything that we left out, or did you take anything from her?"

"No. Pocketbook and everything is still in her car. There was some beer still in the front seat," replied Warren.

Lambert: "Anything else?"

Warren: "Other than saying that I'm sorry that it happened. I didn't mean for it to [happen]. I'm just glad everything's in the open."

Lambert: "Has anybody pressured you in reference to this statement?"

Warren: "No."

Lambert: "This is Lambert. End of statement is twelve-sixteen A.M. The date is July the twenty-first, 1990."

At 12.18 A.M, yet another Coke was brought to

Warren. Lambert asked Warren again if he needed to use the bathroom, but he declined.

Asheville PD's Ted Lambert asked Warren if he would mind going into specific details with investigators from the relevant jurisdictions. "I don't mind. I wanna get this thing over with," replied Warren.

Warren requested to call his wife, Tracey. It was not normal police policy to allow a suspect to leave the interview room to make calls to anyone other than an attorney, and Ted Lambert decided it would not help make Warren any more relaxed and cooperative, so he denied the request.

"You can do that once we're through here, Lesley," Lambert told him.

Every detail of each interview had to be recorded carefully for later use in trials. The investigators agreed between themselves not to discuss anything that had to do with each other's case unless it was unavoidable.

First up were NYSP investigators Bob Cooke and Wayne Corsa. "We introduced ourselves and shook his hand. He was real calm, relaxed, even congenial, very friendly and not antagonistic. The guy was very personable. Absolutely. But I could tell he was a con man," Bob Cooke later recalled.

Lesley Warren was not comfortable on his specially doctored tilting wooden chair. Bob Cooke explained, "It was highly polished, so he kept slipping off it easy, and it had no arms. He had to keep propping himself up." However, Cooke was impressed that, despite his discomfort, Warren continued to give out a relaxed demeanor. Cooke later recalled, "It wasn't like you see on the TV where the guy is being sarcastic. He wasn't crying or showing any emotion. He was real cool."

Warren continued drinking Cokes and Diet Sprites throughout the interviews. Warren even managed a joke when Cooke and Corsa asked him what his home address was.

"Buncombe County Jail," Warren said.

The two NYSP investigators started with gentle questions before moving onto the subject that mattered: Patsy Vineyard's murder.

Warren claimed he'd met Patsy Vineyard in a bar in Sackets Harbor after having been fishing earlier that day with his buddy Tom Walker. He said he couldn't remember the name of the bar, but told investigators it was quiet and he spotted her sitting at a table having a drink. He claimed he and Patsy drank for a while and then left the bar together in his 1980 Mercury Capri. Warren made a point of saying he wasn't on drugs that night and never took any drugs while he was in the army. Warren admitted he was on Range Patrol, which meant he was working at Fort Drum during the entire time Mike Vineyard was away on field maneuvers. Warren also admitted taking Patsy Vineyard's pocketbook and throwing it in Lake Ontario.

Warren said he'd noticed Patsy was wearing two rings, which, he claimed, she took off prior to having consensual sex with him in a deserted spot near "the old military barracks," close to Sackets Harbor. He calmly told investigators Patsy Vineyard had already taken her panties off before they started petting.

Then Warren lowered his voice and said, "After finishing sex, I just killed her for no real reason." He told the detectives he'd choked her. He insisted it was the first time he'd committed murder.

Warren calmly recounted how he dropped her

body in the water. "The water was real shallow, so I carried her out a ways."

Investigators later tested out Warren's version by seeing how far they could wade into that particular stretch of the lake and found that they were able to walk at least 200 feet out into the water.

Warren claimed he took Patsy Vineyard's rings out of her pocketbook and put them in his car. "Then Tracey found them next to the gearshift in the car and took them," said Warren. He admitted that both rings were eventually sold to a jewelry store "on the loop" in Watertown. He insisted he never told Tom Walker about the killing, but he did later tell his wife that he was paid to kill Patsy Vineyard.

Warren had a dig at his so-called friend Tom Walker. "We were friends, but I didn't really like him. He was such a goddamned Goody Two-shoes around his wife. No one ever messed with Denise." Warren admitted he'd bought a gun from Walker for $30 after he'd left the army.

Then Warren took a deep breath and rubbed his eyes before looking up again at the two investigators. "I know what I done ain't right. It's gotta be stopped. All this really bothers me—especially with Jayme. We were friends."

The interview session was exhausting for Cooke and Corsa because they had to take the lead all the time. Warren answered the questions quickly and then there would be silence. The two experienced investigators had to keep coming back to him over and over again.

"Sure, he answered the questions, but he was clearly not giving us one hundred percent." Cooke sensed that Warren was playing psychological games with the two investigators. "It was almost like he'd always gotta be on top. He wanted to feel he was in charge." Cooke continued, "Lesley wanted to maintain that supposed superiority. He was arrogant underneath the surface, but he didn't actually come across that way."

The NYSP investigators knew Warren was lying much of the time. Bob Cooke believed Warren got Patsy Vineyard out of her apartment by telling her that her husband had been injured out on the field. "That girl never left the house alone. She hardly knew anyone," Cooke later explained. "Lesley reckoned he went back to her apartment and had sex with her. That was bullshit."

The NYSP investigators had one big problem: Patsy Vineyard's body when it was recovered was in such a bad state of decomposition that the ME could only speculate that she had been sexually assaulted and then strangled. The detectives had no real physical proof.

Warren admitted transporting Vineyard's body in his car, but he never confirmed that he'd punctured the tire of her car as part of his plan to kidnap and kill her. Cooke and Corsa knew Patsy Vineyard was not a drinker and she would not come out at night. When her photo had been shown round all the local bars, no one had seen her.

Cooke later recalled, "He was playing with us. Playing frickin' mind games with us. A lot of this was his ego. He liked telling us how he met her, saw her and seduced her. He didn't want to admit that he'd tricked her."

During the interview, many of Warren's lies were ignored because, as Cooke explained, "that's part of the game. Then as you come to the end of the interview, you have to bring it to a close by pointing out some of the holes in his story. We said little and listened to him, but some of the things that we felt were not truthful we would ask more questions [about]." When Warren spun the bar story, Cooke shot back with: "Were there a lot of people there that night?' and "What was she drinking?" Warren said he couldn't remember.

The two investigators wanted to keep the interview going, so they ignored a lot of his responses. "We didn't want to intimidate him by saying something like 'you lying son of a bitch,' " Cooke later explained. "And if he kept to the same answer, then we'd move on. We didn't want him clamming up on us."

Lesley Warren showed few real signs of remorse or anger. The emotional void first spotted by the psychiatrists who'd examined Lesley Warren as a child remained firmly in place. "He was confident, maintaining he was the good guy," recalled Bob Cooke. "He was friendly, not sarcastic, not arrogant. Most of his answers were very matter-of-fact."

Cooke tried to turn the calm atmosphere on its head. "Did you take her jeans completely off? Because, as you can see when she was found, she didn't have any jeans. What did you do with those?"

"Oh, I threw them in the water," Warren replied in a matter-of-fact tone.

The two investigators bit their lips and tried to make sure they didn't upset Warren's feelings by injecting any personal outrage into the proceedings. "It was frustrating. We'd have liked to call him every name under the sun but that wouldn't have helped us none," said Bob Cooke. "Sometimes people do volunteer their feelings, but he wasn't volunteering anything. He was a clinical son of a bitch."

Once the interview was completed, Cooke and Corsa of the NYSP got Lesley Warren to agree to pose for a photo with them. In return, the investigators agreed to let Warren call his wife, Tracey.

Today Bob Cooke, recently retired after twenty-six years with NYSP and now an investigator with the Niagara Mohawk Power Corporation in Watertown, still has that photo plus some other mementos of the case—a vast file he's kept on the case, which includes photos of Patsy Vineyard's relatives, girlfriends, Ted Lambert with Cooke in Asheville, plus a series of detailed photos showing the staged office that greatly contributed to convincing Lesley Warren he had no choice but to confess to his appalling crimes.

Sixteen

Spartanburg County Sheriff Investigator Carroll Amory and his colleague Lieutenant Mike Ennis were the next in to see Lesley Warren. The two officers were ordered to leave their walkie-talkies in the main office. They'd already been surprised by the speed with which Ted Lambert had gotten Warren's initial confessions.

Amory later explained, "That really shocked everybody. I was just standing around saying, 'This is unbelievable that he would go and 'fess up so quick.' It was typical of Lesley that he'd go the opposite way from what we expected. He was bright. He had a certain intelligence and charm. But I don't think he ever felt any guilt."

Ted Lambert had already advised Amory and Mike Ennis that Warren was willing to talk about the Velma Faye Gray homicide. Lambert introduced Ennis to the suspected serial killer.

"This is Lesley, Mike," said Lambert.

"Hi there, Lesley," said Ennis.

"Mike's going to advise you of your rights . . ." explained Lambert.

Warren didn't respond. At 2:11 A.M., Ennis read him his rights from a waiver form, explaining the form was in two parts, one advising him of his rights, and the second part where he could waive or give up those rights if he agreed to talk to the detectives. The waiver part of the form stated that he understood he had not been threatened or promised anything, and also referred to his educational level. Warren claimed to have completed eleven years in school and that he had received a GED, the high school equivalency.

Ted Lambert sat in on the interview because he had built up a special rapport with Lesley Warren. He started the ball rolling. "I think the easiest way to do this, Lesley, is just for you to explain to Detective Amory and Lieutenant Ennis what occurred in the death of Faye Gray, and I guess you have to give them some details of how it came about, what the day was like and what led up to it. Just kind of go through it with them."

Warren: "OK. I took the truck from AM-CAN Trucking Company and made a trip to Asheville. I had done it several times before, just really messed around in the truck driving. I was coming down 25, and it was late. It was kind of foggy, and this woman flagged me down. She had run her car into the bank. I didn't go up to the car. I could see where it was at. She asked me for a ride to take her down to use a phone to call help. I took her. It wasn't more than a mile down the road to a convenience store."

Warren insisted he only stopped his truck because he'd almost run her over as he drove up the highway. Warren stated their only conversation had been when Velma Faye Gray told how she'd wrecked her car. Then he said, "Before she could get out of the truck, I grabbed her and choked her."

Warren claimed he couldn't even remember if he'd thrown Velma Faye Gray's pocketbook into the lake when he dropped her body in the water a couple of hours later. He insisted he did not have any sexual relations with Velma Faye Gray. Warren also claimed to the investigators that he later told his wife, Tracey, what had happened. "But I didn't tell her what I had done. I told her somebody else did it, that I just helped them get rid of the body."

Ennis: "Do you remember what she [Faye Gray] was wearing?"
Warren: "I remember she had on shorts. I'm not really sure about the top."
Ennis: "How about her shoes. D'you remember her shoes?"
Warren: "Sandals or flip-flops."

Warren explained how he drove to the bridge by the lake, disposed of Faye Gray's body and then encountered Dorothy Deck. "It was all delivered in a calm, casual voice. No emotion. As normal as apple pie," Detective Carroll Amory later explained.

Lieutenant Ennis asked Warren when he first decided to kill Velma Faye Gray. Warren answered swiftly, "I didn't really know until it was already happening."

Ennis: "Do you remember what you were thinking or what you were feeling at the time you killed this woman?"
Warren: "No."
Ennis: "But you knew at the time that you were killing her?"
Warren: (He nods his head.)
Ennis: "Right?"

Warren: "Yes."

Ennis: "You knew you were doing it? You knew what you were doing? You were killing this lady?"

Warren: "Yes."

Ennis: "You knew it was wrong to take a life?"

Warren: "Yes."

Ennis: "How did you feel after it happened? Do you remember?"

Warren: "Scared."

Ennis: "Did she tell you what her name was?"

Warren: "No, I don't think she did."

Ennis: "When did you first learn what her name was?"

Warren: "On the news."

Ennis: "Had you ever seen this woman before?"

Warren: "No."

Lesley Warren took a deep breath and said, "Just like the others, I'm sorry it happened. I don't know what I was thinking or why. I'm just glad everything's over."

Ennis added, "This ends the statement. July 21, 1990, at two-forty A.M."

During the hours of interviewing that night, Warren was asked if he wanted to go to the rest room six times. It wasn't until 2:41 A.M. that he replied yes to the request. Sergeant Ted Lambert escorted him.

Warren was formally charged with homicide in the High Point and Asheville cases. He was also charged with the South Carolina fugitive's warrant, as well as a felony larceny.

More than 300 pages of statement and over five

hours after they first began, Lesley Eugene Warren
had confessed to four homicides.

He'd even remembered their first names. . . .

Patsy

Faye

Jayme

Kat

He'd seen the reports in the newspapers.

Carroll Amory, believes to this day that Lesley
Warren only 'fessed up to the killings of the women
because their photos were pinned on the walls of
the outer "task force office."

"We sat down and talked about it and concluded
that these are the ones that we knew about and so
he told us. These were the ones with the pictures,
but I always thought there were more that we didn't
know about," explained Amory. "We felt that like
all serial killers, when they get ready to execute him,
he's gonna come up and say he's ready to tell them
about more to prolong the process. He's intelligent;
otherwise, he wouldn't have done what he was doing. He's a crafty son of a bitch."

High Point detectives Mark McNeill and Jerry
Grubb arrived at Asheville PD early next morning
to interview Lesley Warren about the murder of Kat
Johnson. They went straight to the task force interview room and sat down. Up the hall, Warren had
spent a few restless hours in a metal holding cell
with a desk, a water fountain and a window.

Warren, in ankle and wrist chains and wearing a
bright red Buncombe County Jail jumpsuit, was led
in by three deputies. He immediately recognized
Grubb and McNeill and they told him they had spoken to Asheville PD.

"So you're still willing to talk with us, Lesley?" asked McNeill.

"Sure," he replied softly.

The two detectives tried to build an instant rapport with Warren, having arrested him only a few hours earlier in relatively peaceful circumstances. McNeill later recalled, "We asked him if he had an attorney and he said no, and we said did he want an attorney here and he said no." Mark McNeill started the interview while Jerry Grubb injected questions as they tried to clarify certain points. When a man interrupted them by walking into the room, Warren just waved him away. "He wanted to feel he was in charge," McNeill later recalled.

It later emerged that the man had been an investigator from the DA's office. Warren was joking.

McNeill switched on the tape recorder and the detectives tried to throw Warren by going straight into the moment of Kat Johnson's death.

McNeill: "After sex. Did she say anything that made you mad?"

Warren: "Nothing."

McNeill: "Or didn't do anything? She just sat there."

Warren: "Laying on me."

McNeill: "When you started choking her, she didn't act surprised or did she struggle? You don't recall her saying, 'What are you doing?' or 'Quit fooling around' or anything like that?"

Warren: "Nope."

McNeill: "All right, when you were choking her and she was trying to get up from that lying position, what was she doing with her hands?

You remember her shivering and trying to get up. Is that right?"

Warren: "Yes."

McNeill: "But you don't remember what she was doing with her hands? Do you remember what she was doing with her feet?"

Warren (seeming flustered for a moment): "No. No, I don't."

McNeill tried to trivialize the murder to get Warren to confess more details. "Was it very much trouble for you to choke her like that, physically?"

Warren: "No."

McNeill: "Did it take very long before she stopped moving or breathing?"

Warren: "I can't remember at all."

McNeill: "Do you remember when she did stop breathing? Do you remember when she stopped . . . Can you say 'no' so the tape will know?"

Warren: "No."

McNeill: "Do you remember when she stopped struggling?"

Warren: "I don't know. Everything's blurred together."

McNeill: "Did she ever make any sounds, like trying to talk to you or yell?"

Warren: "No, I don't think so."

McNeill: "What made you stop choking her? Was it because she stopped moving?"

Warren: "I guess. That would have been it."

McNeill: "What happened after you choked her? Did she move anymore? Did she talk anymore?"

Warren: "I don't remember."

Less than an hour later, Lesley Warren was given a three-vehicle escort back up Interstate 85 to the parking deck of the Ramada Hotel in High Point. Assembled around Kat Johnson's Renault, detectives had no trouble spotting the blood marks on the trunk handle and the dozens of flies buzzing inside and outside the vehicle. Kat Johnson's car keys were produced.

"And then, *pop*, we had ourselves victim number four," McNeill later explained.

Police found Kat Johnson's naked, decaying body with a bra wrapped around her neck. Warren's fingerprints were found outside the driver's-side door, and his right palm print was found on the outside of the trunk.

The High Point investigators knew it was important not to disturb the crime scene, so police technicians and ME personnel stood by as the keys earlier found in Warren's pocket were used to start the car and drive it onto a waiting flatbed truck. The car and its gruesome cargo were immediately taken to the ME's building on Chapel Hill at the University of North Carolina campus, where Kat Johnson had been a student.

Detective Grubb asked for forensic expert Bill Lennox from the Special Bureau of Investigations in nearby Greensboro to assist the examination. Grubb later recalled, "I knew that he'd be a bit quicker. The moment the lab lifted prints off the back of the vehicle, they told the SBI lab in Greensboro and immediately I knew they'd get going on the autopsy on Katherine."

While the car containing Johnson's corpse was transported across town, High Point detectives Grubb and McNeill got Lesley Warren to give them

a sketchy description of where the killing was supposed to have occurred.

Warren was then escorted back down Interstate
85 to the Buncombe County Jail. Later that afternoon, an investigator with the High Point Police Department served the warrant on Warren in relation
to the death of Kat Johnson. Over at the High Point
Police Department Headquarters on Leonard
Street, detectives began digging out their unsolved
homicides.

At around the same time on Saturday, July 21,
Asheville Police issued a press release about the alleged crimes of Lesley Eugene Warren to the world:

On the 20th of July, at approx 14:20 hours,
High Point police officers effected the arrest
of Lesley Eugene Warren, 22 yoa, of Rt 1, Chandler, NC. Warren was arrested pursuant to outstanding arrest warrants for murder and
kidnapping obtained by Spartanburg County
Sheriff's Department, located in South Carolina. The arrest took place at a residence in the
300 block of Phillips Ave., in the NW section
of High Point. This was incident-free arrest.
Warren was remanded to the custody of
Asheville Police authorities, on an unrelated fe-
lonious larceny charge. At approx 2200 hrs on
the 20th, Warren stated to the Asheville
authorities that he had murdered a woman and
hidden her body in the trunk of her auto which
he had abandoned on the second level of a
parking deck in downtown High Point. He further stated that he had committed this murder
on Sunday, 15 July 1990. High Point officers
located this auto, parked on the second level

of the city parking deck, located in the 100 block of South Main Street.

The body of 21-year-old Katherine Noel Johnson, of — Kensington Drive, High Point, NC, was located in the trunk of the auto. The victim's body and the auto were transported to the NC Medical Examiner's Office in Chapel Hill for examination. The exact cause of the victim's death is pending, awaiting the complete results of the medical examiner's report. The victim's car is in the custodial control of the High Point Police Department pending progress of the case investigation.

This continuing investigation is being conducted by detectives J. Grubb, M.B. McNeill, K.D. Beck, & Lt Nunn. A warrant for the arrest of Lesley Eugene Warren, 22 yoa, of Rt 1, Chandler, NC, charging him with first degree murder; he is presently incarcerated in the Buncombe County Jail, located in Asheville, NC, without privilege of bond.

Asheville local TV station WLOS 13's main news bulletin broadcast that day had the Warren case as lead story and reported the full details behind Warren's apprehension in High Point. Lesley Warren's mother, Phyllis, was watching the TV news. She immediately called Investigator Keith Cochran, who worked in the offices of Warren attorney Scott Jarvis. She said her son had told her if he was re-arrested, then she should contact Jarvis's office.

Cochran established that Warren was being held back in Asheville. He called Asheville Police Department and the Buncombe County Jail and kept Scott Jarvis informed throughout that day. Cochran also insisted he left a message at the Buncombe County

Jail stating that Scott Jarvis was representing Lesley
Warren.

An autopsy on Kat Johnson's remains established
she had died of asphyxia due to strangulation. Her
body, however, had decayed so rapidly in the early
summer heat that she had to be identified through
her dental records.

That same day, July 21, NYSP investigator Wayne
Corsa phoned Mike Vineyard in Tennessee to tell
him about Lesley Warren's confession. The heart-
broken husband of Warren's first-known murder victim, Patsy Vineyard, found all the painful memories
being brought back to the surface by Warren's arrest. Mike Vineyard had stopped talking about his
wife even though he secretly visited her grave regularly to put flowers on it. He'd spent three years
trying to block her out of his mind without success.

Detective Corsa also contacted Patsy's aunt Opal
McCubbins, in Knoxville, Tennessee, and told her
the news.

During that weekend, Corsa and fellow investigator Bob Cooke visited Warren's wife, Tracey, again
and quickly noticed her detached attitude. "We'll
never know how much she really knew about Warren's crimes, but she struck us both as cold and cal-
culated when we interviewed her. She seemed to be
in a complete state of denial about her husband,"
Cooke later revealed.

Tracey gave a three-page deposition after much
discussion with Corsa and Cooke. The statement was
made in the presence of Detective Robbie Hendrix
of the Spartanburg County Sheriff's Department; it
barely scratched the surface of her life with suspected serial killer Lesley Warren.

Spartanburg detective Carroll Amory also encountered Warren's wife, Tracey, in the days following her husband's arrest and described her as "being in a constant state of denial" about her husband's crimes.

That weekend Amory also interviewed Warren's former girlfriend Lisa Lawrence. Initially, she denied any knowledge of Warren and said she did not know anything about him. "Then when we started showing her the danger that she could have been in, she changed her mind," Amory explained.

Lawrence told the investigator how Warren went to Anderson, picked up an AM-CAN truck and then cruised round Asheville before he returned it to the depot. "She was weird," Amory later elaborated. "She didn't seem to understand at first the danger she was in. Then we sat her down in a room one on one. We got to telling her the facts we had against Lesley and the danger she could have been in."

At a press conference on Saturday, July 22, 1990, Lieutenant Ed Grant, the FBI's serial killer profiler, told newsmen he had no doubt that Warren would have struck again if he had not been apprehended. "His mind-set is such that he will kill again."

Dr. LuJuan Gibson, a psychologist and assistant director at the JEC in Swannanoa, told TV and newspaper reporters that Jayme Hurley had taken a special interest in Warren, but she did not believe "the two were romantically involved."

Former JEC social worker Catherine Jenkins was so upset when she heard that Warren had murdered her friend Jayme Hurley that she insisted on giving investigators every detail of her phone conversation with Hurley on the night she died. She even recalled how she had talked about the plot of Stephen King's novel *It.*

Jenkins never read another word of King's novel. As she later explained: "I was unable and unwilling to finish the book. I just kept wondering, after the police contacted me, if Jayme went into the living room and talked to Lesley about me and about me reading about this monster who kills innocent people? It was just a thought, but one that is disturbing to me."

Jenkins told investigators at the time: "It is so sad that Lesley harmed those in his life who have tried the hardest to help and be a friend. I never considered Lesley to be 'normal.' But I trusted Jayme's judgment about him [Warren]."

Jenkins insisted that the Jayme she knew "would never shoot up drugs, at least not willingly." She had no recollection of Warren being involved with drugs while at JEC. Jenkins said, "I wonder what kind of trouble he was in the night of the twenty-fourth. I do know that he would have told Jayme things he would have told no one else."

Seventeen

The weekend of Lesley Warren's arrest, Detective Inspector Jim McCormick of the Royal Canadian Mounted Police requested that his force join the Warren task force because Warren was suspected of at least one killing north of the border. Toronto police even offered the Asheville-based investigators access to their NCIC information to look at other possible Warren homicides in Canada.

Lesley Warren's confession to killing Kat Johnson had come like a bolt out of the blue to the residents of High Point as the report in the local *Enterprise* newspaper detailed on Sunday, July 22.

City police thought they were through with suspected serial killer Lesley Eugene Warren Friday afternoon after they turned him over to Asheville cops.

They thought he was somebody else's nightmare.

But about 10:15 Friday night, Asheville authorities called High Point police to say Warren told them he killed a woman here, local officials said.

During that weekend, Terry Quimby told journalists Warren was not capable of killing four women.

"He's a nice guy, and it's hard for me to believe he did all this," she said. "He's just a friend and I let him stay. I'm still in shock. I won't think about it. I'll put it out of my mind. It's too hard to believe." She continued, "They just went for a motorcycle ride. I can't believe what happened. We were just becoming friends." Then Quimby stated the obvious: "What freaks me out is I could have been next. I mean they say he knew all those girls, too. It's so hard to believe. He was so normal."

Perhaps saddest of all were the first public comments from Warren's father, Doug, who told the press that his son had lived with his mother as a child and he'd had virtually no contact with his father. "I really didn't know him. We separated when he was three or four," said Doug Warren. "We had some problems [with the divorce] and I didn't see much of him after that."

Warren's mother, Phyllis, could not be traced in the hours following her son's arrest. Neither could brother Laron. But Patsy Vineyard's husband, Mike, told newsmen he was stunned when he was told the news about Warren's arrest: "They [the police] stayed on the case when I thought it was hopeless. I mean it's been three years." Mike Vineyard said to reporters he vaguely remembered Warren as a quiet soldier. "He kept to himself. I never associated with him. We never had words." Vineyard couldn't help reflecting on the fact that he continued serving alongside Warren for a year after his wife's murder. "He saw me every day for a year and never gave any sign of what happened," Vineyard said. "If I knew then what I know now, it would've been different."

Over at AM-CAN, where Warren had worked from May to September 1989, personnel described him as a "presentable applicant" and said he left of his own accord. Warren was said to have had no close friends at AM-CAN.

On Sunday, July 22, stories linking Warren to the deaths of two more unnamed women were leaked to the Asheville press. It seemed to many that Warren's current tally of four could rise very quickly. By the following day, the unsolved murder of another local woman was added to the list. Soon other agencies were inquiring about cases on their books that could be linked to the activities of Lesley Warren.

Yet, as news of Warren's arrest spread, officials in Jefferson County, New York—where Patsy Vineyard was murdered—refused to confirm that Warren was their man. District Attorney Gary Miles told newsmen, "We're in a tough position. This press release issued in Asheville is the only thing we have seen on paper. I have not seen any statements, any evidence and photographs. I'm not in a position where I can say I have a prosecutable case."

The NYSP did admit that Warren had been one of the soldiers questioned. Captain Joseph Loszynski, from the New York State Bureau of Criminal Investigation at Oneida, insisted, "There was not one shred of evidence to indicate Lesley Warren was the perpetrator." Loszynski then told reporters, "It could take us three or four weeks to tie up some leads. By no means are we concluded."

In fact, DA Miles had not yet made up his mind whether a prosecution would even be forthcoming. The main reason was that North Carolina had the death penalty while, at that time, New York did not. If a warrant was issued, Warren might never stand trial in New York because he could be convicted and possibly given the death penalty in the North Carolina case. By that evening, warrants had only been

issued for the three other murders so far connected
to Warren.

In High Point, more than a dozen officers
searched the soccer field where Warren said he had
killed Kat Johnson. They located her red high heel
shoes which had her initials in them. When confronted about the shoes, Warren claimed he may
have put them there, but he could not remember
anything after killing Kat Johnson.

In Asheville, Ted Lambert was deeply troubled by
the fact that Warren had indicated he'd killed many
more than four people. That weekend Warren was
taken out on a tour of the area and asked to point
out various death sites, but no more bodies were
located as a result of his information. Some investigators wondered if Warren had made up his claims.

Was Lesley Warren holding back for some reason?

Outside of the Carolinas, Lesley Warren's arrest
was overshadowed by Iraq's massing of troops on
their border with Kuwait. The border buildup coin-
cided with a verbal assault on Kuwait by President
Saddam Hussein and threats of military action. If
Lesley Warren hadn't been kicked out of the U.S.
Army, he might have found himself on a war footing
with a chance to be a hero.

At 2:00 P.M. on Monday, July 23, 1990, the wood-
paneled inner core of the main Buncombe County
Courthouse was packed. Reporters and photogra-
phers were given only a few seconds' notice before
Lesley Warren was led in and the barred floor-to-
ceiling door clanged shut behind him. Dressed in a
red county jumpsuit, feet thrust into thonged scuffs,
Warren stood still for an instant, braced to meet the

sharp slivers of camera lights. He nodded across the room to his mother, Phyllis.

As he moved forward, his ankle chains clanged and scraped against the parquet flooring. Warren seated himself next to his attorney, who waived a reading of the charges aloud. The suspected serial killer sat straight-faced without a hint of emotion. Judge Gary Cash of the district court asked Warren if he understood the charges, and he answered, "Yes, sir."

The court was told that a hearing to determine if there was enough evidence to hold Warren on murder charges was scheduled for August 6. Judge Cash refused to hear any motion for bond because, as he later explained, "in my mind, with all the allegations, no bond would have been appropriate."

Lesley Eugene Warren was formally arraigned and ordered to be held without bail. Judge Cash then set February 27, 1991, as the date for a preliminary hearing requested by his attorney.

Warren got up at the end of the hearing, turned and smiled in the direction of his mother. Then he looked down as he was taken away by three deputies.

Outside the court, Warren's shocked mother emerged in public for the first time to get a message to her incarcerated son. She needed to find out if he wanted her to visit him in the Buncombe County Jail. She defiantly told reporters: "If he doesn't want to say anything, all I want him to know is that I still love him." Phyllis Murray also felt the need to issue a public declaration of love for her son. "I don't uphold what he's done, but he's still my son and I love him," Murray, now forty-two, told reporters. "I want him to know God can forgive him for what he's done. I have said all along my heart goes out to those women and their families. . . . I feel like he has done some of this."

Phyllis Murray later told the local *Asheville Citizen* newspaper that Warren had displayed the same detachment he had since he was four years old. "I don't think he understood the seriousness of the charges," she said. "It was like he wasn't even there. It was like, 'If you said I did it, OK.' "

Murray also claimed her son's unreadable baby face reminded her of when he was a child and she'd tell him things and watch them go right through him. "You would know he heard you, but what you said wasn't going in," she told journalists. Murray had ensured her son was once again represented by attorney Scott Jarvis. She believed Warren would "clam up" because he didn't like his court-appointed lawyers, public defender Robert Hufstader and assistant Robert Clark. Murray also wanted all her son's previous medical records to be made available to his attorneys. "I want them to know the problems he's had," she said.

By Tuesday, July 24, four days after Warren's dramatic arrest, law enforcement agencies from across the country were lining up to question Lesley Warren about unsolved homicides on their books. Prosecutors in High Point believed they'd have a long wait before they could try him for the murder of Kat Johnson.

"It might be a while before he's debriefed and sent for trial anywhere," Guilford County, High Point, district attorney Jim Kimel told reporters. "We'll just try to figure out a way that everybody can get their case resolved in the most efficient manner."

None of the prosecutors from the three states where Warren committed his murders had discussed the order in which the cases would be tried. "I don't know if the death penalty will be involved in any of those earlier homicides," Kimel told reporters. He refused to say if he would be seeking the death penalty for Johnson's killing in High Point.

A few hours later, Detective Jerry Grubb got the one call he dreaded from Kat Johnson's parents, Anne and Bobby, who'd just arrived home from their vacation in the Colorado Rockies. He later said, "Nobody had been able to get hold of them."

The difficult task of identifying Kat Johnson was made fractionally easier because it was agreed that none of the family would have to view her body. David Johnson, her brother, identified the bracelet and watch found on her remains. As Detective Grubb later explained: "If we know exactly who they are, we try to avoid the family having to ID them."

In Asheville, pressure was mounting on the police department to publicly explain why they'd released Lesley Warren before he headed for High Point to murder Kat Johnson. Asheville police chief Gerald Beavers said despite investigators naming Warren as a suspect in Jayme Hurley's death, they didn't have the evidence to hold him.

"If you can't prove there has been a homicide, you certainly can't charge somebody with murdering somebody," said Beavers. "The law and the courts are pretty clear about what you can and can't do, and you can't keep him in jail forever on a couple of piddling misdemeanors. Our system of jurisprudence does not allow us to arrest people for suspicions. Until you can get enough evidence to make a case against somebody, you can't arrest them."

Beavers declined to elaborate on the statements made by Warren at that time or other specific evidence, claiming the cases could be jeopardized. "If there was anything else that could have been done, we would have done it. We had people working around the clock on this case trying to gather the evidence and do the things that needed to be done."

In other developments connected to the Warren case, Guilford County deputies eliminated him as a suspect in the May 1989 death of twenty-five-year-old Vicki Cook Von Cannon at High Point's City Lake Park. But rumors of another victim spread through Asheville's Buncombe County after someone spotted a shallow grave and called the police. Authorities found the carcass of a bear, apparently killed by poachers. Lesley Warren's murderous habits had struck fear into the community.

Naturally, many of Kat Johnson's friends were stunned by the news of her murder. Julia Frost, a former roommate of Johnson, told one local newspaper, "She was a really very intelligent person, very outgoing. One of her best qualities was her honesty and integrity. I know she loved her family a lot."

Noelle Blank, of High Point, another of her closest friends, said: "I can't imagine anybody ever wanting to do any harm to her. She was always concerned with other people and she knew how to make everybody laugh. You just don't take away life from somebody like that."

Meanwhile, Lesley Warren remained in the Buncombe County Jail without bail or bond. He was kept in maximum security under guard as an "escape-prone and violent" prisoner. A grand jury was scheduled to hear the preliminary aspects of the Jayme Hurley case on August 6. Spartanburg County also held a kidnapping and murder warrant for Warren in regard to the death of Velma Faye Gray.

In Watertown, New York, DA Gary Miles of Jefferson County had reviewed evidence and statements obtained during the Vineyard murder investigation and decided it was worth presenting to a grand jury for another indictment. New York State Police finally publicly confirmed that Warren had admitted to the Vineyard killing, although that did not necessarily mean a prosecution would be forthcoming. Most reckoned that North Carolina would try Lesley Warren first.

"It's a very lengthy procedure," a spokesman for the NYSP told journalists. "We would draw up and serve a fugitive warrant in case he walked on a technicality, but then South Carolina would get him first. Their fugitive warrant has already been served."

The *Watertown Daily Times* was furious it had taken so long for Warren's name to be publicly disclosed; it accused Jefferson County district attorney Gary Miles of being "uncooperative in telling county residents about a man unafraid to kill innocent women. He was more concerned that he might be sued if the person named as the serial killer was not involved in Mrs. Vineyard's murder."

On Wednesday, July 25, High Point detectives Mark McNeill and Jerry Grubb plus State Bureau of Investigation agent Ron Padgett reinterviewed Warren at Buncombe County Jail. Warren revealed to the law enforcement officers he'd seriously considered killing the woman parking-lot attendant at the Ramada Hotel. "He said he had an urge to 'off' her as well. But he didn't go through with it for whatever reason," Grubb later recalled.

Warren also claimed he'd slept with Terry Quimby throughout the week before Kat Johnson's murder. "He was kinda proud of it. Like it sorta showed what a ladies' man he was," Mark McNeill later recalled. "All the time we spoke to him, he was extremely pleasant, well mannered and definitely not nervous, although he sure had a character flaw."

Warren ran through the last three days before he killed Kat Johnson and the last twelve tragic hours of her life. Then he verified the model of her car from photographs as well as the site where Johnson was killed. However, Warren was unable to confirm that clothes in certain photos belonged to Johnson. Warren also claimed he could not remember if Kat had been wearing any shoes. When he was shown a photograph of a pair of red high heel shoes, he responded, "I don't know. They could have been."

Later on in the interview, the High Point investigators tried to establish any patterns in Warren's killings, such as use of alcohol and drugs, secluded locations with few, if any, streetlights. Warren ruined it all by telling them he had killed Jayme Hurley in her own bed in her house in Asheville.

Even the way Warren met his victims varied and they certainly did not closely resemble each other in size, hair color or age. While talking about hair color, Warren even referred to his own dyed hair, which was unusually dark with a reddish tint. His moustache and beard were the same color.

Warren also once again insisted he'd had sex with Patsy Vineyard by the lakeshore. Warren proudly claimed he was still having sex with his wife, Tracey, at the time. Warren also mentioned times in 1988 when he suffered memory loss, which lasted a number of days, and suggested that he might have murdered other women during these "blackout periods." Then one of the High Point investigators asked: "Lesley, we've been sitting here talking for quite a while. Do you know, or can you give us any reason, why these women are dead?"

Warren answered, "I don't know."

When asked, "Especially Miss Johnson, why, why did she, uh, die?" Lesley Warren did not reply.

Deputies from Oconee County, South Carolina, interviewed Lesley Warren in the Buncombe County Jail on July 26, after linking him to the 1988 death of Daisy Snieder, a forty-two-year-old woman, whose body was found in a remote section of woods near the Oconee Power Station on November 26, 1988. Snieder had been shot, strangled and sexually assaulted.

"We had someone [Warren] confessing to some murders in other areas and we had a similar unsolved murder on our hands," explained one senior Oconee investigator. "He's not a particularly strong suspect in the case, but we're following all the leads, touching all the bases."

In Asheville, officers fielded numerous calls from yet more agencies wanting information about the cases against Warren. Investigators considered that the six months from May to September 1989 may well have been Warren's prime killing time. It was during that period Warren worked as an interstate truck driver traveling all over the Carolinas, to California, along the Eastern Seaboard and north into Canada.

The following day, July 27, journalists located and interviewed Sharon Carver, the cousin of the neighbor Warren attacked back in 1983. Carver had knocked down Warren with a right-hand punch, which probably saved the other woman's life. Carver said, "A lot of women might be alive today if something had been done about Lesley a long time ago."

Lab analysis on numerous items collected by police during the last month of investigations showed dozens of links between Warren and the murders he'd confessed to.

On August 1, Sergeant Ted Lambert of the Asheville PD interviewed Lesley Warren once again about a drug transaction that he'd told authorities he'd been involved with. Warren claimed he'd acted as "backup" to a man named Stanley Morgan on three or four occasions. Warren gave Lambert details of one particular incident that he claimed involved two men from Georgia. Warren said that as the drug deal was being concluded, the two men from Georgia fired at Morgan, who returned fire, killing both of the other men. Warren told Lambert that he had helped bury the two men. It was virtually impossible to prove Warren's claims and some investigators believed that his "confession" was a ruse to try and gain sympathy.

New York State Police decided not to file charges of first-degree murder in the death of Patsy Vineyard until Warren had been tried on the North and South Carolina charges. However, they considered the Vineyard case closed. Lesley Warren was their man.

All serial-type killings that occurred between 1985 and 1990 could, in theory, be connected to Lesley Warren's activities.

On August 6, 1990, Lesley Warren was indicted by a Buncombe County grand jury on charges of first-degree murder connected to the killing of Jayme Hurley. That same day, Sergeant Ted Lambert of the Asheville PD once again visited Warren in

Buncombe County Jail where Warren said that in August 1988 he met a Mexican migrant worker named "Mary" with whom he had sex. He claimed he and Mary went to his New York boardinghouse, watched movies together and then went to bed. When Warren was next aware of his surroundings, he told Lambert, Mary was dead. He claimed that he later buried Mary's body in a field. Warren also stated he'd killed a woman called "Ronnie," whom he'd picked up and taken to South Carolina while working as a truck driver for AM-CAN.

Warren claimed he suffered from regular blackouts and memory loss, and that the next time he became aware of his surroundings he was in Tennessee. Warren then noticed Ronnie next to him and she was dead. He told Lambert he left the body in the woods.

Just a few days earlier, Lesley Warren had been linked to only three killings. Now it looked as if his true toll could well go into double figures.

By August 7, investigators became convinced Warren was responsible for the death of twenty-two-year-old blond Donna Medford, whose eyes were so green that she was known to friends as "Jade." Donna, from Watertown, had often spent time in the bars of Sackets Harbor.

At the end of July 1987, Donna Medford had rented a boat and gone out on Lake Ontario on the opposite side to Sackets Harbor. She had sex with a man, who then choked her. She was wearing jeans and sandals at the time.

Another potential victim was thirty-nine-year-old Raquel Westfall, who was murdered in Pennsylvania. Then there was the unsolved homicide of twenty-one-year-old Clare Gravel from Salem, Massachusetts. The Salem State College student had been strangled by her own shirt. One witness recalled seeing a white pickup driving near the scene of the killing.

On August 8, investigators in Orange County, Virginia, announced that Lesley Warren was the chief suspect in the strangling of a sixty-two-year-old woman called Ethel Sarah Kidd in Burr Hill, Virginia. She had been murdered right in the middle of Warren's spree on April 12, 1989. Over in Essex County, South Carolina, the unidentified body of a woman found in May 1988 was also being linked to Warren's activities.

In Allegheny County, Pennsylvania, Detective Nick Bruich was convinced that Warren was responsible for the homicide of yet another unidentified woman in her early twenties, who'd been walking along a railroad track next to a housing project when her killer struck. She had been strangled and suffered a fractured skull. But, unlike Warren's modus operandi, this victim had been cut from her chest to her vagina.

Another unsolved homicide linked to Lesley Warren was that of Sherry Lynn Armstrong, thirty-three, killed on November 10, 1989, after suffering multiple stab wounds in Newport, Kentucky. Warren's name was linked to another homicide victim, twenty-five-year-old Tammy Charles, from Cary, North Carolina, who had been missing since February 28, 1990.

As one of the Warren task force team members pointed out: "These calls from other agencies were pouring in. It was pretty terrifying to know that so many unsolved murders by homicidal maniacs across the continent had been committed. It felt like there had to be at least half a dozen other blood-lusting serial killers out there at any one time."

In High Point, a grand jury indicted Lesley Warren in connection with the slaying of Kat Johnson.

Eighteen

In November 1990, Lesley Warren was caught up in what Buncombe County Jail officials called a "small disturbance" just before he was due to be transferred to High Point, North Carolina, in connection with the Kat Johnson murder. Inmates in a unit for dangerous prisoners where Warren was housed set a pile of clothing afire.

Sergeant Charles Wyatt, spokesman for Buncombe County Sheriff's Department, later explained: "Warren was participating; he wasn't the one that did this particular act of setting the fire." Wyatt said Warren was "raising hell in general. It was nothing out of the ordinary for this particular block, the type of people we have in it. From time to time, we do have problems with some of these inmates."

Warren did not face any criminal charges in relation to the incident, but jail disciplinary action was a certainty. Warren was transported within hours to High Point to make the court appearance for the Johnson killing. In a brief hearing at superior court, Guilford, North Carolina, Judge Howard R. "Rick" Greeson appointed assistant public defenders Randy May and John Bryson to defend Warren.

While in court, Lesley Warren responded to Judge Greeson's questions with a soft "No, sir" and "Yes, sir." His skin was pale, and his hair, now blond and cut closely on the sides and top, hung to his shoulders. He sported a small goatee and stared across the courtroom audience between questions.

DA Jim Kimel said the Warren case would be treated as a capital case in which he may seek the death penalty. That decision would be dependent on the outcome of Warren's trial in Asheville for the Jayme Hurley murder. A conviction in that case would probably give the state the aggravating factor it needed to seek a death penalty.

After the brief hearing, a reporter pushed his way through the crowd outside the courthouse and asked Warren if he had confessed to the killing. He did not reply. Deputies then drove Warren back to the Buncombe County Jail.

An army of psychologists lined up to talk with Warren in prison. Dr. Bruce Welch made a point of allowing the suspected serial killer to describe the offenses he had been charged with. "The importance lay in finding out what he was thinking before, during and after everything happened," Dr. Welch later explained. "It's what we call state of mind at the time of the offense and, of course, it's very important for someone like me to find out what they were thinking at the time."

Welch concluded that Lesley Warren "seemed to have holes in his memory about what happened. It seems legitimate that he doesn't remember a lot. That's not at all uncommon." Warren even admitted to Welch that he must have committed the killings. "He remembered that he certainly must have done it, and he acknowledged to me that he had. It's just that he can't come up with the details."

But Warren did tell Dr. Welch that for at least two days before the Jayme Hurley killing he had been doing a large amount of intravenous cocaine. Warren claimed he was addicted to cocaine. He was also drinking alcohol at the time and he claimed that had clouded his memory.

The bottom line was that Lesley Warren could barely recall his crimes. He told Welch he put his hands around Jayme Hurley's neck and that he did strangle her.

"But I don't know why I did," Warren told Welch.

Lesley Warren was yet again having trouble coming to terms with his actions. What Welch later called "a transient amnesic disorder due to chronic cocaine and alcohol injection" meant that he only recalled what he wanted. Welch insisted Warren was not fully aware of his environment, so he could not relate to anything that happened. Lesley Warren had acute problems for virtually his entire life. All the clues had been sitting there since he was four years old. Welch also referred to the fact that Warren had been completely knocked unconscious twice in his life, although he insisted there was no residual effects from those injuries.

Early in 1991, Sergeant Ted Lambert was celebrating promotion to lieutenant when he called up the NYSP senior investigator Bob Cooke to tell him that it was hoped Warren's trial for the Jayme Hurley killing would go ahead later that year. But Lambert knew the projected start date was an optimistic long shot.

In Buncombe County, DA Ron Moore had his plate full with other murder cases, having just completed his office's third back-to-back murder trial. He had seven other murder cases scheduled ahead of the Warren trial. However, Moore made it clear he'd be seeking the death penalty because the strangulation of Jayme Hurley had "been such an atrocious way to kill someone." Buncombe County public defender Robert Hufstader and assistant Robert Clark were also swamped with cases because they were handling more than half of that summer's projected murder trials.

Jayme Hurley's family, still devastated by her death, demanded a swift trial for Lesley Warren. Lee Hurley, her brother, told reporters, "You had to know her to understand how great the loss was. It's still unbelievable." Jayme Hurley's elderly father said, "It's been a depressing thing all the way through. I'd like to see it finished soon. So would a lot of other people in the two other states who are waiting to see what's going to happen here. But all I can do by trying to push them might be to get myself more excited and upset, so I just leave it up to them."

Warren's mother, Phyllis Murray, told reporters it was "unfair" for her son to face a long stretch in jail without a trial. "It's ironic that a person can be charged for keeping an animal penned up in a small cage without exercise, when that's what's happening to my son," she said. "It's indecent to take a human being and lock him up without letting them get out in the sunshine."

Murray was particularly upset because her son had lost a lot of weight in jail and had started needing glasses to read his favorite Stephen King and Dean R. Koontz novels. She also claimed he'd been suffering appalling nightmares since his arrest, including one recurring dream in which snakes were crawling all over him.

"It worries me, but what can I do?" Murray told one reporter. Others demanded that Lesley Warren start facing up to his real-life nightmares and head for the death chamber as swiftly as possible.

In June 1991, all the agencies originally involved in the Warren investigation met up once again to swap information to ensure the case against the suspected serial killer was airtight. New York officials agreed that as capital punishment did not exist in their state, they might never prosecute Warren if they were satisfied with the punishment he got down South.

Prosecutors and investigators from all four jurisdictions connected to the victims of Lesley Warren agreed South Carolina would definitely be allowed to try him first. Prosecutors wanted each conviction, should there be one, to be used by subsequent jurisdictions as aggravating factors in asking for the death penalty. This guaranteed Lesley Warren would die for the crimes he had committed.

In early August 1991, Warren made a brief appearance in the Buncombe County District Court where he was informed he would be shipped to South Carolina to stand trial for the Velma Faye Gray killing unless he planned to contest his extradition. He had ten days to challenge the ruling. Governor Carroll Campbell of South Carolina had already issued a governor's warrant for Warren. He was extradited on August 23, 1991.

Carl Allen, a criminal defense lawyer in Greenville, was assigned to represent Warren and it was predicted that Allen would need at least four to five months to prepare the case. Warren was immediately denied bond and kept in the Greenville Detention Center. It was agreed that at a later date he would spend some days in the state mental hospital in Columbia, South Carolina, for psychiatric evaluation.

But that supposedly imminent trial never materialized and by the following February 1992, Greenville County had delayed Warren's first trial for the Velma Faye Gray killing because they did not want to pay for the high-priced defense experts required to give testimony on Warren's behalf. His furious defense attorneys then threatened to delay the trial until the county agreed to foot the bill for witnesses.

Back in the Greenville County Jail after yet another psychiatric evaluation, Warren was bemused by the whole situation. Court officials predicted a delay of at least a year and it emerged that Greenville County was only one of three South Carolina counties refusing to pay for the supposedly high-priced defense experts. Local media had a field day. Greenville's Channel 13 TV evening news reported, "The murder trial of confessed serial killer Lesley Warren is on hold tonight. . . . Two years have now passed since police arrested Warren and he still hasn't gone to trial."

Velma Faye Gray's brother George Jackson vented his family's frustration in an interview with Channel 13. "I am concerned that the information is getting old. Some of the witnesses may forget when this thing finally comes to trial." Channel 13 reporter Judy Fleming pointed out to viewers, "Prosecutors say as soon as the state agrees to pay defense attorney fees the case against Warren is ready for trial. When that will be—no one can say."

The row over who would pay for the specialist witnesses for Warren's defense got to the core root of criminal trials, according to DA Ron Moore of Buncombe County, back in Asheville. Taking aim at the testimony that would be offered by psychologists and psychiatrists in the Warren case, he said, "One of these days, defense lawyers will realize the collective wisdom of twelve persons [in a jury] is a lot more intuitive than that of a Ph.D. pointy head."

The use of such experts came with a hefty price tag, which had to be paid out of the taxpayer-funded court system. Naturally, defense attorneys and psychologists insisted that mental-health professionals should be brought into the Warren trial to give objective opinions about the defendant's mental state at the time the crime was committed. The influence of such testimony on the jury was of paramount importance to defense attorneys. But the DA prosecuting Warren intended to outweigh any such testimony.

Experts would be called to testify whether he knew right from wrong when he killed Velma Faye Gray. DA Ron Moore believed such mental-health professionals were "hired guns" who charged by the hour to tell jurors what the defense wanted them to hear. "It sickens me to sit in a trial and listen to this," Moore later explained. "There's evil in this world, and in these cases that's what we're dealing with, evil people doing evil deeds."

Defense attorneys naturally disagreed. "Often people who commit heinous offenses have some type of mental illness and most times that's the only explanation for their conduct," said one of Warren's counsels in Greenville. There were also genuine fears that prosecutors might distort the findings of a psychologist during cross-examination "because they often take specific components of an evaluation and emphasize that as opposed to the objective tests as a whole."

Finally, on April 9, 1992, to counter any efforts by Warren's defense attorneys, Lesley Warren was given a full psychological test, which resulted in him being pronounced "beyond any doubt sane." But the row about who would pay the cost of Warren's defense witnesses continued into the late summer of 1992, provoking further anger and resentment among the families of his victims.

Brother Lee Hurley said, "I'm disappointed he has not been brought to trial. The most disgusting part of this whole thing is that the state of South Carolina is bickering over who will pay for his defense fees. I'm really bitter he's getting his three meals a day and is being taken care of. . . ."

Lee Hurley and the rest of Jayme's family remained stunned by the JEC connection between his sister and Warren and how it probably cost her her life. "My sister was very openhearted. She befriended everyone. She helped Lesley tremendously. She was trusting, too trusting. It's unbelievable, really pathetic. It is always happening to someone with a future."

By early December 1992, Greenville County court officials predicted Warren's trial for the murder of Velma Faye Gray would finally go ahead "by late January or early February" the following year. Warren's attorneys were put on notice that prosecutors intended to seek the death penalty. On December 11, Asheville police investigator Ted Lambert called NYSP colleague Bob Cooke and said: "It's gonna happen in January."

But January, February and March 1993 passed without any agreement between prosecutors and defense attorneys over those controversial witnesses. In April, Faye Gray's furious brother George Jackson vented his family's frustration. "In my opinion, he ought to be put to death. Me, my family and thousands of our friends believe he should be put to death. He doesn't deserve to live." But when would the trial actually go ahead?

The state supreme court decided Greenville County taxpayers would pay the cost of Warren's defense witnesses. Two new lawyers were assigned to his case. A local court official announced, "If everything goes as planned, Warren will leave the detention center and face his first trial this summer."

On July 23, 1993, Judge C. Victor Pyle, the circuit judge of the 13th judicial circuit, disappointed prosecutors in Greenville County by ruling there was not enough evidence to prosecute Warren for kidnap in the murder of Velma Faye Gray. George Jackson was incensed. "I think it's a win for the criminal. If I were going to commit murder, I would come to South Carolina to do it because they're not going to try you for the death penalty."

Greenville County prosecutor Warren Mowry told newsmen, "We knew it was a close call on the kidnapping. There wasn't a whole lot of evidence that we could substantially use to show a kidnapping had occurred, which we needed for an aggravating circumstance to seek the death penalty."

However, prosecutors were extremely confident of convicting Warren of murder and predicted a short trial of just a few days. They also knew the death penalty issue would remain in the forefront at Warren's next scheduled trial for the murder of Jayme Hurley in North Carolina. As one legal expert explained, "That's because if he's convicted of murder in South Carolina, it will be easier for North Carolina prosecutors to seek the death penalty against him."

On July 23, Bob Cooke of the NYSP heard from Ted Lambert at Asheville PD once again. Warren was offering to plead guilty on the South Carolina case if North Carolina would give assurances they would not seek the death penalty. The deal was immediately turned down by North Carolina prosecutors who had every intention of seeking the death penalty against Lesley Warren.

The selection of a jury for Lesley Warren's first trial finally began in early September 1993. As Lee Hurley, Jayme's brother, said, "It's long overdue. I feel sorry for the victim's [Velma Faye Gray's] family having to wait so long, as we are having to wait so long in Asheville."

There was great disappointment from many of the families of Warren's victims when the court announced in advance that Warren would not face the death penalty if found guilty.

Warren's Greenville attorney, county public defender John Maudlin, expected to pick a jury and begin testimony all on the first day of the trial. He refused to say ahead of the trial if Warren would be testifying in his own defense. "I feel it's inappropriate for attorneys to talk about their cases beforehand," he said.

Behind the scenes, prosecutors in South Carolina remained convinced a guilty verdict would be an aggravating factor in asking for the death penalty in Warren's trials in Asheville and High Point. In Asheville's Buncombe County, Judge C. Walter Allen of the superior court cleared the way for three county residents to testify in South Carolina. They were Warren's onetime girlfriends Bronya Owenby and Saundra Davis and friend Jerry Wayne Rogers.

Warren's assistant public defender in Buncombe County, Bob Clark, knew full well that the outcome of the South Carolina case would have a big influence on his client's eventual fate in Asheville.

Back in Greenville, the prosecutor, Warren Mowry, said he expected no one to mention the other charges against Warren during the South

Carolina trial unless "the defense try to depict him as the all-American boy next door."

On Monday, September 13, 1993, Lesley Warren finally found himself facing trial for one of the murders he'd committed. However, the judge's pretrial rule not to allow in evidence that might have brought Warren the death penalty continued to outrage the relatives of his victim Velma Faye Gray. "I consider him like a rodent; I'd like to squash him. He doesn't need to exist. He shouldn't live," Gray's brother George Jackson told reporters outside the court.

In the courtroom, prosecutor Warren Mowry opened proceedings by telling the Greenville jury he had no eyewitnesses to Gray's slaying, but promised to create a "full and complex" jigsaw puzzle with other witnesses. John Maudlin, the public defender, suggested that some of the pieces of the jigsaw puzzle might be missing and urged the jury to see Warren as innocent until proven otherwise.

The judge reminded the jury, "Now, ladies and gentlemen, there will be some television coverage. There will be some newspaper coverage. Again, I remind you don't read that. Don't watch it. Don't listen to anything about the case or discuss it tonight. And if you'll come back in the morning, then we'll pick up till we get the whole case together and give you a chance to deliberate at that point in time."

The following day, Tuesday, September 14, the court heard how Warren had confessed to the murder of Velma Faye Gray immediately after his arrest in 1990. Spartanburg County detective captain Mike Ennis read Warren's statement from the witness

stand and quoted him saying he had picked up Gray
in northern Greenville County after her car ran off
the road.

According to the statement, Warren admitted
Gray asked for a ride to call for help and that he
drove her in a tractor-trailer to a convenience store
a short distance away. "Before she could get out of
the truck, I grabbed her and choked her," the statement said. Warren was quoted as then telling investigators how he later placed her body in the trunk
of his car and drove her to Lake Bowen, where he
tied Gray's hands behind her back with shoelace.
He had been intending to attach something heavy
to the body so it would stay at the bottom of the
lake, "but I couldn't find anything to weight her
with."

Next in the witness stand was Asheville Police Department Lieutenant Ted Lambert, who testified
that Warren had confessed to killing "many more"
than four people. Lambert conceded that many of
Warren's claims might never be fully substantiated.

Pathologist Dr. John Wren told the hushed courtroom about the injuries inflicted on Velma Faye
Gray. He said an injury to her neck was "consistent
with throttling, strangulation or a small concentrated blow." Wren stated that Gray had died from
a lack of oxygen, which could have occurred under
different scenarios, including drowning and strangulation.

Motorist Katie Manchester, a key prosecution witness, was asked to identify Lesley Warren as the man
she saw alongside the AM-CAN truck the night of
Velma Faye Gray's disappearance. She immediately
confirmed it was him, but then admitted under defense questioning she had seen Warren before when

she was summoned to sit in the court during a pretrial hearing.

Warren's defense attorney, John Maudlin, also pointed out to the court that Katie Manchester had not correctly identified Warren in the days following the Gray homicide. She had also admitted seeing Warren's photo on TV. Maudlin even asked the judge, "Your Honor, under those circumstances I would move to have the jury instructed to disregard any identification by this witness. I would ask that her description of the truck driver, as was laid out in her statement, remain. I will not contest her in-court identification and allow that to be stricken under the circumstances."

The following day, state prosecutor Mowry insisted in his closing remarks to the jury that no promises were made or force used to obtain Warren's statement. But public defender John Maudlin attacked the credibility of his client's confession by once again pointing out that Warren told police he'd killed "many more" people, but in numerous cases no actual proof of a crime was ever found.

That same day, the six-man, six-woman jury deliberated for just under three hours before finding Lesley Warren guilty of murder. Under the terms of his life sentence, he would be eligible for parole in twenty years. Both prosecutor and defense attorney agreed that Warren's confession played a key role in the jury's decision. Public defender John Maudlin immediately said he would appeal the verdict.

Police and prosecutors hoped that Warren's next courtroom appearance would end in the death penalty.

Nineteen

North Carolina authorities immediately applied to move Warren to Asheville to face his next trial for the murder of Jayme Hurley. DA Ron Moore was anxious to get custody of his man as quickly as possible. "When we get our trial started depends on how long it takes South Carolina authorities to get him here and for us and his lawyers to get ready," he told reporters following Warren's first conviction.

But once again the wheels of justice moved at a snail's pace, and by March 1994, it had become clear to prosecutors and investigators that Warren's Asheville trial was a long way off. Moore hoped it might go ahead by Christmas 1994, but he admitted it was more likely to start in 1995.

On Tuesday, April 26, 1994, Lesley Warren was finally transferred back to Buncombe County Jail to await his trial for the Hurley murder in Asheville. Warren's attorneys were once again warned by DA Ron Moore that it would be months before the trial commenced. He explained that "we want to give the defense enough time to get ready, and we also have other murder trials lined up to do."

Warren's incarceration was costing Buncombe County taxpayers $28 per day, but the move to the county jail was essential because it enabled Warren to talk to his defense lawyers. Ron Moore remained adamant Warren should face the death penalty and he planned to use Warren's 1993 South Carolina Velma Faye Gray conviction as an "aggravating" circumstance in his quest for the death penalty.

Meanwhile, Lesley Warren's lawyers began seriously considering an insanity defense for his upcoming trial for the Jayme Hurley murder. On Thursday, May 12, 1994, Lesley Warren, sporting a full beard and a tight white T-shirt, walked into the Buncombe County Courthouse a very different person from the timid, smiling country boy arrested by police back in July 1990.

Judge C. Walter Allen of the superior court gave public defender Robert Hufstader sixty days to file motions, including the insanity defense. Warren looked cold and unemotional as he stood in silence in the dock. DA Moore assured the court that the trial for the Hurley killing would go ahead within six months.

On August 23, 1994, there was yet another postponement to Warren's upcoming trial. Judge Allen signed an order effectively stopping the clock on the deadline for holding Warren agreed upon at the earlier hearing. In January 1995, DA Moore was obliged to publicly reiterate that he was still seeking the death penalty against Lesley Warren, despite all the delays.

It wasn't until Monday, February 6, 1995—the date of Jayme Hurley's birthday—that Lesley Warren finally appeared in court to face trial for her murder. As he stood handcuffed and pleaded guilty to first-degree murder in front of Judge William Freeman of the Buncombe County Superior Court, Warren showed little emotion. Judge Freeman warned the now twenty-seven-year-old alleged serial killer he faced a mandatory minimum of life in prison or the death sentence.

One of the first witnesses to testify was Asheville PD's Lieutenant Ted Lambert. He told the court how one of Hurley's friends had told him Warren had been at the victim's home the day of her disappearance. Lambert then explained that Jayme Hurley's purse was found during the search of Warren's 1968 Chevy van and how investigators eventually located her body in a shallow grave off Highway 151 in the western part of Buncombe County.

The court heard how Warren was already serving a life sentence for killing Velma Faye Gray and that he had been held at the Buncombe County Jail since April 1994 in connection with Hurley's death. The public defenders Bob Hufstader and Bob Clark were in agreement with prosecutors that Warren was mentally competent for court proceedings.

DA Ron Moore informed the judge he intended to seek the death penalty against Warren, and the judge scheduled May 1 as a date for Warren's sentencing hearing. During that same court appearance on February 6, 1995, Warren also pleaded guilty to larceny for the unrelated theft of a set of rings from a relative valued at $8,000. The judge informed Warren he could get a maximum of ten years in prison for the larceny. It was part of a plea agreement struck between prosecutors and his defense attorneys.

That agreement stated: "The state does not have evidence of course of conduct and therefore no evidence of additional alleged crimes will be offered by the state unless such evidence becomes relevant to cross-examination of defense witnesses at the capital sentencing hearing."

On May 1, 1995, a judge rescheduled Warren's

sentencing hearing to September 18 that year. A jury would decide whether Warren should live or die. Prosecutors intended presenting evidence of Hurley's murder as well as details of aggravating factors relating to Warren's murder conviction in South Carolina.

Just before Warren's sentencing trial in September 1995, his twenty-six-year-old wife, Tracey, admitted to reporters she was haunted by the charges against her husband. "You never get to forget it," she said to one local newspaper, before going on to describe her husband's life as a "Dr. Jekyll and Mr. Hyde" story. "The person I know is totally different from the person people tell me he is," she said, insisting Warren was "a quiet, shy and considerate husband." But Tracey Warren knew she had to accept whatever happened during the sentencing hearing. "He did it, they proved it and he's got to be punished," she added.

Public defender Bob Hufstader made a motion to question jurors individually—because of the pretrial publicity—on the first day of selection, September 18, 1995. It was to be a painstakingly slow process. Prosecution and defense attorneys were allowed to question each prospective jury member one at a time instead of in groups of twelve.

Warren's attorneys claimed news reports of the other crimes connected to Warren were "prejudicial" to him. To prove their point, they submitted to the court an article from the previous Monday's *Citizen-Times* that mentioned broadcasts on the local TV station. Judge Ronald Stephens granted the defense motion, but he denied another defense motion to sequester the jury once it was selected.

On the evening of September 19, psychiatric evaluator Dr. Bruce Welch interviewed Warren at the Foothills Correctional Institute. Warren was given a sodium Amytal interview, which involved administering a form of barbiturate called amybarbitol sodium. The hour-long procedure involved Warren lying down and being covered up and receiving an intravenous solution containing the barbiturate. The intention had been to "kick start" Warren so that he would talk more openly about his feelings and emotions.

Warren's interview under the influence of those barbiturates gave the impression he was completely apathetic about his life. Initially, Dr. Welch asked Warren about his state of mind when he was committing the murders.

Welch: "Did you think about your mother then?"

Warren: "Sometimes I do. Sometimes I don't."

[Warren hesitated before telling Welch his mother was always asking him to do things around the house, and that was a hassle.]

Warren: "It was an inconvenience for me to always have to be doing these things."

Welch: "Do you feel like she was on your back?"

Warren: "Yes, she was on my back."

Welch: "Do you want to get her off?"

Warren: "Yeah."

Warren talked at length about his mother. He felt she was always riding him, she was always demanding a lot of performance from him, and she had high expectations that he had difficulty fulfilling. Warren didn't specify what his mother expected of him, but it was the only time he seemed to give the doctor something approaching an emotional response.

He said he felt like she was always pressuring him and he didn't like the way that felt. Suddenly, he sounded frustrated, even angry, about his childhood. As Dr. Welch later admitted, "To me, that's a sign that the interview may not be going in the right direction because someone's fighting it."

Welch later claimed the primary reason for administering drugs to Warren was because he had consistently been unable to recall any of his emotional thoughts, feelings, the spots and open holes in his memory. Welch also believed that Warren's excessive use of cocaine might have caused some level of residual memory loss.

Dr. Welch later admitted it was the first time he had ever had a patient personally administered with sodium Amytal. He refused to elaborate any more about the specific subjects raised.

"It's not something you use to provide information directly to the court. It was never intended for that purpose. I was hoping to get new information from Lesley Warren. Up to that point, no new information had been developed with him."

Back in court the following day, attorneys completed the initial selection of twenty-two potential jurors, five of whom were dismissed by the state, three by the defense. The court then excused another twelve. Each side was allowed to excuse fourteen people for the jury and one alternate.

It wasn't until Thursday, September 28, that the twelfth juror was seated for Warren's sentencing hearing. Jury selection continued another day as attorneys tried to select two alternates. In all, more than eighty people had been questioned by lawyers and each interview had taken up to forty-five minutes as prosecutors and defenders probed the backgrounds of potential jurors and their views on the death penalty.

On Friday, September 29, the six men and six women of the jury were finally seated and Judge Ronald Stephens allowed the prosecution and defense to make their opening statements. Assistant DA Kate Dreher began by showing jurors a large photograph of Jayme Hurley, a person they had only known by name during jury selection. "This case calls for the imposition of the death penalty," Dreher calmly told the jury, then wrapped up the relevancy of the five witnesses the prosecution intended to call.

In an even shorter opening address to the jury, Bob Hufstader, Warren's lead attorney, conceded his client's guilt and how Warren had told authorities about the homicide early on. "What I ask is that you keep an open mind and you listen attentively to all the evidence," Hufstader said to the jury. After the jury had been dismissed for the weekend, Judge Stephens ruled that the prosecution could introduce into evidence photographs of the area where Hurley was found as well as photos of Velma Faye Gray.

First witness was Jayme Hurley's friend Catherine Jenkins, who testified she had spoken on the phone to Hurley for fifty-seven minutes the night before she was reported missing. "She told me Lesley Warren came there; he needed help and she told him he could sleep on the couch," Jenkins informed the court.

The physical evidence used to link Warren to Hurley's murder was introduced during the testimony of Captain Ross Robinson of the Asheville Police. Back then he was a sergeant in the department's crime scene unit. The evidence included Hurley's pocket-book, along with fibers found at the makeshift grave that were identical to fibers found in Warren's van, in bedsheets found near Hurley's grave and in a pillowcase in Warren's van that matched what was found at Hurley's home.

During Captain Robinson's testimony, prosecutors presented a videotape of the disinterment of Hurley's body from her shallow grave. Jurors showed no external signs of being disturbed by the video as they carefully watched investigators slowly remove the dirt around Hurley's body.

Lesley Warren's defense attorneys called to the stand psychologist David Evers, who'd evaluated fourteen-year-old Lesley Warren in 1982. "In my opinion, he was severely emotionally disturbed," Evers told the court. "I think he was a danger to himself and to others." Evers said Warren had been unable to deal with everyday stress as a teenager. Evers testified that Warren's mother had told him that his father had abused Lesley from infancy and how Warren had watched as his father burned down their trailer home. The psychologist then told the court how Warren had been committed for a long period to Broughton Park State Hospital. He pointed out it was highly unusual for a teenager to be kept in such an institution for a long period of time.

Prosecutors then began to try and punch holes in Evers's testimony during cross-examination. Assistant DA Kate Dreher told the court the main source of the child-abuse story was Warren's mother. She even suggested to Evers that the information was exaggerated. The prosecution also questioned Carol and Betty Pressley, Lesley Warren's neighbors when he was a teenager. They testified that they never heard screams or other sounds from the Warren home, which would have indicated if a child was being beaten. Prosecutor Dreher also challenged the reports of Warren watching his family's trailer burn to the ground in a fire set by his father. The Pressleys testified that Lesley Warren's father, Doug, was the only person they saw outside the trailer on the night of the fire. Betty Pressley told the court that Warren's mother, Phyllis, had told her she and the kids spent the night at Lesley's grandparents' house thirty yards in front of the Warren trailer. Dreher even introduced a report from the local fire department that listed the cause of the fire as "undetermined."

Across the courtroom, Spartanburg detective Carroll Amory glanced at Lesley Warren as he sat listening to the detailed evidence. Their eyes caught each other for a millisecond; then Warren turned away again. "It was almost as if he didn't want to be reminded of what he'd done," Carroll Amory later recalled.

Warren's main defender in court was psychiatrist Dr. Bruce Welch, who'd interviewed him on at least five occasions, including just a few days previously. Welch described the defendant as a wooden statue, a person who was so detached from his own emotions that he appeared cool and aloof. Welch also pointed out that Warren was not only taking cocaine but was also smoking marijuana and drinking alcohol at the time he killed Hurley. "He was taking enough cocaine on his own account that it would be an overdose to the average person," Welch told the court.

But Dreher disagreed when she began cross-examining him. "There is no evidence that Lesley Eugene Warren used cocaine except for the history provided by Lesley Warren," Dreher said. Welch insisted he'd learned of Warren's drug use from other sources, including his relatives and Asheville PD. Dreher pointed out that all police records were based on what Warren himself had said and she told the court that Warren's time in the U.S. Army indicated he used marijuana only once in his life.

Then Warren's first- and second-grade teachers testified that his mother had told them of abuse in the home. Under cross-examination, they said Lesley Warren was an average student. His third-grade teacher, Charlotte Spence, told the court that Warren's report card showed no indication of behavioral problems.

Summing up, prosecutors described Warren as an "opportunist killer" who would strike again if he was not sent to death row. Prosecutors recounted to the jury the testimony of a defense witness who'd walked in on Warren at the juvenile detention center in 1983 just after he'd tried to hang himself.

"When they resuscitated him, he said he needed to die because he was going to hurt somebody someday," Assistant DA Kate Dreher told the court. "He saw the writing on the wall even then."

During her forty-five-minute presentation to the jury, Dreher even acted out Warren putting his hands around Jayme Hurley's throat, dragging her body through the woods and digging a grave near Mount Pisgah. "You have to picture it; you have to know what you are dealing with," she told the jury.

Dreher's closing arguments evoked tears from several of Hurley's and Velma Faye Gray's relatives and friends sitting in the courtroom. "If he ever gets an opportunity to kill again, he will do it," she said. DA Ron Moore said in his closing address to the jury: "The only way to keep Lesley Warren from doing it again is to impose the death penalty."

Warren's defending counsels insisted their client was a battered child who was mentally disturbed. They argued that jurors should spare Warren's life because of his childhood abuse and the fact he had developed severe mental disorders at the time he strangled Hurley. Robert Hufstader told the jury that abuse allegations, questioned by prosecutors during their closing statements, were true. He repeated testimony from Warren's uncle who'd told the court that Warren was beaten by his father.

Defender Hufstader also referred to 1973 court documents from the divorce of Warren's parents that spoke of Warren being abused. "He had immense problems and those problems contributed very much to what he did, which was a tragic thing," said Hufstader. "We are not asking for forgiveness; we're asking for him to be put away for the rest of his natural life." Fellow defense attorney John Barrett told the jurors, "At the time of the crime, he was operating with a mind that was misshapen since he was little."

Warren's defense attorneys Robert Hufstader and John Barrett carefully pointed out the mitigating facts that had to be considered in relation to granting the death penalty for the Jayme Hurley killing:

1. It was committed while Warren was under the influence of mental or emotional disturbance.

2. Warren's ability to conform his conduct to the requirements of the law was seriously impaired.

3. Warren's young age at the time of the crime.

4. Warren was an unwanted child and his upbringing by his parents reflected that.

5. Warren's mother attempted to give him away to an aunt.

6. Warren was physically abused by his father.

7. Warren's first years of life were in a home in which his father abused his mother.

8. Warren's father left him and the rest of the family when Warren was very young.

9. When he was five years, four months old, Warren saw his home and belongings burned and was told his father burned the home.

10. Warren was in need of psychotherapy at the age of seven.

11. Warren was in need of further psychotherapy at the age of ten.

12. Warren was in need of further psychotherapy at the age of thirteen.

13. As a juvenile, Warren was so disturbed he tried to hang himself.

14. Warren's father rejected him again when he was a teenager.

15. At the age of fourteen, Warren was diagnosed as being severely emotionally disturbed.

16. At the age of fourteen, Warren had to be hospitalized for over a year in a mental institution.

17. Warren had already pleaded guilty to the murder of Jayme Hurley.

18. Warren had been a good inmate in the Buncombe County Jail.

19. Warren had admitted he had taken the life of Jayme Hurley to Ross Robinson.

The jury was dismissed to consider whether Lesley Warren should die for the murder of Jayme Hurley, the only person in Warren's entire life who'd genuinely seemed to care about him. The mental-health experts who testified on behalf of Lesley Warren during the Hurley trial charged a total of $12,500.

Early the following morning, October 9, 1995, jailers found a weapon inside Lesley Warren's cell at the Buncombe County Jail. Security at the Buncombe Courthouse where he was about to appear to hear the jury's verdict on his sentencing was immediately heightened.

Deputies were ordered by the sheriff's department to keep friends and relatives off the first row of benches behind the defense and prosecution. Jailers had recovered a ten-inch piece of metal, sharpened at one end, inside an air shaft in a cell Warren shared with another inmate.

The weapon had been found during a routine search. Captain Randy Ray later told reporters that such weapons, known as "shanks," were sometimes found in the jail. They were usually made by inmates out of pieces of metal that had been either discarded or torn from fixtures. They were then sharpened on the jail's concrete floor, explained Ray.

Twenty

On October 9, 1995, a superior court jury was impaneled and recommended a sentence of death on Lesley Warren for the murder of Jayme Hurley. The Buncombe County jury had deliberated for three and a half hours before sentencing Lesley Warren. He showed no emotion as the sentence was announced.

Judge Ronald Stephens set an execution date for December 15, knowing the death sentence would be automatically appealed to the North Carolina supreme court. The verdict brought tears to the eyes of one juror and several of Hurley's and Gray's relatives and friends who were in the courtroom. "It's been a long five years," commented brother Lee Hurley after the verdict. "I think we paid the debt we owed to Jayme and Velma Gray."

None of Lesley Warren's relatives were in court to hear the verdict. "We were disappointed, but we're certainly not angry at the jury," said one of Warren's public defenders, John Barrett. Warren was immediately dispatched to Central Prison in Raleigh. It was unclear whether he would be returned to South Carolina to continue his life sentence for the Gray killing before his trial for the murder of Kat Johnson.

"This has been a long time coming, and we're

glad this day is finally here," said DA Ron Moore after the verdict. "I think Lesley Warren is one of the most dangerous people who has come through our courtroom. He kills people with his bare hands, innocent women who have done nothing to provoke him."

On Tuesday, October 31, Lesley Warren appeared in court to plead not guilty to the first-degree murder of his last-known victim, High Point student Kat Johnson. During an initial superior court hearing, Judge Russell G. Walker Jr. of Asheboro set November 27 as the deadline for any prearrangement motions and referred to a possible trial date of January 22 or February 19, 1996.

Wearing a red prison jumpsuit, leg shackles, no socks and orange sandals, Warren sat stone-faced, giving a long, calm stare to each person who spoke during the proceedings. Occasionally, his eyes wandered across to the handful of courtroom spectators.

Warren's defenders, John Bryson, an attorney in private practice, and David May, a Guilford assistant public defender, initially asked Judge Walker to postpone Warren's arraignment until later in November. Bryson explained, "Mr. Warren has returned to High Point for the first time since 1990. This is the first time we've been able to work with him as a client. Any defenses we would be pursuing . . . that would require filing motions prearrangement, we have not had a chance to do so."

But High Point prosecutor Richard Lyle told the judge that Warren's case was not complex, noting that he'd already been convicted in Greenville and Asheville. "It's time for the [High Point] victims to have their day in court," Lyle said. "They've been waiting five years."

The judge sided with Lyle, and Bryson entered the not guilty plea on behalf of Warren. That same day, Judge Walker also held a mandatory hearing to determine whether prosecutors could go ahead with Warren's trial as a capital murder case. Citing Warren's previous murder convictions, Walker said prosecutors had sufficient evidence to pursue a death penalty upon conviction.

In North Carolina, Guilford County DA Jim Kimel was planning to team up with High Point prosecutor Richard Lyle. "We are seeking the death penalty," Kimel told reporters, referring to the upcoming Warren trial for the killing of Kat Johnson.

With a buzz cut and moustache, Lesley Warren looked very different from his earlier court appearances when he was escorted into the Guilford County Courthouse for the first day's hearing. He'd put on weight and was allowed to wear civilian clothes as opposed to the red prison jumpsuits normally given to prisoners considered high-security risks.

Judge Howard R. "Rick" Greeson of the superior court ordered the Greenville courtroom to be emptied when Lesley Warren entered for the first time on March 26, 1996, for jury selection. Anyone entering Greeson's courtroom during the trial was patted down and bailiffs with hand-held metal detectors inspected every visitor. Baggage and pocketbooks, even coats, were thoroughly searched as well. Each person reentering the court was searched again as they walked back in.

Judge Greeson also ordered bailiffs to lock the courtroom doors once proceedings began and no one except court personnel was allowed to enter or leave. At the start of the trial, Greeson explained to attorneys, "I want to apologize for this, but I do it in all capital cases. I've tried seven capital cases in three years, and haven't had a disturbance yet." Greeson genuinely feared that the emotions of the families involved could run high.

Initially, attorneys for both prosecution and defense dealt with perhaps the most crucial part of the Katherine Johnson murder case: photographs of the victim. Warren's defense team filed a motion to limit the photographs that prosecutors could enter into evidence and show to the jury. "Our concerns are this, Judge, the relevance of the photos, and the fact that the prejudicial effect outweighs the probative value," John Bryson told Judge Greeson of the Guilford superior court.

As the photos were shown to the two defense attorneys, Lesley Warren tried to look away, choosing instead to look down at the yellow legal pad he frequently wrote on.

Of the twelve photos, two were of Johnson alive and ten were taken after police found her body. Seven of those ten pictures were from the autopsy. Judge Greeson agreed to prohibit use of one autopsy photograph, but he said that prosecutors had the right to show any view that's relevant, "even if it is gory."

Judge Greeson helped matters greatly at one stage by covering some points with the whole jury pool, rather than letting the lawyers do it during the individual screening. Meanwhile, Lesley Warren busied himself writing in the notebook on his lap.

As DA Kimel prepared to talk about the photos, he made a point of telling Johnson's parents in the spectators' gallery, "You probably don't want to see this part." The Johnsons left the courtroom and waited outside until Greeson recessed the court. Both sides also agreed to throw out several pages in Warren's forty-four-page statement to detectives taken in 1990 that referred to Warren's reaction to questions about the Johnson killing.

Jury selection was done with painstaking precision by both sides who eventually agreed on the final panel of twelve jurors after challenges and choices had exhausted the pool of forty-two potential jurors with which they began the day. Jurors were also screened on an individual basis with regard to pre-trial publicity and their opinions on the death penalty. Warren's defense team made a point of telling prospective jurors that Warren wasn't guilty of first-degree murder, but he admitted being guilty to second-degree murder.

On Monday, March 25, 1996, several of the jury threw Warren steely glances of disgust as they were shown autopsy photos of Johnson's decomposing body. Evidence from witnesses who were with Warren the day he met Johnson told the court that Warren had boasted of "having her" before the night was through.

Defense attorney John Bryson insisted his client had been too drunk to form the intent to kill, which made him guilty of second-degree murder, not first-degree. "Lesley was clearly very, very drunk that night," Bryson said, citing that earlier witness testimony.

"Does anybody believe that when he said that [he would have Johnson before the night was through] that he was saying he was going to kill her? The evidence in this case is that it was a spontaneous act brought on by drunkenness."

But Bryson's words were shot down by DA Kimel's argument that everything Warren did from the time he drove into High Point on his stolen motorcycle on Friday, July 13, 1990, until he was arrested the following Friday, was part of a plan. Kimel reminded jurors of the medical examiner's testimony that, on average, a person loses consciousness about ten to fifteen seconds after strangulation starts and dies within three to five minutes.

"Let's just take the average case, but remember, Katherine Johnson wasn't just average," Kimel said, putting a blue egg timer on the edge of the jury box and setting the timer at four minutes.

Then he counted aloud to ten"

"ONE.

"TWO.

"THREE.

"FOUR.

"FIVE.

"SIX.

"SEVEN.

"EIGHT.

"NINE.

"TEN.

"Katherine's just lost consciousness," Kimel said. "She looked at him as long as you just looked at me." Kimel kept talking to the jury as the egg timer continued pouring sand. "He's still strangling her, all this time," he said. Then he said nothing. All eyes were on the egg timer. After about three minutes had passed, Kimel said, "Why is he still strangling her now if he didn't intend to kill her?"

With just a few grains of sand left in the timer, Kimel added, "Time's winding down for Katherine Johnson."

The timer rang out.

"She's dead."

DA Kimel and assistant DA Cole ended the presentation of their case by playing an audiotaped statement of Warren confessing to killing Johnson. "I choked her," Warren was heard saying in a Southern drawl that sounded weary after several hours of intense questioning by detectives just a few hours after his arrest.

The Guilford County jury took just twenty-eight minutes to convict Lesley Warren of the first-degree murder of Kat Johnson.

Brother David, sitting between parents Anne and Bobby Johnson, moved forward in his seat before the verdict was handed to Judge Greeson. As the clerk read the word "guilty," David Johnson raised both fists upward before dropping his head, and a whispered cry of "Yes!" escaped from him. There were tears of relief from his parents and their friends, seated around them. "We just want to express our appreciation to our family and friends who have helped us through this time," Anne Johnson told reporters outside the court. "It's been a hard ordeal for all of us. We're pleased it's almost over."

On Wednesday, March 27, jurors filed back into the jury box to consider whether Warren should be sentenced to death. Not one of them looked in the direction of Lesley Warren. Jurors were immediately told about Warren's prior convictions on two other murders, but they were not told he'd been given a death sentence on one of those.

The jurors saw photos of those other two victims Hurley and Gray, despite fresh objections from Warren's court-appointed attorneys, Bryson and May. "The photos are not relevant; they're highly prejudicial and inflammatory," Bryson told Judge Greeson.

But Guilford County DA Jim Kimel had no doubt the photos were essential evidence. "Warren committed especially heinous and particularly shocking crimes. He's the one that buried Jayme Hurley's body; he's the one that threw Velma Faye Gray in the lake. He can't complain about it now."

In his closing argument during the sentencing phase, Kimel said Warren's two previous murder convictions were more than enough to justify a death sentence. "We don't ask for revenge," Kimel told the jury, pacing in front of a board in which he had pinned photos of the three women's dead bodies. "It's not proper; it's not right. You're the voice of the community. You say what's acceptable, what the punishment is. By your recommendation, you know what you can do? . . . You can take [the body photos] down and bring back some degree of dignity."

Kimel picked up a photo of Kat Johnson taken the last day her parents saw her alive, July 4, 1990. "The thing you remember most is not that," Kimel said, taking down an autopsy photo of her body, replacing it with the July 4 photo, "but this."

Warren's attorneys Bryson and May argued that their client had adapted to prison life and belonged there for the rest of his life. "Look in your soul before you pass judgment on this man," May told the jury, "because you'll not be able to look back again."

The following day, Thursday, March 28, the seven-man, five-woman jury found themselves hung up on a confusing sentence in the judge's recommendations that determined whether there was an aggravating factor that warranted giving Warren the death sentence. Thirty minutes into the deliberation, Judge Greeson sent the jury home until the following morning.

When they returned on March 29 to sentence

Warren to death, it became clear they had ignored any mitigating circumstances, such as his voluntary confession in the hours following his arrest.

In his subsequent appeal, Warren objected to photographs shown to jurors and argued that the other murder case should not have been considered as a factor in his sentencing since he had committed the murder but not been convicted of it at the time Hurley was killed. On Friday, November 7, 1997, the state supreme court upheld Lesley Warren's death sentence for the killing of Jayme Hurley.

Now Lesley Warren finds himself on the death row of Central Prison, part of the North Carolina Department of Correction, where at least 190 other killers are given a round-the-clock guard.

In order for Warren to make one of his regular psychiatric evaluations at the state mental hospital, prison rules require the following conditions:

1. one armed and experienced correction officer in a lead vehicle,

2. two armed and experienced custody staff; one sergeant and one correction officer in the vehicle with condemned inmate,

3. one armed and experienced officer in a chase vehicle.

On all of Warren's trips outside prison, the sheriff of the county plus the police department where he was being transported to for standby assistance had to be notified. It was also required that the hospital police be notified and they in turn would often request standby assistance.

During the early part of his incarceration, there

were major security concerns about transporting Warren; it was felt that as a death row inmate he knew he was to be executed and had nothing to lose by attempting to escape. There was also concern that any leak of information to Warren concerning his movement schedule or the location of where he was being transported would increase the chances that he might try and set up outside assistance to try and escape.

As a result, Warren had to be escorted by experienced staff, but there were not enough certified staff (two years or more) to cover key areas with Central Prison in addition to the special assignments for outside transportation to hospital and court appearances. There was also a genuine fear that if Warren got wind of his movements, his family and friends might choose that moment to turn up at the prison to see Warren, resulting in custody staff being overwhelmed.

No chances were to be taken with Lesley Warren.

Endnote

In the case of Lesley Warren, the triggering factors that provoked him to kill were scarily unpredictable. One victim was killed because she tried to run away, while another was slain because she allegedly provided him with sex too easily. By her agreeing to his demands, Warren felt his control was being threatened.

But there was no way of knowing what would send Lesley Warren into a murderous frenzy. Essentially, Warren was a combination of two types of serial murderer as defined by experts. He qualified as a hedonistic killer because he seemed to have little motive beyond his own pleasure. He killed because it felt good. Inflicting death provided Warren with the ultimate high—a source of intense, primarily, sexual pleasure. But there was also an element of the power seeker about him because he seemed to need to assert his supremacy over a helpless victim, to compensate for his own deep-seated feelings of worthlessness by completely dominating another human being.

Now that you have absorbed the appalling catalogue of crimes committed by Lesley Eugene Warren, this breakdown of the different phases that a serial killer evolves through will cement the impression that Warren was a classic animal of his species:

THE WOOING PHASE. Some killers strike without warning, but not Lesley Warren. He didn't want to snatch someone off the street or break into a house and slay all those inside. Warren knew he would derive more pleasure from luring his victims into his clutches, lulling them into a false sense of security by tricking them into lowering their defenses. Clean-cut and polite, he had no trouble with his first victims. He knew how to charm them.

THE CAPTURE PHASE. The next step was to spring the trap that ensnared his victims. Seeing the full horror on their faces made the game all worthwhile to Lesley Warren. This was the moment when—having accepted a ride—the would-be victim realized she may be at the point of no return. That was when Lesley Warren assaulted them and said he had no intention of releasing them—ever.

THE MURDER. In Lesley Warren's case, the killing and the sex usually occurred simultaneously—the moment at which he strangled the last breath out of his victim became the ultimate climax. This was the acme of pleasure that he'd been building toward since the first time he fantasized about murder. Strangulation was the death of Warren's choice. It was the only way that he could get any real pleasure.

THE TOTEM PHASE. Just like a sexual climax, the killing was an intense and transient pleasure for Lesley Warren. To prolong that experience and help him relive it in later fantasies, he often removed some jewelry from the body. That became a souvenir or "totemic" object associated with the victim. Sometimes he took a purse as well.

THE DEPRESSION PHASE. In the aftermath of the killing, Lesley Warren undoubtedly experienced some emotional letdown—the equivalent of what the French call *postcoital tristesse*. In Warren, it sometimes left him with such severe headaches that he seriously considered suicide. But once that feeling had passed, he renewed his desire to murder again—an insatiable need for a fix of fresh flesh.

Serial and thrill killings are a U.S. epidemic that began toward the end of the nineteenth century with the Industrial Revolution and exploded into the nation's headlines in the 1970s. The so-called thrill killers seemed for years to be confined to the big cities of the North and West: Los Angeles with Charles Manson, Richard "Night Stalker" Ramirez and "The Zodiac Killer"; New York with "Son of Sam"; Chicago with John Wayne Gacy; Texas with Henry Lee Lucas; Seattle and vicinity with Ted Bundy, Edmund Kemper and the "Green River Killer"; Milwaukee with Jeffrey Dahmer.

But then along with the urbanization and migration in the South came the serial killers. During the 1990s, no less than three serial killers—including Lesley Warren—have passed through North Carolina.

Michael Sonner, now thirty, dropped out of Northwest Guilford High School and worked several odd jobs, including two in Warren's killing field of High Point. After his second escape from Davidson County Jail in 1993, Sonner killed a Nevada state trooper. He was already awaiting trial for slaying two people outside a truck stop in Texas. Sonner told investigators he'd also killed two women in California.

Sean Patrick Goble, an Asheboro truck driver, confessed to killing two women in Tennessee and one in North Carolina. He dropped that victim's body off near Greensboro while driving a tractor-trailer for a Winston-Salem trucking company. Police believe that Goble is responsible for dozens of interstate slayings throughout the Eastern Seaboard and Midwest.

As you will have discovered reading about the life and crimes of Lesley Warren, serial killers are not analytical geniuses, beyond good and evil, like Friedrich Nietzsche's superman. They aren't even homoerotic headcases with sex-change obsessions, like something out of *The Silence of the Lambs*.

Most, like Warren, are white loners. Few are legally insane. They drink beer and work blue-collar jobs, have wives or girlfriends (or both), and not many of them have psycho-killer tattoos on their foreheads. But the serial killer epidemic is American through and through.

Seventy-five percent of the world's serial killers are found within our shores. They are nearly all white men aged between twenty-four and thirty-five, which made Lesley Warren a "baby" in every sense of the word. Criminologist Michael Newton, who compiled the stories of 544 serial killers in his book *Hunting Humans—An Encyclopedia of Modern Serial Killers*, says that at least one-third are like Lesley Warren, nomadic transients wandering the country and killing.

Experts who examined Lesley Warren were never able to truly nail down his real motives for killing because he did not select and stalk his intended victims in the way that most serial killers do. And while there were strong sado-sexual overtones in his murders, in at least half his killings he actually befriended most of his victims before exterminating them.

There is even doubt that Warren fed off his victims' fear and agony like most known serial killers. It seems that the only power he thrived on was after they had died.

And Finally. . .

One day at 12:01 A.M., in the not too distant future, Lesley Warren will be taken from his holding cell in the death house of the state penitentiary in Central Prison. He will be strapped to a hospital gurney in North Carolina's brightly lit, cobalt-blue execution chamber.

As the witnesses file into the death room, Warren, clad in a denim shirt and his favorite jeans, will ramble through a final statement that thanks his family, friends and supporters. He'll no doubt mention he will never forget them. Then the intravenous tubes will be inserted into Warren's arms. The tubes lead to a room shielded by a one-way mirror; the twenty-first century's version of the hooded executioner will say, "We're ready."

As the lethal mix of sodium thiopental, pancuronium bromide and potassium chloride courses through his veins, Warren will take his last, long breath, shut his eyes and briefly snort. For a few moments, the only sounds in the death chamber will be pens on paper as the media chronicles the life being extinguished before them. Lesley Warren will be pronounced dead by 12:20 A.M.

The only pain he will have felt? The prick from the insertion of the needles. . . .

HORRIFYING TRUE CRIME
FROM PINNACLE BOOKS